IMAGINE
THERE'S NO
COUNTRY

Poverty, Inequality, and Growth
in the Era of Globalization

IMAGINE THERE'S NO COUNTRY

Poverty, Inequality, and Growth in the Era of Globalization

Surjit S. Bhalla

INSTITUTE FOR INTERNATIONAL ECONOMICS
Washington, DC
September 2002

Surjit S. Bhalla is managing director of Oxus Research and Investments, a New Delhi-based economic research, asset management and emerging-markets advisory firm. He taught at the Delhi School of Economics and held various positions at the Rand Corporation, the Brookings Institution, the research and treasury departments of the World Bank, Goldman Sachs (1992-94), and Deutsche Bank (1994-96). He is the author of research papers on a wide range of topics including farm productivity and agricultural policy; poverty and inequality; the determinants of growth, with emphasis on the separate roles of economic and political freedom; inflation and capital account convertibility; and determination of interest rates, exchange rates, and stock prices. He is also a regular contributor to newspapers and magazines on economics, politics, and cricket.

INSTITUTE FOR INTERNATIONAL ECONOMICS
1750 Massachusetts Avenue, NW
Washington, DC 20036-1903
(202) 328-9000 FAX: (202) 659-3225
http://www.iie.com

C. Fred Bergsten, *Director*
Brigitte Coulton, *Director of Publications
  and Web Development*
Brett Kitchen, *Director of Marketing*

*Typesetting and printing by
  Automated Graphic Systems, Inc.
Cover design by Itu Chaudhuri Design*

Printed in the United States of America
04 03 02   5 4 3 2 1

Library of Congress Cataloging-in-Publication Data

Bhalla, Surjit S.
    Imagine there's no country : poverty, inequality, and growth in the era of globalization / Surjit S. Bhalla.
        p. cm.
    Includes bibliographical references and index.
    ISBN 0-88132-348-9
    1. Poverty. 2. Income distribution.
3. Globalization. I. Title.

HC79.P6 B4827 2002
339.4′6—dc21
                                2002027329

For Simran and Sahil
Enjoy this ever new and better world

Contents

Tables

Figures

Preface

Poverty in the poor countries of the world is one of the most crucial issues of our time. Hundreds of millions of human beings exist on standards of living that would be unthinkable in the rich countries. New policies to address global poverty, in both rich and poor countries, have again moved to the top of the world agenda, though their implementation and ultimate results remain very much in doubt.

It is thus surprising that there is intense and, in fact, growing disagreement over the extent of world poverty, and even whether it is rising or falling. These disputes turn partly on highly technical, but politically critical, questions of how "poverty" is measured both at any given point and over periods of time. They also turn on central conceptual questions, such as whether our concern for "world poverty" should give priority to numbers of countries or—as argued in this book—to numbers of people.

This study addresses all these questions and concludes that much of the "conventional wisdom" surrounding the global poverty issue is wrong. Author Surjit Bhalla argues that absolute poverty levels are about one-half as great as suggested by the World Bank and other authoritative sources. He demonstrates that the dramatic growth and poverty reduction in China and India, with by far the largest populations in the world, have also reduced global income inequality sharply. Indeed, Bhalla believes that there has been—and will continue to be—steady convergence between the richer and poorer segments of the global family. As the world commences another extensive effort to improve the lot of the poorest among us, we hope and believe that this hopeful new analysis can make a major contribution to the understanding of the problem and thus greatly strengthen the foundation for a constructive policy response.

The Institute for International Economics is a private nonprofit institution for the study and discussion of international economic policy. Its purpose is to analyze important issues in that area and to develop and communicate practical new approaches for dealing with them. The Institute is completely nonpartisan.

The Institute is funded largely by philanthropic foundations. Major institutional grants are now being received from the William M. Keck, Jr. Foundation and the Starr Foundation. A number of other foundations and private corporations contribute to the highly diversified financial resources of the Institute. About 31 percent of the Institute's resources in our latest fiscal year were provided by contributors outside the United States, including about 18 percent from Japan.

The Board of Directors bears overall responsibility for the Institute and gives general guidance and approval to its research program, including the identification of topics that are likely to become important over the medium run (one to three years), and which should be addressed by the Institute. The Director, working closely with the staff and outside Advisory Committee, is responsible for the development of particular projects and makes the final decision to publish an individual study.

The Institute hopes that its studies and other activities will contribute to building a stronger foundation for international economic policy around the world. We invite readers of these publications to let us know how they think we can best accomplish this objective.

C. FRED BERGSTEN
Director
September 2002

Acknowledgments

While it took longer than expected, I must confess to considerable enjoyment while conducting the research for this book, including the quite predictable nightmares about the data being wrong, the method being wrong, or the analysis being incomplete. And just as I was beginning to enjoy the writing—the moment just after dawn—the deadlines started encroaching. But the pinch was almost not felt due to the constant support and encouragement from the Institute for International Economics, and especially from John Williamson. Thanks. And thanks again for patience, discussions, suggestions, and comments on previous drafts.

Montek Ahluwalia, Suman Bery, Ravinder Kaur, and Arvind Virmani have had to bear the brunt of my seemingly interminable discussions on poverty and inequality. Homi Kharas, Farrukh Iqbal, and Robert Lawrence were part of the magnificent, but critical, seven. Angus Deaton always provided a helpful ear and even more helpful comments. Sanjiv Kumar took time off from discussions about world markets for discussions on the politics and economics of research on poverty and inequality. Constructive criticism from all came in loud and clear, as did the encouragement and support. Thank you—it is much appreciated.

The book has been in preparation for almost three years now and its findings have been discussed at various institutions. It is difficult to thank all the participants individually, but I am grateful to the institutions for providing the opportunity, and to the participants for their interest and comments—the Carnegie Endowment for International Peace, June 2000; the International Monetary Fund and the World Bank, June 2000; the Institute for International Economics, October 2000 and

July 2001; Princeton University, October 2000; the Rajiv Gandhi Institute, New Delhi, January 2001; United Nations, New York, July 2001, Asian Development Bank, August 2001; the National Council of Applied Economic Research, New Delhi, February 2002; OECD, Paris, June 2002; and the World Bank, June 2002.

The seminars were a great forum for exchange of ideas; even when there was disagreement, the intellectual support received was of immense value. Several individuals provided helpful comments: Orley Ashenfelter, Yves Balcer, Fred Bergsten, Nancy Birdsall, Angus Deaton, V. Gnanathurai, Farrukh Iqbal, Shafiqul Islam, Nanak Kakwani, Homi Kharas, Art Kraay, Branko Milanovic, Gobind Nankani, Omar Noman, Arvind Panagriya, Pronab Sen, Lyn Squire, and Roberto Zagha. I hope I have done justice to your concerns. Thank you in any case! Discussions with Nanak Kakwani on Lorenz curves, and Prabhu Ghate and Nadeem ul-Haque on the structure of economic research were especially useful.

Several individuals provided comments on the penultimate draft (November 2001) and the final draft (May 2002); detailed comments by Richard Cooper, Art Kraay and an anonymous referee were most useful. These comments did not necessarily imply agreement. Special thanks, therefore, to Nancy Birdsall, William Cline, Richard Cooper, Art Kraay, Jim Gordon, George de Menil, Dani Rodrik, Martin Ravallion, Nirvikar Singh, and Clas Wihlborg; and warm thanks to an anonymous referee on his critically constructive comments.

Research is never easy, and especially one involving numbers; worse, when numbers themselves are controversial. The team at Oxus helped me wade through the sea of information and reduce it to a useable dataset. Many thanks to Shekhar Aiyar, Dipankar Basu, Nabhojit Basu, Rohit Chawdhry, Arindom Mookerjee, and Suraj Saigal; and to Ashok Aswal, Swati Kaura, and Abhijit Shankar for pitching in. Thanks also to Itu Chaudhuri for consistently being an intellectual and always willing to engage in debate—and for providing creative titles at short notice (including the title of this book!).

Thanking one's life partner is conventional, perhaps even mandatory. But my debt and gratitude to my wife, Ravinder Kaur, is heartfelt. This book would not have been possible without the support of my family, and the intellectual support of Ravi. It helps that our interests in research coincide, and it helps even more that she is able to bring a sociologist's perspective, and even yet more given our slightly different ideological persuasions. The completion of my book should now make possible for Ravi to complete *her* book, and I am looking forward to changing places.

Our two children were also supportive. I missed helping Simran with her homework, and I am sure she missed our jam sessions on rock music, especially of the sixties variety. It is good to see the music live on. Our son, Sahil, a bit too much like me, was not quiet about my mental absence from the family, and especially the acute absence over the last year. Missing his workaholic dad, he prophesied that this book would never be completed, but it has! I have not played cricket with him for over a year. It is time to make up.

SURJIT S. BHALLA
September 2002

RECEIVED WISDOM ON POVERTY, INEQUALITY, AND GROWTH

Overview: New Results on Poverty, Inequality, and Growth in the Era of Globalization

According to received wisdom in the international community, we are told that during the past 20 years, the period of globalization, there has been a large increase in world inequality. I find the opposite to be true. Not only has inequality not increased, it has actually fallen, and by the end of 2000 was at its lowest level in 50 years. Moreover, by the end of this decade, the level of inequality is likely to be equal to that prevailing 100 years ago.

We are also told by the World Bank[1] that instead of convergence, or even conditional convergence, there has been divergence in the world economy. Translated, this means that poor countries have grown at a slower pace than rich countries. I reach the opposite conclusion. As a group, poor countries have grown more quickly. Further, if the unit of observation is not the poor country but the poor *individual*, then the growth rate has been considerably faster than ever before, and considerably higher than the growth rate in industrialized economies. The globalization period has been the golden age of development.

We are told that global poverty reduction has stagnated—that it was about 33 percent in 1985, 28 percent in 1987, 24 percent in 1998, and 23 percent in 1999. Thus, over 14 years (1985-99), when the per capita incomes of poor countries[2] grew by 51 percent, the percentage of poor people

---

1. The World Bank is the major source of information on levels and trends in absolute poverty. What is described as received wisdom on poverty has often been conveyed in, or by, World Bank documents. See *World Development Report*, 1980, 1990, and 2000.

2. The classification followed throughout the text is as follows: the industrialized world includes high-income Western nations and other high-income countries; and the developing

declined by only 10 percent. In the earlier preglobalization period of 1960 to 1975 (which included the oil-shock year of 1973), poverty declined by 13 percentage points, from 51 to 38 percent, and this at a time when per capita income increased by 47 percent. According to this view, then, the globalization period witnessed higher growth and a smaller decline in poverty—so there is no chance that globalization has been good for poverty reduction.

The reality is the opposite. Poverty not only declined from 1985 to 2000, but did so at a faster pace than at any time in world history. Using the popular $1-a-day poverty line, the percentage of poor people in the developing world declined by 25 percentage points from 1985 to 2000—from 37.4 to 13.1 percent.[3] From 1960 to 1975, the decline was considerably lower, at 8 percentage points.[4] During the previous 50 years, from 1910 to 1960, the decline was a comparable 22 percent.[5]

Can the World Bank's results on marginal poverty decline during the era of globalization—and especially marginal given the high growth rates in per capita income—be possible? Surely not. Yet the conventional wisdom is so called because it has passed several tests of credibility, and because the facts have been vetted at distinguished forums by international experts. Because prominent economists and other researchers have come to believe that the so-called globalization period of the past 20 years was not good for equality, growth, or poor people, these views have achieved the status of wisdom.[6] In this book, I claim that this "wisdom" is not only wrong, but manifestly so. At this point, the reader may say,

---

world, or poor countries, are those that do not belong to the industrialized world or are not part of the former Soviet Union or in Eastern Europe. Four countries of Central Asia—Kazakhstan, Kyrgyz Republic, Mongolia, and Uzbekistan—are included in the "developing world" classification.

3. The World Bank estimate of 23 percent in 1999 is for a *lower* poverty line of $1.08 a day at purchasing power parity 1993 prices, from survey data; the estimates presented here are for a 39 percent higher poverty line of $1.50 a day, at 1993 prices, from national accounts data for consumption expenditures.

4. It should be emphasized that the closer one gets to the floor of poverty (0 percent), the more effort it takes. In other words, a 10-percentage-point movement from 50 to 40 percent requires considerably less per capita growth than a movement from 20 to 10 percent. See Bhalla (1988) and Asian Development Bank (2002) for the details and further discussion.

5. See Bourguignon and Morrisson (2001, table 1.0).

6. For an extended, and extensive, exposition of the antiglobalization view by a prominent economist and policymaker, see Stiglitz (2002). Some excerpts: "It has become clear not to just ordinary citizens but to policymakers as well, and not just to those in the developing countries but those in developed countries as well, that globalization as it has been practiced has not lived up to what its advocates promised it would accomplish. . . . In some cases it has not even resulted in growth, but when it has, it has not brought benefits to all . . . the net effect of the policies set by the Washington Consensus has all too often been to benefit the few at the expense of many, the well-off at the expense of the poor." (p. 20).

Table 1.1 Some new and different results for poverty, inequality, and growth in the era of globalization, 1980-2000

Topic	Previous results	New results
World poverty (head count ratio)	Level estimated to be 28 percent in 1987, 29 percent in 1990, and 23 percent in 1999	Level estimated to be 44 percent in 1980, 30 percent in 1987, 25 percent in 1990, and 13 percent in 2000
Millennium Development Goals (head count ratio)	Target of half the ratio observed in 1990 or 15 percent head count ratio to be reached by 2015	2015 target of less than 15 percent poor already reached, and exceeded, in 2000
World individual income inequality	Somewhat flat in the 1980s; significant worsening in 1988-1993	Large improvement in individual inequality; by end 2000, world individual inequality was at its lowest level in the post-World War II period
Intracountry inequality	Broadly constant as measured by change in quintile shares or inequality indices like Gini; one study (Cornia-Kiiski 2001), however, finds a significant worsening	Overwhelming evidence that intracountry inequality worsened
Growth (per capita income)		Developing-country average annual growth almost double that experienced by the industrialized world: 3.1 percent versus 1.6 percent
Propoor growth		If poor defined as fraction of population in 1980, then for each 10 percent rise in consumption by the nonpoor, consumption by the poor rose by 18 percent

"Surely, he can't be right." But I just might be. The facts that are presented, analyzed, and interpreted below speak for themselves. (See table 1.1 for a brief summary of some of the different results).

The Issues

Poverty, inequality, and growth are three subjects of major interest to development economists and policymakers in developing countries. These three subjects are studied in different orders by different people, with differing emphases. One's emphasis is perhaps an indicator of research interests, or the results obtained, or, for lack of a better word, ideology. My ordering is growth first, poverty second, and inequality a distant third. Many (including Marx) have it in exactly the reverse order.

But then came globalization, and the threesome became a foursome. What affects what? And did this new force represent good, or evil, especially where the already dismal fortunes of poor people were concerned? This book is about the evolution of policy concerns with respect to the threesome for the period after World War II, from 1950 to 2000, with special emphasis on the role of globalization.

But what is "globalization"? For many, it is an undesirable force; for many others, it is a process that has been good for rich countries and terrible for poor nations. Above all, globalization is a phenomenon, a sequence of events, a pattern of technological progress. In the main, this progress has meant a stupendous decline in transportation costs; a massive reduction in costs of communication; a lowering of production costs;[7] a large increase in intercountry competitiveness; and a breaking down of barriers between countries—barriers of protection, of the flow of knowledge, and of the transfer and absorption of culture. Of major interest to many, and myself, are the consequences of this process. This book is about the economic fallout; the examination of cultural consequences (e.g., the proliferation of McDonalds) is best left to anthropologists and pop psychologists.

But when did globalization happen? Obviously, it is happening continuously, so giving it a precise date is empiricism gone bad, if not mad. For purposes of analysis, however, a "structural" break point is needed, not least because an assessment is needed to measure what happened during the periods before and after globalization. Most researchers time the advent of the new phase of globalization to the 1980s. Two favorite turning points are the beginning of the Uruguay Round of trade talks in 1983, and the fall of the Berlin Wall in June 1989. Another important candidate for dating this worldwide event is Mikhail Gorbachev's perestroika starting in 1984. No matter what criteria are used, the mid-1980s is the "last" date for the advent of globalization. This means that 1980 is a conservative starting point for the new "era of globalization."[8]

However, the following (as quoted in Beck 2000) should temper any exaggerated claims about the newness of globalization:

> [The] exploitation of the world market has given a cosmopolitan character to production and consumption in every country.... All old-established national

---

7. This is why there has been very little world inflation for the past decade and why there will be very little for the next decade or so. As long as there are 1.3 billion Chinese and 1 billion Indians playing catch-up, it is a bit difficult to visualize world inflation.

8. See Rodrik (1997); Friedman (1999); and Clive Crook, "Globalisation and Its Critics," *The Economist*, 2001. These are all excellent, and very different, studies of globalization. Both Rodrik and Friedman correctly point out that globalization is a long, ongoing phenomenon that got interrupted by the Cold War.

industries have been destroyed or are daily being destroyed. They are dislodged by new industries, whose introduction becomes a life and death question for all civilized nations.... In place of the old local and national seclusion and self-sufficiency, we have intercourse in every direction, universal interdependence of nations. And as in material, so also in intellectual production. The intellectual creations of individual nations become common property. National one-sidedness and narrow-mindedness become more and more impossible. (Karl Marx and Friedrich Engels, *Communist Manifesto*, 1848)

The Framework and the Data

Once globalization is situated chronologically, a framework for its analysis naturally suggests itself. The control time period before globalization consists of the years before 1980. It is convenient to use periods of equivalent length, so the years from 1960 to 1980 form a 20-year period when globalization as we know it was *not* present. There is a period of the same length after the advent of globalization, from 1980 to 2000.

With both control and event periods set, one can begin to evaluate the effects of globalization. Among its many different consequences, three types of changes are of major interest: changes in growth rates, changes in inequality, and changes in poverty (the head count ratio of poverty, and the number of poor people). Note that these three types of changes cover practically all areas of interest to an economist, either directly or indirectly. That is why they constitute an all-important triad.

Several pressing questions are explored in the following chapters. Has globalization made the world grow at a faster rate? Has it made rich countries relatively better off? Has inequality in the world worsened during this period? Has poverty been reduced at a faster pace during globalization? If yes, why? If not, is it because the growth rate was lower, or inequality worsened, or both? Who precisely gained from globalization? Was it elites, in both the industrialized and developing worlds? Besides poor people and elites, how did the middle class benefit (or lose) from globalization?

Framing questions is easy. But how can they be answered? By definition, answers to questions involve numbers, and lots of data. At a minimum, consistent data are needed for at least three variables: income, consumption, and population. These data would be easy to find. But data are needed for the 50-year period from 1950 to 2000.[9] Now that is a bit more difficult. And data are needed not only in local currency terms, but also in purchasing power parity (PPP) terms that are equivalent across nations. That is considerably more difficult—but doable. But the availability and

---

9. As is documented in appendix A, the data for the period 1950-60 are not as accurate as the other data. Hence, though most of the important data are for the entire period, 1950-2000, most of the analysis is for the 40-year period 1960-2000.

processing of such data cannot answer any question pertaining to "who benefits"? Is it rich people? Rich people in rich countries? The middle class in rich countries? Elites in the developing world?

For such questions, one needs data on the distribution of income within countries—both at a point in time and, because intertemporal questions are being asked, across time. Now things get very problematical, especially if questions on absolute poverty also need to be answered—for absolute poverty is defined in consumption terms. And what happens if both income and consumption distribution data are not available for the same country, let alone available for the same country at least once during the preglobalization period and once during the globalization period itself?

This is where the work really begins. And this book is the outcome of an extensive research effort. Appendix A documents how, for all the countries of the world, data have been assembled on population, per capita income, per capita consumption (in both PPP and local currency terms), and their distributions (when available) for 1950 to 2000. Although many numbers are presented, the emphasis is always on presenting the big picture of what happened before and after globalization. And the big picture is at some variance with received wisdom.

A Bird's Eye View

This book is organized in three parts: the received findings, methodological considerations (an examination of assumptions, data, and methods), and new results. Part I, chapters 1 through 4, reports (in as detailed a manner as possible) the received wisdom on the triad of growth, inequality, and poverty. Part II begins with chapter 5, a critical summary of the state of knowledge today. The rest of part II, chapters 6 through 8, discusses this knowledge; data and methodological issues pertaining to the analysis of the triad; and the development of a system of analysis, the simple accounting procedure (SAP). Part III, chapters 9 through 13, presents new results based on the SAP methods.

Chapters 6, 7, and 9 explain how it has come about that the two estimates of world poverty—the one in the marketplace and the one estimated using SAP—vary so much, and vary especially during the period for which explicit results of conventional wisdom are available, the 12-year period from 1987 to 1999.[10] Chapter 8 is concerned with the methodological

---

10. Just as the final draft of the book was being readied for publication (the end of April 2002), the World Bank, after an unprecedented gap of 3 years, released preliminary data for world poverty in 1999. (Estimates for 1998 had been released as early as 1999.) These data showed that the stagnation had continued; as a fraction of the population, poverty declined by 1 percentage point in 1999; the number of poor people declined by only 50 million. And this occurred during what is generally acknowledged as a sharp recovery year in developing countries, a year for which the official Government of India estimates of poverty recorded a decline of 160 million. In contrast, the World Bank estimates for 1999

issues of how to estimate the distribution of income from limited data. The chapter explains why detailed distribution data (at the percentile rather than quintile level) are necessary for generating credible estimates of world poverty, inequality, and convergence or divergence and for assessing how the world and poor people have fared during the globalization era.

Part III looks at the same issues, but within an integrated framework made possible through the assembling of a "new" dataset on poverty, inequality, and growth. Methods, assumptions, and definitions are revisited and reexamined. This part presents estimates according to SAP—on inequality, on poverty, on the middle class, on catch-up, and on living standards.

A More Detailed Overview

Chapter 2 discusses the pattern of growth (according to several classifications of countries) during the past 50 years. Chapter 3 assembles the available evidence on inequality, and chapter 4 does the same for poverty. Chapter 5 summarizes the available evidence—data and conclusions that supposedly "prove" that something was markedly wrong with the world during the globalization period. According to this view, growth in developing countries slowed down, inequalities (measured according to several dimensions) increased, and poverty reduction stagnated. Perhaps the antiglobalization forces, from Seattle to Washington to Western Europe, were right all along—capitalism had failed to deliver growth, especially to those most in need of high growth in incomes and improvement in living standards. Perhaps the policies of the Washington Consensus,[11] "forced" on the developing world by such international organizations as the International Monetary Fund and the World Bank, had not proved to be correct.

A new look, with the same (but larger) dataset, is warranted, and this integrated, rigorous methodological framework is described in chapter 8. (Actually, not much is new in this method, as is revealed by its name, again, simple accounting procedure.) The chapter documents the attributes of this dataset and methodology. In particular, it explains why the study of inequality should be conducted at an individual, rather than a country, level. It also explains how the conventionally estimated relationship between poverty reduction and economic growth is heavily flawed. Because correction for this misspecification leads to an estimated elasticity

---

suggest a decline of only 32 million for *all of South Asia*. Thus, all of the book's conclusions pertaining to the questionable nature of the available world poverty estimates remain.

11. See Williamson (1990) for the details on the content of this evocative phrase. There is little discussion of development policy in the world that does not at some point have to explain its differences, or similarity, with the Washington Consensus.

that is often more than *double* what the literature documents, it is not surprising to obtain the conclusion (contrary to chapter 4) that the globalization period witnessed a large reduction in poverty, and not stagnation.

Throughout the book, the evolution of world poverty is the subject of concern—especially in chapters 6, 7, 9, and 10. Chapters 6 and 7 examine the consensus on the triad of issues with both a broad brush and a microscope. Although backed by authoritative research and institutional credibility, the research findings to date on divergence in per capita incomes, inequality change, and stagnation in poverty levels during the high-growth globalization decades do not pass a test of credibility.

Results on Absolute Poverty

Chapter 6 documents how the conventional-wisdom estimates of poverty (provided by the World Bank) are based on recently released PPP exchange rates for consumption for only one year, 1993.[12] The sine qua non of any proper analysis of poverty is that there be an accepted definition of how to convert individual country currencies into a global currency, and that there be an accepted, and constant, poverty line. Neither attribute is present in the results communicated by the World Bank.

This book uses *published* annual estimates of PPP exchange rates, exactly the same definition of poverty (a poverty line equal to a daily income of $1.08), the same data, and the same method (survey distribution and survey means)—in short, an exact replication of the World Bank's methods—to reach the finding that there were 400 million *fewer* poor people in 1999 than what the bank estimated. Thus, there were 766 million poor people, not 1.15 billion (a World Bank estimate based not on official PPP exchange rates but on recently published "consumption" PPP exchange rates). And using this book's data and methods (see chapters 6-9), the head count ratio of poverty, rather than being 23 percent, is shown to be 14 percent in 1999 and 13 percent in 2000. The number of poor people in 2000 is estimated to be 650 million. The 2000 head count number of 13 percent is put in perspective by noting that the famous Millennium Development Goal is to halve poverty by 2015 (compared with the early 1990s), that is, to reach 15 percent.[13]

---

12. This PPP consumption exchange rate has only very recently been published on the World Wide Web (and so far not in the World Bank's *World Development Indicators*), and that also for only 1993. In contrast, the PPP income exchange rates have always been published in *World Development Indicators*, and are available for every year, for every country, after 1960.

13. Regarding social indicators like infant mortality, school completion rates, etc., it is documented (see Asian Development Bank 2002) that it is virtually impossible to reach the targets set for 2015. The reason for this "impossibility" is that such indicators follow a highly decreasing returns profile—e.g., it is much easier to reduce infant mortality from 100 to 50 than it is to decrease it from 50 to 25. What appears to have happened is that the

Chapter 7 discusses the major source of differences in poverty estimates between those of the World Bank after 1990 and those of other researchers (including ones at the World Bank before 1990). (This difference is independent of, and in addition to, the problem of the use of consumption versus official PPP exchange rates mentioned above.) The source pertains to a megamethodological, almost philosophical, difference. There is only one source for distribution data: the national household surveys of income and expenditure. But there are two different sources for data on the *means* of these distributions. The World Bank, since the late 1980s, believes in using only survey data; but before then, the bank believed in using the national accounts system estimates for the means. How great a difference this change in data source makes is revealed by the estimates of global and regional poverty, made in chapter 9 for a 50-year period, 1950-2000.

Results on Propoor Growth

The lower than expected reduction in poverty led to an emphasis on identifying policies that would enhance the poverty reduction yield. The methodological issue is one of isolating the poverty reduction component of a given amount of growth (e.g., if observed growth in incomes is 10 percent, and if this growth is neutral, then how much reduction in the head count ratio should one expect—10 percentage points, less, or more). Chapter 10 offers a method to translate income[14] growth, ceteris paribus, into declines in the head count ratio of poverty.

To date, economists have inferred a "trickle-down elasticity" (i.e., the percentage change in poverty that is expected to occur, given a percentage change in average incomes) from a simple model relating observed change in poverty to observed change in incomes. Typically, this elasticity has been estimated to be between 1.5 and 3, with the most-preferred, central estimate being 2;[15] that is, a 10 percent increase in average income is expected to result in a 20 percent decline in the head count ratio. This might appear large, but it is not; the reason is that the change in poverty is measured as the percentage change in the head count ratio (the percentage of poor people). A decline in the percentage of poor people from 40

---

target setters used simple Club of Rome extrapolations without taking diminishing returns into account.

14. The terms "income" and "consumption" are sometimes used interchangeably, even though calculations on poverty change always pertain to consumption levels. As is well known, a preferred measure of income welfare is revealed by consumption (more related to permanent income, and therefore permanent welfare) rather than by income. For various reasons, discussions of country welfare are always done in terms of changes in income (GDP per capita) rather than consumption (private final consumption expenditure per capita).

15. See Ravallion and Datt (1999), Collier and Dollar (2000), and Kakwani and Pernia (2000).

to 20 percent is a 69 percent (log) change, so such a decline would typically require per capita income to increase by (log) 35 percent.

As was indicated in a report on Malaysia from the World Bank (1991),[16] and further developed in Bhalla (2000b) and Bhalla (2001a), such methods are plagued with statistical and specification errors. The shape of the income distribution, and the incidence of the poverty line (at the tails or in the fat of the curve) relative to the incomes of the poor, are critical parameters in the estimation of the trickle-down elasticity. The correct estimation of this elasticity shows it to be about twice as high as the incorrect estimates of 2 found in the literature. The theoretical correction has, therefore, a very large empirical impact. Once these corrected elasticities are available, it is a relatively simple procedure to forecast poverty levels in 2015, given assumptions about region-specific per capita economic growth.

The world has already achieved the 2015 goal of less than 15 percent poverty; in 2015 itself, only about 10 percent of the developing world is expected to be poor. This forecast is for a poverty line that is almost double the one in use today ($2 a day vs. the $1.08 a day commonly accepted by international agencies).

Has Globalization Worsened Inequality?

Chapter 11 discusses most of the cross-sectional evidence on country inequality. It uses the method outlined in appendix B, which helps to break down five quintile shares of income (data that are most often reported by official household survey agencies) into 100 percentile levels of income.[17] This expansion allows a much more refined construction of global income inequality. Of course, the expansion may contain significant errors.

The chapter provides evidence that the method is exceedingly accurate, however. This evidence is based on comparing the SAP estimate of the Gini coefficient with official published estimates ostensibly based on the entire sample of households (rather than five quintiles) contained in close to 1,000 surveys. The chapter estimates inequality in several regions of the world, as well as the world itself, and concludes that inequality actually decreased in the 1980s and 1990s—and that world inequality today, with a Gini index of 65.1, is at its lowest ever, or at least since 1910.

---

16. This report primarily involved Homi Kharas and myself on the chapters pertaining to poverty and inequality—and the report was the first to document the importance of "where the poverty line is" relative to the distribution of income for obtaining estimates of the effect of growth on poverty reduction. Chapter 10 fleshes out this hypothesis.

17. This procedure is essentially an extension of the method outlined in Kakwani (1980).

Has Globalization Been Good for Poor People?

Chapter 12 presents data on several aspects of development and growth for both the preglobalization era and the past 20 years. Data on educational attainment, infant mortality, monetary poverty, and so on are all aspects of living that show a larger improvement during the globalization period. The chapter discusses the consequences of globalization for convergence, and the consequent effect on global inequality and poverty. It is observed that the forces of globalization have immensely benefited both poor people and elites in developing countries, and have led to a fair amount of convergence—which means that large numbers of individuals from poor countries are now competitive with the middle class (the 30th to the 80th percentiles in the income distribution) in the industrialized world. Hence, it is not surprising that the middle class (e.g., union members) in industrialized countries may be leading the antiglobalization charge.

Chapter 13 concludes that there seems to be little doubt that living standards of poor people have increased during the past 20 years at a pace faster than average living standards; and that globalization has been a force for higher growth and prosperity for most—especially for those in the bottom economic half of the world's population. That this is not conventional wisdom is discussed in terms of methodological roads not taken, and of the forks in the methodological roads that have led to false conclusions.

Research and Monopolies

To date, the generation of poverty estimates has been a monopoly of quasi-governmental organizations, and primarily of the World Bank. This has been a natural monopoly because of the large effort involved in the generation and collection of household data—an effort aided by the reluctance of most governments to release such data to individuals who are not from quasi-governmental organizations. The monopoly has been partly vindicated by the tremendous number of research and policy initiatives that the World Bank has undertaken on the important issues of economic development and poverty alleviation. Former World Bank president Robert McNamara's initiative, and the leadership of economists like Hollis Chenery and Montek Ahluwalia, allowed the bank in the mid-1970s to initiate, sponsor, and fund research on the then-new issue of poverty and inequality.[18] What had been an almost exclusive concern of economists in India became an international obsession: How much poverty is there? How can it best be reduced? And so on. Tomes of (non-

18. At that time, the World Bank was exclusively a project-financing and technical assistance institution.

Indian) research and extensive international policy concern owe a great deal to that first effort.

This monopoly had its predictable effects. There is some evidence that the monopolists got sloppy; that results (on convergence, on poverty, on inequality) that have been disseminated, and accepted, do not pass the test of credibility. The story of the nature of research, of monopoly aspects of funding this research, and so on, is even more involved than the debate on trends in inequality and poverty.[19] Like all monopolies, however, even this one is ending. Until 2 years ago, there was only the World Bank estimate of world poverty. Then, the *first* alternative to the World Bank's estimate of world poverty was presented by Bhalla (2000d), an estimate indicating that there was substantially less poverty in the world than the "official" World Bank figures.[20]

---

19. See Bhalla (2002b) for an exploration.

20. Revised Bhalla estimates are presented in chapter 8.

2

The Pattern of Economic Growth, 1950-2000

Growth is good. Growth makes the world go around. Growth is a many-splendored thing. All you need is growth. Yes, but how do you get it?

Growth is the core of economics. Inequality may be its heart, but growth is its soul. Adam Smith talked about the wealth of nations; differences in wealth brought about by different *rates* of long-run growth. The world is divided into countries, and the preoccupation of every born-again economist, and politician, is how to achieve faster growth for *her* economy. Every country, irrespective of ideological persuasion, has worshiped at the altar of growth.

Growth is therefore the key to the kingdom. It brings about the wealth of nations, it can help bring about justice. Though one might argue about the importance of the nonmaterial things in life, it is clear that without growth on the table, such discussions will remain just that—armchair arguments. And without growth, concerns about poverty and inequality will only become greater concerns. The first concern, therefore, is with what happened to average incomes in different parts of the world during the past half-century, 1950-2000.

But how should levels of living be compared across countries? National accounts data are in local currency, and one needs an exchange rate to compare incomes. The conventional US dollar exchange rate provides one such method of comparing incomes across countries; though useful, this method is deemed incorrect mostly because governments intervene in foreign exchange markets and set exchange rates, and these exchange rates may not reflect comparable purchasing power. Exchange rates set by the "market" can and do go out of whack with distressing regularity.

It is unlikely that East Asia suffered a decline in average levels of living of 50 percent or so within a few months during the 1997 crisis.

Precisely in recognition of this problem, the International Comparison Programme[1] was initiated in the late 1960s by the United Nations and the World Bank. This project yielded a new currency—purchasing power parity or PPP—and several volumes of research. It is the bread and butter of practically every economist interested in cross-country analysis—among research *projects*, this one is *the* Nobel prize. But not everyone thinks the same, including the authors of some UN reports.[2]

For an evaluation of growth, two estimates are possible: growth in local currency terms and growth in PPP dollars. The two need not be identical. Most regions of the world show similar trends according to the two measures for the period 1960-80, and approximately 0.5 percent show *lower* growth for the PPP measure, 1980-2000. Thus, if PPP dollar estimates are used (as they are throughout, because intercountry comparisons of *levels* of living are made), it should be recognized that they are lower-bound estimates of the growth that citizens of the world enjoyed, and especially a lower bound for the second period, also called the globalization period, 1980-2000.

Two major conclusions emerge from the intertemporal comparison of growth rates. First, the world as a whole showed a mild acceleration of 0.15 percent a year in the second period, as the average annual *country* growth rate[3] increased from 2.5 to 2.65 percent. But second, the fruits of this extra growth were not shared equally; in particular, poor countries (also known as the developing world) increased their average growth by a full percent a year, while the industrialized world witnessed a large 1.7 percent decrease in its annual growth rate during the ostensibly pro-industrialized-world period of globalization—from 3.3 to only 1.6 percent a year. These data provide the first hint that the globalization era was a golden era for the average citizen of a poor developing country.

Data and Methods of Estimating Growth

Given the large set of countries for which local currency and PPP data on incomes are available (between 160 and 180 countries), it is useful to summarize the data by regions. Thus, data are presented for several different classifications—the world, industrialized countries, the develop-

---

1. Hence, the original term for purchasing power parity prices was ICP prices or Kravis dollars, named after the project leader, Irving Kravis (see Kravis et al. 1975; Kravis, Heston, and Summers 1982).

2. In the UN *Human Development Report 1999* for the national accounts estimates of purchasing power, the US dollar exchange rate—warts, overvaluation, and all—is preferred.

3. Unless otherwise stated, all levels and growth rates are weighted by population size.

ing world (this includes all countries not part of the industrialized world and not part of Eastern Europe or the former Soviet Union). Data are also reported for regions—Asia, South Asia, East Asia, sub-Saharan Africa, the Middle East and North Africa, Latin America, and so on.

In the interests of full disclosure, results are also reported for the developing world *excluding* India and China. The share in world population of these two countries is almost 39 percent, a level that has stayed constant since 1980. And as a proportion of the developing-world population, these two large countries constitute almost half, or 46 percent. Thus, it does not make much sense to look at the world while excluding India and China, or even worse to look at the developing world excluding India and China.[4] Nevertheless, statistics are reported because justified concern can be with what is happening in the world outside of these two economies—the *other* half of the developing world.

The concern in empirical research is not whether any system, or method, reveals the "truth," but whether it reveals the unknown truth better than any other available estimator. Errors of exaggeration (e.g., output and/or output growth being greater than the unknown reality) or errors of pessimism (e.g., prices or values being lower than the unknown truth) will be present with all estimators. So the choice is not between perfect and imperfect; it is between different approximations.

Two different sources of data provide this approximation, and each source has its advantages. PPP data allow for meaningful comparisons of absolute levels of income for different countries (i.e., the purchasing power of a person in India can be compared with that of a person in the United States). Local currency (national accounts) data allow for a more accurate representation of what happened within a particular country, at a point in time and over time. How comparable are the growth rates according to the two sources? (The levels of income, by definition, are not comparable.)

Table 2.1 presents results for the period 1960 to 2000.[5] Regardless of the region or the period, the local currency (sometimes referred to as system of national accounts, or NA) and PPP growth rates are close to each other for the period 1960-80. The average growth for the world is the same—2.50 percent a year (PPP) versus 2.48 percent a year (local currency). Two of the poorest regions, South Asia and sub-Saharan Africa, show divergence from the constancy pattern between the local currency

---

4. It is important to remember that the two largest regions of the developing world (outside of Asia)—sub-Saharan Africa and Latin America—together have only *half* of the population of China plus India.

5. Though data are available for the period 1950-2000, the first decade is generally ignored in most (but not all) of the data presented. This choice was dictated by data accuracy considerations (for both national accounts and PPP) for the period 1950-59.

Table 2.1 Annualized per capita growth rates according to various measures of GDP

Region[a]	1960-80 period		1980-2000 period	
	1993 PPP[b]	National accounts	1993 PPP[b]	National accounts
East Asia	2.85	2.59	6.12	6.57
South Asia	0.55	1.11	3.00	3.42
Asia	1.98	2.02	4.86	5.29
China and India	1.74	1.84	5.75	6.11
Sub-Saharan Africa	1.29	0.85	−0.58	−0.29
Middle East and North Africa	3.21	2.73	0.15	1.22
Latin America	3.13	3.15	0.08	0.53
Developing world	2.12	2.07	3.11	3.60
Developing world, excluding China and India	2.51	2.33	0.69	1.18
Eastern Europe	4.03	4.04	−1.88	−1.43
Nonindustrialized world	2.32	2.27	2.84	3.33
Industrialized world	3.27	3.34	1.55	2.00
World	**2.50**	**2.48**	**2.65**	**3.12**

PPP = purchasing power parity

a. For the classification of regions, see appendix C.

b. Nominal PPP data, 1993 base, have been converted into constant PPP data, 1993 base, using the US GDP deflator, a practice followed in World Bank, *World Development Indicators*, 1998.

Note: Growth rates are in logarithmic terms. Regional averages are population-weighted means of individual country growth rates.

Sources: World Bank, *World Development Indicators*, CD-ROMs, 1998, 2001; Maddison (2001); Penn World Tables, various years.

and PPP estimates. For the second period, the PPP growth estimates are about 0.5 percent a year lower for almost all the regions.[6]

This relatively close correspondence between PPP and NA should not be surprising because NA estimates of growth are major inputs into the construction of PPP estimates. Therefore, accusations of relatively larger inaccuracy cannot be leveled against PPP estimates without doing the same against the NA estimates. What all this means is that one can proceed with a reasonable degree of confidence with the PPP estimates of both levels, and growth, of income per capita; and that one can use such estimates for both intertemporal and cross-country comparisons. Further, world poverty and world inequality calculations constructed with PPP

---

6. The reasons for the near uniform divergence between PPP and local national accounts estimates for 1980-2000 is beyond the scope of this book. A 0.5 percent annual difference translates into a 10.5 percent difference over 20 years. One explanation is provided by the fact that the US dollar depreciated with respect to PPP dollars by 9 percent from 1980 to 2000.

Table 2.2 GDP of global regions, 1950-2000 (millions of PPP dollars per day)

Region[a]	1950	1960	1980	2000
East Asia	1,120	1,697	5,052	20,473
South Asia	1,019	1,522	2,697	7,369
Asia	2,139	3,219	7,749	27,842
China and India	1,425	2,091	4,146	18,022
Sub-Saharan Africa	537	846	1,907	2,640
Middle East and North Africa	506	924	3,230	5,089
Latin America	1,302	2,105	6,263	9,007
Developing world	4,900	7,773	20,584	45,561
Developing world, excluding China and India	3,475	5,682	16,437	27,539
Eastern Europe	1,896	3,002	7,986	6,591
Nonindustrialized world	6,381	10,097	27,135	51,169
Industrialized world	10,623	16,411	36,192	56,337
World	**17,004**	**26,508**	**63,327**	**107,506**

a. For the classification of regions, see appendix C.

Note: Nominal purchasing power parity (PPP) data, 1993 base, have been converted into constant PPP data, 1993 base, using the US GDP deflator, a practice followed in World Bank, *World Development Indicators*, 1998.

Sources: World Bank, *World Development Indicators*, CD-ROMs, 1998, 2001; Maddison (2001); Penn World Tables, various years.

data are also reliable and indeed are *overestimates* of "true" poverty (measured in local currency) and "true" inequality.

Global Levels of Income and Growth

Tables 2.2, 2.3, and 2.4 (and figures 2.1 and 2.2) present results on global and regional levels of living and growth (all PPP 1993 data). The pattern suggests that considerable progress has been made since 1950. Per capita income in the developing world has gone up almost fourfold (269 percent, or by a factor equal to 3.69), and the industrialized world has lagged behind by about 40 percentage points. The time pattern, though, is quite different. The golden age for the industrialized world was in the *preglobalization* phase, with developing economies more than catching up in the past 20 years. In the 1980s and 1990s, per capita growth in developing countries was double the rate experienced by the industrialized world (3.11 vs. 1.55 percent; table 2.1). The net effect of the favorable impact of globalization on the fortunes of the developing world can also be gauged from the following statistic: In 1980, the mean incomes in developing economies were 12.6 percent of those of the industrialized world; in 2000, these relative incomes had increased to 14.0 percent.

Table 2.3 Population of global regions, 1950-2000 (millions)

Region[a]	1950	1960	1980	2000
East Asia	958	942	1,422	1,894
South Asia	471	562	903	1,355
Asia	1,430	1,503	2,325	3,250
China and India	1,107	1,102	1,669	2,284
Sub-Saharan Africa	177	223	381	662
Middle East and North Africa	102	132	227	375
Latin America	166	218	362	519
Developing world	1,942	2,159	3,408	4,937
Developing world, excluding China and India	835	1,057	1,739	2,653
Eastern Europe	276	315	385	414
Nonindustrialized world	2,150	2,392	3,679	5,219
Industrialized world	545	630	752	852
World	**2,695**	**3,022**	**4,321**	**6,071**

a. For the classification of regions, see appendix C.

Sources: World Bank, *World Development Indicators*, CD-ROMs, 1998, 2001; Maddison (2001); Penn World Tables, various years.

Table 2.4 Per capita daily income of global regions, 1950-2000 (dollars per day)

Region[a]	1950	1960	1980	2000
East Asia	1.17	1.80	3.55	10.81
South Asia	2.16	2.71	2.99	5.44
Asia	1.50	2.14	3.33	8.57
China and India	1.29	1.90	2.48	7.89
Sub-Saharan Africa	3.03	3.79	5.01	3.99
Middle East and North Africa	4.96	7.00	14.23	13.57
Latin America	7.84	9.66	17.30	17.35
Developing world	2.52	3.60	6.04	9.23
Developing world, excluding China and India	4.16	5.38	9.45	10.38
Eastern Europe	6.87	9.53	20.74	15.92
Nonindustrialized world	2.97	4.22	7.38	9.80
Industrialized world	19.49	26.05	48.13	66.12
World	**6.31**	**8.77**	**14.29**	**17.71**

a. For the classification of regions, see appendix C.

Note: Income is in 1993 purchasing power parity (PPP) dollars. Nominal PPP data, 1993 base, have been converted into constant PPP data, 1993 base, using the US GDP deflator, a practice followed in World Bank, *World Development Indicators*, 1998.

Sources: World Bank, *World Development Indicators*, CD-ROMs, 1998, 2001; Maddison (2001); Penn World Tables, various years.

Figure 2.1 Average per capita daily incomes of global regions, 1960, 1980, and 2000 (1993 purchasing power parity dollars)

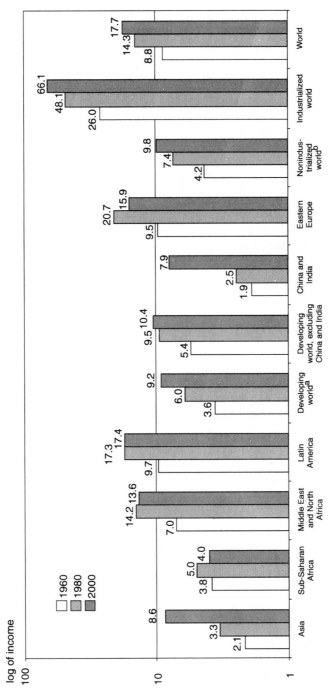

a. The developing world is the world excluding the industrialized world and Eastern Europe.

b. The nonindustrialized world is the world excluding the developed industrialized world.

Note: For the classification of regions, see appendix C. The bars represent logs of average incomes; the numbers above each bar indicate the average per capita per day income in that region in 1993 purchasing power parity dollars.

Sources: World Bank, *World Development Indicators*, CD-ROMs, 1998, 2001; Maddison (2001); Penn World Tables, various years.

Figure 2.2 Annual per capita income growth before and during the globalization era (percent)

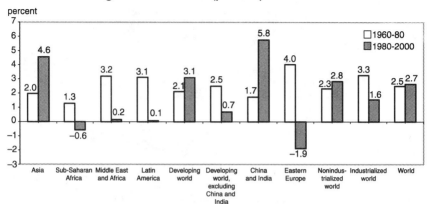

a. The developing world is the world excluding the industrialized world and Eastern Europe.

b. The nonindustrialized world is the world excluding the developed (industrialized) world.

Note: For the classification of regions, see appendix C. The "globalization era" is defined as 1980-2000, and the "preglobalization" period as 1960-80. Period growth rates are logarithmic terms. Regional averages are population-weighted means of individual country growth rates.

Sources: World Bank, *World Development Indicators*, CD-ROMs, 1998, 2001; Maddison (2001); Penn World Tables, various years.

That China and India are important players in the developing-world growth sweepstakes is not surprising—excluding them for 1980-2000 reduces the average growth rates by 2.4 percentage points to a rate of only 0.7 percent a year. For Eastern Europe, the globalization period was one of hard adjustment; per capita income levels today are less than three-fourths of the levels prevailing in the mid-1980s. However, some countries have actually benefited from the radical change in their economies—the Czech Republic, Hungary, and Poland, to name a few. This is on the economic side; all of Eastern Europe has benefited enormously in political freedom.

There is considerable diversity in development. It is interesting to go back to the 1960 levels of income. That was the time of the "Asian Drama." Economists were pessimistic on this the poorest region in the world—yes, poorer than even sub-Saharan Africa, and poorer by a wide margin; the average African had twice the income of the average Asian in 1960. Globalization has been extraordinarily good to Asians. The average Asian's income has grown fourfold (this is not in nominal PPP dollars!) since 1960, an annual increase of 3.7 percent per capita. The inhabitant of the industrialized world could only increase her income by 2.3 percent a year.

These "simple" calculations do not even hint at the suggestion that globalization has been bad for poor people; the poor Asian's rate of growth of income was 4.9 percent during the period 1980-2000, a rate of annual growth approximately two and a half times the preglobalization average of 2.0 percent a year. Today, Asians make up half of the world's population, and more than two-thirds of the population of the developing world.

The other third of the developing world was not so lucky with globalization. The globalization period was not good for either Latin America or Africa. After almost doubling per capita income from 1960 to 1980, Latin American economies barely maintained their 1980 levels, and that too over a 20-year period. Africa did worse, as its per capita incomes declined by 12 percent during the past two decades.

In 1960, the average Asian had an income equal to half that of an African, and one-fifth of a Latin American. In 2000, the Asian had incomes almost double that of an African. The incorporation of the Asian experience lends credence to the "conditional convergence" hypothesis, a hypothesis according to which "poor" countries grow at a faster rate than "rich" economies (e.g., an Asian economy grows at a faster rate than an African economy, because it was substantially poorer at the "beginning" in 1960). But that should mean that an African economy should grow faster than a Latin American economy—clearly something that did not happen. But that is because the hypothesis pertains to ceteris paribus conditions, and what is being stated is a mutatis mutandis phenomenon!

Thus, there are several "mixed" answers to the single question of what has happened to developing-world economies during the past 40 years. Nor do the answers get simpler if the examination is done on the basis of two 20-year periods. A mixed conclusion is the correct conclusion. The average country showed a mild acceleration (0.15 percent a year) in the era of globalization, but the pattern of this increase was mixed. Further, the developing-world growth rate exceeded that of rich nations by an average of 1.6 percent a year, in contrast to a deficit annual growth rate of 1.1 percent in the 1970s and 1980s. The positive swing with globalization was therefore a large 2.7 percent a year during the period 1980-2000.

What seems clear, therefore, is that the period of globalization was associated with a *relative* improvement in the living standards of poor countries. It is likely, therefore, that the poor also benefited in considerable measure from this extra growth. However, the differing pattern of this growth in various countries, and the different inequality experiences within poor countries, make it impossible to state with any precision what happened to poor *individuals* in poor *countries*.

Globalization: Divergence

In striking contrast to the above result, several "divergence" studies have concluded, with little ambiguity, that things have worsened for the poor economies of the world and, by extension, for the poor people of the world.

The conventional wisdom at present is that global income inequality has worsened during the past decade or two; this deterioration is a reversal of the previous presumed trend toward equality; and this reversal is causally related to globalization. The punch line of this new wisdom is that divergence runs counter to the expectation of the natural, normal "capitalist" trend of growth and development—that is, runs counter to the expectation of convergence.

The most popular version of the convergence hypothesis states that poor nations will have a *natural* tendency to steadily *approach* the income levels of industrialized countries; this "approach" implies a higher growth rate. Why? Because eventually—in a world with the free movement of goods, capital, and labor—factor prices (and hence wages, and hence income levels) will have to equalize. The only way this can happen is for nations with lower productivity to grow at a faster rate for consistently long periods of time (i.e., catch-up). And if catch-up is a natural phenomenon, then poor nations will grow at a higher rate, and the world will have a tendency to become more equal.

This central idea of convergence deserves emphasis. Growth theory (both new and old) tells us that countries with lower technology and incomes will, via openness and sharing of the same global technology, grow at a faster rate than rich economies; that is, their productivity growth will be higher, often considerably more than that experienced by the "frontier" industrialized economies (e.g., the United States). The assertion that globalization *should* lead to greater global income equality is therefore admitted to by most Washington Consensus economists.

This conclusion holds when world income is defined as the incomes of individuals (and households) in the world. Lack of data on these individual incomes has forced researchers to couch their convergence tests in terms of the only unit of observation that is easily available, namely a country. And if average growth rates of countries are not weighted by population (as they should be), "odd" results are easily obtained.

Baumol, Nelson, and Wolff (1994), in one of the first detailed analyses on the subject, conclude thus about what one should expect from a converging world:

> Thus, convergence, in one or another of its senses, is surely a key matter for our evaluation of the world economy's well-being. A world of convergence is in a felicitous state, with poverty eroding and international disparities declining. If not offset by detrimental developments of other sorts, it is a desirable condition and a state of affairs in which one of the most intractable of economic problems, inequality among countries in the distribution of income, is improving. (p. 5)

Baumol and his colleagues, being experts on the subject, are not ambiguous; and their forecast is that globalization will lead to a decline in international inequality, and a faster decline in poverty.

But the fear of several people (some of them perhaps unfairly called antiglobalizers) is that there is an increase in world inequality, and perhaps even an increase in absolute poverty. At best, it is feared that the decline in absolute poverty is not commensurate with the increase in per capita incomes that the developing world has experienced. As is suggested by table 2.4, the developing world experienced an increase of 53 percent in per capita incomes during the 1980-2000 period. For the 1987-99 period, this increase is 30 percent. But according to World Bank figures, absolute poverty declined by only 5 to 6 percentage points during these 12 years. And according to Milanovic (1999), world inequality increased between 1988 and 1993. So what happened to convergence?

There are very few people who argue that the industrialized world is getting richer and that the developing world is getting absolutely poorer. Whether world inequality has increased or decreased is the concern of a major part of this book; this chapter will discuss some indirect evidence on the subject, with the idea of assessing what our a priori assumptions should be, given what we know or intuitively feel about world growth and globalization and world inequality. In other words, the assessment (for now) will be at an intuitive level, rather than at a relatively intractable level of inequality among the citizens of the world and the trends in this inequality (questions to which some answers are given in the next two chapters).

Evidence of Convergence or Divergence

Although the evidence on levels of average income suggested a confusing picture (some poor nations grew fast, some showed a decline in real incomes), other sets of evidence point to a consistent divergence interpretation of the experience of the past 50 years. This evidence, popularized by Pritchett (1997, 2001), consists of looking at *relative* incomes of the richest and poorest countries at different points in time. Using data on per capita incomes for several countries, he documents the reality of not only no convergence but of divergence, and divergence that he claims has most likely increased:

> First, divergence in output per person across countries is perhaps *the* dominant feature of modern economic history. The ratio of per capita income in the richest versus the poorest country has increased by a factor of 6 and the standard deviation of (natural log) GDP per capita has increased between 60 percent and 100 percent. The increasingly sophisticated econometric testing of conditional convergence with the thirty or so years of conveniently available, internationally comparable data should not obscure that fact. (Pritchett 2001, 3)

Because of its elegant simplicity, this procedure has found many followers and deserves to be examined in a serious fashion. The Pritchett method and data are summarized in figure 2.3. If the United States is taken as a "representative" rich economy, if not the richest, then the trend in the ratio between its per capita income and that prevailing in a poor economy is indicative of convergence, or its lack.[7] The statistics on divergence are frightening. If the poorest economy is taken as a reference, then an average American was about 50 times richer in 1950 and 1960; today, she is more than 70 times as rich. If instead of the poorest country the 10th-poorest country is taken as reference (a crude attempt to remove outliers) the American is less relatively rich, but still becoming richer. Indeed, by this yardstick, a greater trend in divergence is observed—the ratio was about 23 in 1960, and today, at 45, is almost double that relative level.

There clearly is a problem with the comparison between the richest and poorest countries. Consequently, *World Development Report 2000/2001: Attacking Poverty* advocates a comparison between the richest 20 countries and the poorest 20 countries. No matter—the divergence story still holds. The ratio for the richest to poorest 20 countries increases from 23 in 1960 to 36 in 2000. However, if the calculation is done on the *same* set of countries as constituted the poorest and the richest in 1960 (keeping the sample constant in statistician's terms, or comparing apples to apples), a radically opposite result is observed. Instead of divergence, there is sharp convergence. The ratio of richest to poorest declines markedly between 1960 and 2000—from 23 to 9.5 (i.e., the rich-country inhabitant is less than half as relatively rich in 2000 as she was in 1960).[8] This is not divergence (figure 2.4).

But if this last piece of evidence is ignored (we will come back to it in chapters 11 and 12) then these numbers document in simple terms the kind of divergence that has taken place. A 50 percent increase in relative incomes over 20 years implies an excess growth rate of 2 percent *each year*; that is, the industrialized-world resident had an (average) extra growth of this amount for each of the past 20 years.[9] It will not be an understatement to state that this statistic (relative income of an American with that of the poorest or poor country) has caught the imagination of several researchers, especially those at think tanks and international organizations.

This imagination and reasoning were echoed by the United Nations *Human Development Report 1999* (p. 3):

---

7. This automatically follows from the fact that the level of income at any point in time is a function of growth from a prior given initial level of income.

8. Clearly it matters for this calculation whether large countries like China and India are among the 20 (China is; India is not). That is precisely the problem with the (mis)calculation of convergence/divergence. The correct calculation has to be for a constant *fraction* of people, something attempted in the second half of this book.

9. But the data given in table 2.1 suggest just the opposite, i.e., that the developing-world resident had an excess annual growth rate of 1.7 percent!

Figure 2.3 Ratios of mean income of the United States and of the poorest country

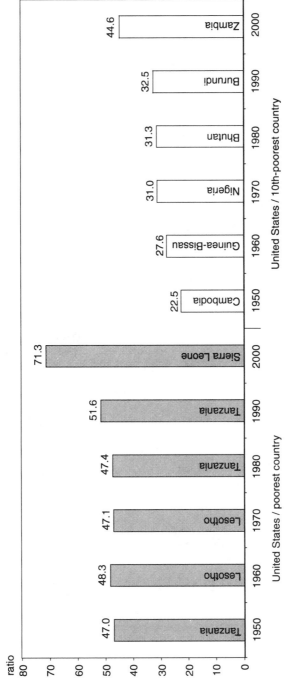

Note: Mean incomes are in constant purchasing power parity (PPP) dollars, 1993 base. The poorest and 10th-poorest countries were chosen on the basis of per capita income, 1993 PPP, for the selected years.

Sources: World Bank, *World Development Indicators*, CD-ROMs, 1998, 2001; Maddison (2001); Penn World Tables, various years.

Figure 2.4 Convergence or divergence? It depends

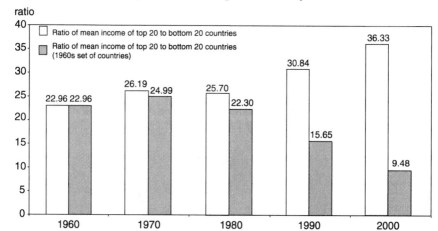

Note: For each year, the unshaded bar represents the income ratio of the mean-to-20 poorest countries in that year; the shaded bar represents the constant set of 20 richest and poorest countries in 1960.

Sources: World Bank, *World Development Indicators*, CD-ROMs, 1998, 2001; Maddison (2001); Penn World Tables, various years.

> Inequality between countries has also increased. The income gap between the fifth of the world's people living in the richest countries and the fifth in the poorest was 74 to 1 in 1997, up from 60 to 1 in 1990 and 30 to 1 in 1960. In the nineteenth century, too, inequality grew rapidly during the last three decades, in an era of rapid global integration: the income gap between the top and bottom countries increased from 3 to 1 in 1820 to 7 to 1 in 1870 and 11 to 1 in 1913.

And they were echoed by the International Monetary Fund (IMF 2000, 2):

> The gaps between rich and poor countries, and rich and poor people within countries, have grown. The richest quarter of the world's population saw its per capita GDP increase nearly six-fold during the century, while the poorest quarter experienced less than a three-fold increase. Income inequality has clearly increased.

And further echoed by Stewart (2000, 27):

> The impact of globalization seems to have been unequalizing between nations as well as within them.

And also echoed by the World Bank in *World Development Report 2000/2001*:

> The average income in the richest 20 countries is 37 times the average in the poorest 20—a gap that has doubled in the past 40 years. (p. 3)

On page 51 of *World Development Report 2000/2001*, two contradictory statements about trends in world individual inequality are made. First:

"Available estimates indicate that there have been some *increases in worldwide inequality between individuals* in past decade." (emphasis added). Second, a paragraph or two earlier, an equally definitive statement is made: "Trends in worldwide inequality between individuals reflect trends in both inequality between countries and inequality within countries. . . . In China for example, rapid growth from a very low base has helped a fifth of the world's population halve the gap in average per capita incomes with the world as a whole, significantly *reducing worldwide inequality between individuals*" (emphasis added).

Divergence stated differently, but equivalently, means an increase in inequality. Data on divergence per se cannot indicate whether poor people are getting poorer in absolute terms. For that to be determined, data on both the distribution and level of income are needed, an exercise reported in chapter 11. For the moment, it is important to note that the data marshaled by various experts, *all* the quasi-governmental organizations, and several academics are strongly suggestive of divergence. Although the average developing-world resident experienced a faster growth than her rich-country counterpart (as predicted by the theory of convergence), it is suggested that this may not have been the experience of the poorer residents of the developing world.

It is suggested that an increase in inequality was a concomitant of this faster growth. So the globalization period probably was associated with an increase in the size of the pie (something good) but a worsening in the shares that accrue to different sets of people (possibly a bad outcome). And if distribution worsened enough, then the case of the poor being absolutely worse off, despite growth in average incomes, is no longer theoretical.

Given this overwhelming "evidence" for divergence, it is not surprising to note that the concern should be shifted from one of poor people getting rich at a slower pace (the strict implication of divergence) to poor people getting poorer in absolute terms. One antiglobalization leader said this just before the World Trade Organization meeting at Doha in November 2001. When asked about why demonstrations were being planned, she stated, and I paraphrase: "Globalization leads to the North getting richer, and the South getting poorer. . . . This is a direct consequence of globalization, and we need to stop this from continuing."

3

Inequality as We Know It

Inequality is a subject of inquiry for every brand of social scientist—philosophers, economists, sociologists, psychiatrists, and even politicians. It is unclear what the net value added of all the opinion is. On one related issue, however, there is agreement: What is most important, both in moral and in practical terms, is that *equality of opportunity* is a goal worthy of pursuit.

The dichotomy, both conceptually and for policy, between concern with inequality and concern with equality of opportunity is stark and obvious. There is very little one can, or should do, with either inequality or trends in inequality.[1] The reason one should do little is partly on practical grounds; moralists have devised ingenious ways to tax the rich so that inequality is altered, and ingeniously have the wealthy avoided taxation (including bribery, of course). The other objection is philosophical: Reducing inequality implies knowledge of a preferred inequality *level* and a preferred dynamic path. This may seem laughable now, but the popularity of central planning and loco parentis (the state knows better) in the 1960s, 1970s, and 1980s was due to the presumed power of the state to achieve whatever goal it desired. This brings us back to the original problem: if one wanted to change inequality levels, and inequality trends, what policies would one implement? What confidence would one have in the goals? And do the unequal even care?

The concern with inequality is not new; indeed, it has commanded the attention of social scientists for several centuries. Philosopher Immanuel

---

1. Although facts are stressed throughout this book, this is much more in the nature of opinion.

Kant (as quoted in Dahrendorf 1968) called "inequality among men a rich source of much that is evil, but also of everything that is good." But the sociologist Dahrendorf admits to failure in making any progress in doing anything about inequality:

> So far, however, as far as the problem of inequality itself is concerned, this history [of sociological research] has achieved little more than given it a different name: what was called in the eighteenth century the origin of inequality and in the nineteenth the formation of classes, we describe today as the theory of social stratification—all this even though the original problem has not changed and no satisfactory solution to it has been found. (1968, 152)

Over the years, several prominent economists (e.g., Adam Smith, Friedrich von Hayek) have agreed with the observation that there is no easy solution to be found; indeed, given its confusing complexity, perhaps no solution need be found. Marx thought he had found the solution: perfect equality. History has judged that notion to be extremely problematical, and thrown out the sage, along with his followers. Nowadays, economists generally tend to be more concerned with the growth in the pie than in its distribution; for many of them, the economics of inequality per se is not much different from the "economics of envy."

Rawls (1958), in his classic essay "Justice as Fairness" (later published in an expanded form as *A Theory of Justice*, 1971), outlined the *maximin* principle of justice (and equality). This principle argued that the concept of justice dictated that policies that improved the position of the least advantaged member of society should be preferred over all others. (Obviously, it would follow that among competing policies, those that improved the lot of the least advantaged more would be preferred.) In 1971, I criticized this principle on the grounds that it ignored the role of inequality, and inequality trends, in a person's utility function, something that was likely to be prominent among the citizens of industrialized economies (Bhalla 1971).

At a minimum, therefore, it is a moot question whether inequality per se, at the world or country level, is important. No doubt it is important for politicians because populism is almost exclusively based on the economics of envy. But is it important for policy? Do poor people really care about inequality or do they care more, much more, about absolute standards of living? Very likely, concern for inequality is a highly income-elastic superior good—the more one becomes richer, the more one is (naturally) concerned with the Joneses and the Veblins who have more.

The fact remains that inequality, and its study, remains an intellectually fascinating and emotive issue. One of the most profound insights into what actually happens to inequality within a society was provided by Simon Kuznets in the mid-1950s. In one of the most justifiably celebrated articles, Kuznets postulated that inequality charts out an inverted U-curve with development; that is, as economies develop, inequality first increases (the left leg of the inverted U) and then declines. Research over the years, which is documented extensively in this chapter, supports this result. However, it should be emphasized that the Kuznets inverted U-curve applies to what happens *within* countries over time; what happens to inequality among the collection of individuals in the world, over time, is quite another story. Indeed, it is theoretically possible (and empirically true!) that each country can experience a worsening of inequality and yet overall improving inequality—a possibility, and finding, missed by most research to date.

Measuring Inequality

This chapter discusses issues relating to the measurement of inequality, and it introduces such concepts as the Lorenz curve and the inequality Gini index. After measurement is out of the way, the chapter goes on to discuss perhaps the most important development in the study of the economics of inequality during the past 50 years—the Kuznets inverted U-curve, which relates the path of inequality to the path of development.

This inverted U-curve can be tested in a variety of ways. The chapter reviews the results of the various tests and reaches a threefold conclusion: During short periods of time (a decade or so), inequality does have a tendency to worsen. During long periods, it appears that the level of inequality on the right side of the inverted U is approximately equal to that on the left. And data for the past 20 years indicate that, on average, country inequality has definitely worsened.

The study of income distribution is a study of shares in the pie—who has what amount. The best-known of the descriptions of the pattern of income distribution is the Lorenz curve: If the population is ordered according to income, the Lorenz curve plots the cumulative share in income (*y*-axis) versus the cumulative share in the population (*x*-axis).

By definition, therefore, the Lorenz curve starts at zero and ends at unity (figure 3.1 plots such a curve for three different years—1960, 1980, and 2000). If incomes are equally distributed, then the Lorenz curve is described by the diagonal (i.e., the share of income at each point is equal to the share of population). If all the income in society accrued to just one person, then the Lorenz curve would be the zero line (A to B) and then at the end the share would "spike" up to 1 (B to C). The Gini coefficient[2] is equal to 1 in the latter case (perfect inequality) and 0 in the former (perfect equality). For the curve shown in the figure (world distribution in 2000), the Gini coefficient is 0.651 (or 65.1).

---

2. The Gini coefficient is the "area between the Lorenz curve and the diagonal, relative to the whole triangle below the diagonal, or half the mean difference relative to the mean" (Atkinson and Brandolini 1999, 6).

Figure 3.1 World Lorenz curve, 1960, 1980, and 2000

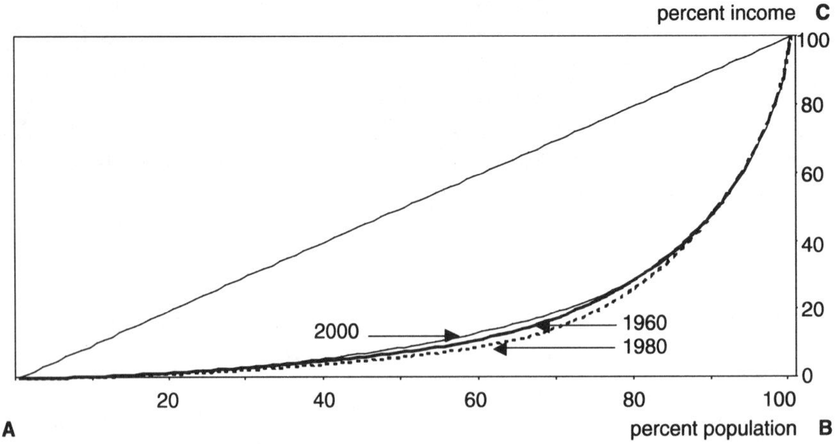

Note: World income inequality is computed by the simple accounting procedure (SAP) method of aggregating individual country data on distributions of incomes into a world distribution of individuals; see chapter 11 for the details.

Sources: Deininger and Squire (1996); World Income Inequality Database, available at http://www.wider.unu.edu/wiid; Asian Development Bank (2002); Milanovic and Yitzhaki (2001).

Measuring Intertemporal Inequality

Along with the Gini, researchers have used other definitions of inequality—the share in incomes of a particular quintile (e.g., the bottom 20 percent) or the ratio in incomes of different groups (e.g., the ratio in incomes of the top vs. the bottom decile). This logic has even been extended to the study of incomes of the richest country relative to the poorest country, as we saw in the previous chapter. Decile or quintile shares are descriptions or summary statistics for different *parts* of the Lorenz curve.

The trends in these components can be used to reveal whether the incomes of a particular quintile are growing at a faster or slower rate than the average. A faster rate implies that the *share* of that group in total income is increasing, a slower rate that the *share* is decreasing. This is definitional and studies of inequality that look at changes in shares are *equivalent* to studies of inequality that look at relative rates of growth in incomes. In economic terms, the much talked about *unitary* elasticity of incomes of poor people with respect to average income ("elasticity of connection," according to Timmer 1997) is the same as a *zero* elasticity of the share of income with respect to income growth.

Simple Inequality Mathematics

Country data are often presented in the form of quintile and mean incomes. Knowledge of the mean income at each point in time allows one to compute absolute levels, and changes. The *absolute* income at any point in time is revealed by a simple formula:

$$(U*N)/(Y*100) = X \qquad (3.1)$$

where N represents the number of percentiles, U the mean income of these percentiles, Y the mean income of the population, and X the share in income of U percentiles. (A population has 100 percentiles, and each quintile has 20.)

For an N with a value of 20, or the bottom 20 percent, the equation becomes

$$U*20 = X*Y*100, \text{ or}$$
$$U = (100/N)*X*Y$$
$$U = k*X*Y \qquad (3.2)$$

In log terms, the equation becomes

$$\log(U) = \log(k) + \log(X) + \log(Y)$$

In (log) rate-of-growth terms, the above equation reduces to

$$u = y + x \qquad (3.3)$$

where lowercase u represents the rate of growth in incomes for a particular quintile (or decile or percentile), y is the rate of growth in average income of the population, and x is the growth in share in income of this particular classification (decile, percentile, etc.). Equation 3.3 is important to appreciate because it underpins a considerable part of the simple accounting that is needed to talk about inequality changes. The equation is an identity—it must hold, and no assumptions are required.

The simple computations involved in equation 3.3 allow one to interpret, at a glance, whether the incomes of the poorest quintile have grown at a faster (increase in share) or slower (decrease in share) rate than the richest quintile or the middle quintile, or whatever. Note that the coefficients of both y and x are unity. In other words, *if there is no change in inequality (shares are constant, or* x *is zero) then the rate of growth of incomes in the particular quintile is equal to the growth in average incomes.*

Data for China can be used to illustrate the ease, and power, of equation 3.3. In 1985, the share of the bottom quintile was 7.7 percent, which declined to 5.6 percent in 1995. This decline is a (log) change of -16.4 percent. The average per capita income during the same period rose from purchasing power parity (PPP) $1.95 (at 1993 prices) to PPP $3.62, or a 61.8 percent (log) increase. According to equation 3.3, the change in income of the first quintile, u, is equal to the change in average income (variable y), plus the change in inequality (variable x). The value of y is 61.8; that of x is -16.4. Hence, the increase in income of the first quintile is equal to $61.8 + (-16.4)$, or 45.4 percent.

Armed with this simple inequality mathematics, one can begin to analyze various relationships. The decline in share of income of the first quintile is analogous (equivalent) to lower relative growth (45.4 vs. 61.8 percent); this decline is also analogous (equivalent) to the elasticity of incomes of the group (defined as poor people or the first quintile) being lower than 1; in this case, the elasticity is equal to 0.73 (relative growth rates, or 45.4 divided by 61.8). Because the growth in incomes of poor people was lower than average growth, we can state with some basis that growth was antipoor; in other words, the term "propoor growth" is nothing more than a restatement of the fact that the incomes of poor people rose at a lower rate than average income.[3]

Inequality: Kuznets Curve and Data Requirements

On the basis of the data available, Kuznets observed that rich economies displayed lower inequality than poor countries. If this observation is combined with assumptions about rural-to-urban transformation—with the smaller urban sector growing faster (due to industrialization) than the larger rural sector[4]—one would logically observe inequality increasing, and upon "maturation" of the economy, observe decreasing inequality. Hence, the inverted U-shaped pattern.

When Kuznets posited his hypothesis about income distribution worsening with development, he had very little data on income inequality in developing countries—countries for which his hypothesis had relevance. As a part of its drive to study inequality and poverty in detail, the World Bank launched its Redistribution with Growth project in the mid-1970s. This project consisted of compiling existing data, analyzing these data (among the earliest efforts in this regard are the pioneering papers by Ahluwalia and Chenery and their associates: Ahluwalia 1974, 1976; Ahluwalia, Carter, and Chenery 1979), and encouraging, financially and otherwise, developing countries to conduct household surveys. The dataset used by Ahluwalia (1976) was published in a book by Jain (1975). This

---

3. Actually, as we will see in chapter 10, the correct derivation of whether growth has been propoor or not is more, much more, than observing this simple relationship. Indeed, the elegance and the "obviousness" of the simple relationship has prevented researchers from correctly identifying whether a particular process of growth was propoor or not.

4. This pattern of growth has also been argued by Lewis (1954); an elegant mathematical formulation, and simulation, of the inverted U-curve hypothesis is contained in Robinson (1976).

compilation of data, warts and all, was to be a major input for the analysis, and debate, over poverty, inequality, and growth. This dataset had expanded the earlier collection by Adelman and Morris (1973) and Paukert (1973).

Ahluwalia put the Jain inequality data through several tests and concluded thus:

> There is strong support for the proposition that relative inequality increases substantially in the early stages of development, with a reversal of this tendency in the later stages. This proposition holds whether we restrict the sample to developing countries or expand it to include developed and socialist countries. Furthermore, it appears that the process is most prolonged for the poorest group ... the cross section results do not support the stronger hypothesis that the deterioration in relative inequality reflects a prolonged absolute impoverishment of large sections of the population in the course of development. The cross country pattern shows average absolute incomes of the lower percentile groups rising as per capita GNP rises, although slower than for upper income groups. (1976, 338)

Ahluwalia's paper was the first extensive study of inequality and development. This seminal effort set off a flurry of research, in both data collection and replication. The conclusions also appear to have stood the test of time, though some not as strongly as first identified. The "prolonged" experience, when it has occurred, has not necessarily been particular to the poorest group; and the lower percentile groups have not necessarily had a lower elasticity of growth, as Ahluwalia's own concurrent research (1974) had shown.

It is important to note what this important cross-sectional result (the inverted U-curve) does and does not indicate. It does not indicate that worsening inequality will happen. It does indicate that developing countries (at lower levels of income or development) were *observed* to have lower shares in income of the first quintile. If it is now assumed that developing countries would follow, *over time*, the pattern of income shares observed at *a point in time*, then and only then can one conclude that the Kuznets curve is predictive.[5]

The Ahluwalia data, and results, were subjected to intense scrutiny and analysis by Anand and Kanbur (1993a, 1993b), who demonstrated that data inaccuracies and misspecifications (e.g., mixing household data with individual data, and consumption surveys with income surveys) may have had a considerable effect on the finding of the inverted-U-curve result. Further, if these data were corrected for such measurement mistakes, instead of an inverted U-curve, a normally shaped U-curve was found; that is, developing countries tended first to show a decline in

---

5. The brilliance of Kuznets's insight is underlined by the fact that his observation about the inverted U was based on very limited data. Starting with Ahluwalia (1976), there have been scores of important studies on the Kuznets curve. The conclusion 40 years later and with tons of new data is that it is one of the most remarkably accurate "forecasts" in economics.

inequality before a subsequent increase. Anand and Kanbur were silent on what could be generating this anomalous finding, because the theory about inequality first worsening due to the rural urban transformation seemed to be intuitive and plausible.

The increased availability of distribution data also led to an analysis of "spells" of experience (i.e., noting what happened to inequality and levels of development for the *same* country over time).[6] The conclusions of these studies were mixed, but they broadly supported the proposition that inequality stayed relatively constant, within a country, over time (i.e., they rejected the Kuznets curve).

Thus, by the early 1990s, the received wisdom on country inequality and changes therein was that inequality levels in developing countries had stayed relatively constant; some countries had improved, others had deteriorated, but there was no major story either way. Anand and Kanbur's conclusions, while technically correct, were more in the nature of a statistical, not economic, result. The reality was of a moderately Kuznetsian variety. Further, whereas data availability and documentation had improved considerably since the mid-1970s, there was still a relative paucity of data for some of the poorest countries in the world, especially those in sub-Saharan Africa.[7]

There are three other stylized facts pertaining to income distribution. First, consumption distributions tend to be more equally distributed than do income distributions, often by about 10 to 15 percent. This result can be verified by observing the data for the same country for the same point in time. Both Berry, Bourguignon, and Morrisson (1981) and Deininger and Squire (1996) suggest that the consumption Gini is about 6 points lower than the income Gini—a result also corroborated by our data. Second, after-tax distributions tend to be more equal than before-tax distributions. Third, inequality appears to be region specific. The industrialized world and Asia show low levels of inequality, and sub-Saharan Africa and Latin America show very high (almost "double" the Gini level of Asia) levels of inequality.

Recent Evidence on Country Inequality

For the study of trends in inequality, researchers have used essentially two different methods—either a study of the change in shares of income of different quintiles (and/or changes in the Gini), or the analysis of the elasticity of the mean income of a particular income group (e.g., the first

---

6. See Fields (1980); World Bank, *World Development Report 1990: Poverty and Development*.

7. E.g., by the end of the 1970s, results for only three sub-Saharan African economies were available, compared with more than 16 surveys for the five major countries in South Asia.

quintile) with respect to average income in the economy. As was discussed in the context of the equations above, the two yield identical results: a zero change in shares is equivalent to a unitary elasticity of quintile income.

Underlying all of this analysis is the Kuznets framework (i.e., how is inequality related to development). The variable of interest is an *index* of inequality, for example, the Gini, or the share of income of a particular quintile, or the ratio of incomes of two deciles (the income of the top 10 percent relative to the income of the bottom 10 percent, etc.), and the relationship of the chosen economic variable to economic growth.

The first important post-Ahluwalia and post-Anand and Kanbur result about inequality trends was provided by Deininger and Squire (1996). They assembled the second large inequality dataset (the first was that of Ahluwalia and Jain), subjected it to various tests, and found that inequality does not change much *within* countries over time. To be sure, there are problems with the data,[8] and there are exceptions to the rule; but the fundamental trend was one of little change.

This new dataset was analyzed further by Li, Squire, and Zou (1998), who ran several regressions with the Gini coefficient as the dependent variable. Their conclusion was the same: income inequality was relatively stable within countries over time. *In other words, there was no support for the Kuznets hypothesis.*

Cornia and Kiiski (2001), using a third compilation of data (the World Institute for Development Economics Research, or WIDER, dataset[9]) on inequality, conducted detailed tests of inequality changes within countries, and particularly the analysis of changes during the globalization period. Their conclusion: "Over the last twenty years, this trend towards equality was halted in parallel with the emergence, consolidation and diffusion of a new economic paradigm often referred to as the 'Washington Consensus'."

Cornia and Kiiski's analysis was in the spirit of "spell analysis," that is, looking at individual countries' changes in inequality. Using the larger WIDER dataset (which includes 73 countries with spells, as compared with the 49 countries with spells used by Li et al.), Cornia and Kiiski

---

8. The Deininger and Squire (1996) dataset, along with a corresponding assembling of data by the United Nations University's World Institute for Development Economics Research (the World Income Inequality Database, available at http://www.wider.unu.edu/wiid), and the data collected by the Asian Development Bank (RETA-5917, Research Project on Developing a Poverty Database), forms the core of the income distribution data used for this study. There are definite problems with the non-Asian Development Bank distribution data, and better documentation and "cleaning" would be warranted. E.g., for some observations, the quintile shares are inconsistent (i.e., a poorer quintile being shown to have a larger share of income than a richer quintile, a definitionally impossible situation). Atkinson-Brandolini (1999) point out several problems with these datasets.

9. This dataset expands on the observations contained in the Deininger and Squire (1996) dataset.

reveal that the conclusion of Li and his colleagues of "no change in inequality" was somewhat inaccurate; that there are trends not caught by the simple model of Li and his colleagues, but captured by their non-linear techniques. These techniques suggest that within-country inequality declined between 1950 and 1970, and increased thereafter. However, during a much longer period (1960-2000), there was little change in intracountry inequality, thus reaffirming the conclusion of Deininger and Squire and of Li and his colleagues.

The results are indicative of one simple fact: When the hurly-burly is done, little change in inequality is observed in most countries—the ones that started off unequal stayed unequal, and the ones that started equal stayed equal.[10] Of course, some striking changes are observed (e.g., the large increase in inequality in China), and after a century of constancy, a large increase in inequality in the United States in the late 1980s. But these are exceptions. The norm is small long-term changes in country inequality.

The Evidence Once Again

The method developed to analyze inequality at an individual level, through construction of Lorenz curves, is outlined in appendix A. Construction of the dataset required the use of data for more than 1,000 household surveys and is possibly the most exhaustive dataset of its kind. This dataset covers, for most countries, all the years between 1950 and 2000 for four major variables: population, real PPP income, real PPP consumption, and income (and consumption) distribution.

Does this new dataset suggest any "new" results on inequality levels and trends? Let us reestimate the relationship between inequality and development. Table 3.1 reports the results for income distribution data for selected countries and regions. Three years are selected—1960, 1980, and 2000.[11] The results, according to the Gini inequality index, is that for a large set of countries inequality *has* worsened over time. The worsening inequality is particularly noticeable for the United Kingdom, United States, China, Nigeria, and Russia. The initially highly unequal economies like Brazil and Mexico buck the trend, and show significant improvement in inequality. This "equality convergence" pattern has not gone unnoticed, and has been commented upon by Benabou (1996), Roemer and Gugerty (1997), and Ravallion (2001b).

---

10. Or as T.S. Eliot might have said: "We arrive where we started, and know inequality for the first time."

11. If a survey was not conducted in a particular year, data for the nearest year prior to the year in question were used. If there was no survey earlier, then the result of the first such survey subsequent to the year in question was used.

Table 3.1 Country and regional inequality; Gini and quintile income shares

Region or country	Gini[a] 1960	Gini[a] 1980	Gini[a] 2000	Share of 1st quintile 1960	Share of 1st quintile 1980	Share of 1st quintile 2000	Share of 5th quintile 1960	Share of 5th quintile 1980	Share of 5th quintile 2000
Industrialized world									
United States	36.3	39.7	45.7	4.8	4.3	3.6	41.3	43.6	49.4
United Kingdom	27.7	27.4	36.2	9.4	10.2	6.6	36.9	37.6	42.9
Australia	32.0	39.3	35.4	6.6	4.6	5.9	38.8	43.4	41.3
Germany	27.3	32.1	30.1	10.5	6.6	8.2	37.7	39.0	38.4
Sweden	40.0	32.7	25.1	4.4	7.0	9.6	44.0	39.5	34.6
Developing world									
Bangladesh	37.4	35.3	45.1	6.9	7.4	6.2	44.5	42.9	52.1
Brazil	49.7	57.9	52.1	3.8	2.9	3.5	54.0	61.6	56.2
China	29.5	29.5	40.5	7.9	7.9	5.9	36.7	36.7	46.6
South Korea	35.5	40.0	31.7	5.8	5.1	7.5	41.9	45.4	39.3
Mexico	56.0	56.2	51.8	4.4	3.1	4.0	61.4	60.2	56.6
Malaysia	37.4	51.3	49.3	6.5	3.7	4.4	44.0	55.8	54.3
Indonesia	40.2	40.5	37.6	6.5	5.9	7.3	47.0	46.8	45.5
Russia	24.7	24.7	35.9	9.5	9.5	6.7	34.0	34.0	42.4
Nigeria	44.7	44.7	56.9	4.7	4.7	3.3	49.6	49.6	61.2
Industrialized world				6.1	6.4	6.8	42.1	40.5	42.2
Developing world				6.7	6.5	5.7	45.2	45.8	49.2
World				**6.8**	**6.7**	**5.9**	**43.7**	**44.1**	**47.7**

a. Gini is computed by the simple accounting procedure method and not "published" estimates because there are problems with some of these Gini estimates; see chapter 8.

b. In many cases, income distribution data are not available for 1960, 1980, or 2000. In such cases, the table presents either the closest earlier year for which data are available, or, where earlier data are not available, data for the earliest later year. E.g., if the latest survey took place in 1995, the 2000 figures reflect these values; if the first survey took place in 1975, the 1960 figures reflect those values.

Sources: Deininger and Squire (1996); World Income Inequality Database, available at http://www.wider.unu.edu/wiid; Asian Development Bank (2002); Milanovic and Yitzhaki (2001).

Not reported in table 3.1 is the pattern of distribution for consumption. The pattern is the same, except that four economies with relatively large populations, all in Asia, grew at an accelerated pace during the globalization period and yet did not show any trend in consumption inequality: India, Indonesia, South Korea, and Vietnam. On a probability basis, all these economies are due for a worsening; when and whether it will happen, and why inequality has not worsened for 20 years, is a subject for research and perhaps another book!

The result for trends in regional inequality as measured by quintile shares is consistent with the result observed for individual countries. Among the regions, the industrialized countries show a decrease in inequality (see the figures for the first quintile) from 1960 to 2000, despite the fact that such countries as the United States and United Kingdom significantly worsen.[12] However, the fifth decile also gains, suggesting that the Lorenz curves are "crossing." The developing world shows a similar pattern—little change in inequality from 1960 to 1980, and a large increase in inequality from 1980 to 2000. Note that the above results hold regardless of which measure of inequality is used—share of the first quintile or share of the fifth quintile.

The final "screening" calculations on the data are reported in figure 3.2. The averages for the annual (log) change in inequality income and consumption distribution changes are reported for three classifications of data and two time periods: all changes experienced during the very short term (less than or equal to 3 years), medium-term changes (between 4 and 8 years), and long-term changes (9 to 15 years). For the 1960-80 period, there seems to be a definite trend toward equality, and the change is larger, and more positive, the larger the time frame of observation. For the next 20 years, there is a complete reversal. Now there is a trend toward greater inequality, and the magnitude is again larger the longer the period of observation.

Thus, the conclusion that *country* inequality worsened during the past 20 years appears to be fairly robust. These results directly contradict the findings of Deininger and Squire and Li and his colleagues and are more along the lines of the results reached by Cornia and Kiiski.

Tests of Inequality Change

The large number of countries for which data on distributions exist for more than 1 year allows the *direct* estimation of the time profile of inequality. Individual quintile income levels (derived from a multiplication of quintile shares with mean income) can be regressed on mean income and the "elasticity of connection" observed. If the elasticity is equal to 1, it follows that inequality did not change for a typical country.

This 45-degree method (so named because the result obtained is a 45-degree line between average income of the first quintile and average income in the economy), which is quite the rage today, was first used by Ahluwalia in 1974. He regressed the growth rate of income of the lowest 40 percent on the growth rate of GNP for 13 developing countries, and he failed to find any strong pattern; that is, he found a unitary elasticity between the growth in incomes of poor people (defined as the bottom 40 percent of the developing world) and the growth in average incomes of

---

12. Regional figures for the first and fifth quintiles are obtained by weighting the quintile shares of the countries by their population in the region. This cannot be done with the Gini; for what happened to regional Ginis, see chapter 11.

Figure 3.2 The time dimension of world inequality change, 1960-2000

1960-80

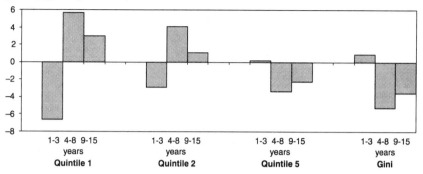

percent (log) / change[a]

1980-2000

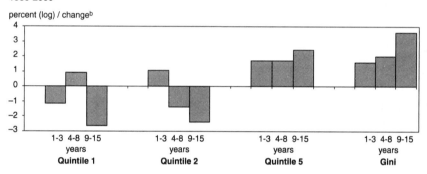

percent (log) / change[b]

a. Percent changes, all in log terms, reflect the *total* changes over each period, rather than annual changes.

Note: For each measure of inequality—income/consumption shares of quintile 1 (Q1), Q2, and Q5, and income/consumption Gini—(log) changes are calculated over various time frames with reference to each year—(t, t-1), (t, t-2), (t, t-3) . . . (t, t-15). The mean is then calculated, for each year, for sets of changes, i.e., the 1-year, 2-year, and 3-year changes are one set; 4-year to 8-year changes are another set; and 9-year to 15-year changes are a third set. (The shorter (1-3 years) and longer (9-15 years) sets give, respectively, the short- and long-term trends in inequality.)

Once obtained, these figures are averaged for the two time periods, 1960-80 and 1980-2000, to see whether there has been a shift in the *direction* of inequality change between the preglobalization (1960-80) and globalization (1980-2000) periods. In most instances, the results are dramatic and conclusive.

Sources: Deininger and Squire (1996); World Income Inequality Database, available at http://www.wider.unu.edu/wiid; Asian Development Bank (2002); Milanovic and Yitzhaki (2001).

Figure 3.3 Elasticity of incomes of poor people (bottom 20 percent) with respect to average incomes

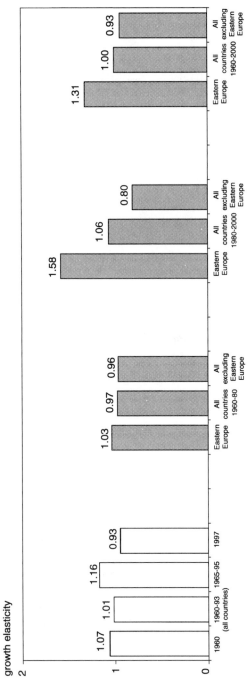

Note: Income elasticities are computed by regressing the (log) average income of the 1st quintile as a function of the (log) average income, at 1993 purchasing power parity prices. Differences in these estimates are due to differences in the choice of countries and time periods, as well as to different methods of estimation. The simple accounting procedure results are for the countries in the nonindustrialized world. The estimation method incorporates fixed effects with robust standard errors.

Sources: Unshaded bars: All countries, 1960–93: Roemer and Gugerty (1997); 1965–95: Gallup, Radelet, and Warner (1998); 1997: Timmer (1997); 1960: Dollar and Kraay (2000). Shaded bars: Simple accounting procedure method.

the entire economy: the predicted line was one of 45 degrees (Ahluwalia 1974).

Three studies undertaken at the Harvard Institute of International Development (HIID) in 1997 and 1998 (Roemer and Gugerty 1997; Timmer 1997; Gallup, Radelet, and Warner 1998) used the newly available Deininger and Squire dataset to update, and methodologically improve upon, Ahluwalia's regressions. Except for one regression by Timmer, which used dummy variables for each decade of analysis, all the regressions reported in the HIID papers show the first quintile elasticity to be not significantly different from unity. The period covered by the HIID studies was mostly the years after 1960, and the studies used data for approximately 30 to 60 countries (depending on the author and analysis).

A few years later, Dollar and Kraay (2000) subjected the same distribution data to additional tests and reached the same conclusion as the HIID studies. They found that "growth was good for the poor" because poor people shared equally in the fruits of average growth (i.e., the 45-degree line).

Thus, a strong result emerging from these log-log studies is that the average country has not witnessed any change in inequality during the past 40 years—a "flat" U-curve. The bottom 20 percent of individuals in a typical country experienced the same growth, or fall, in incomes as the average person. In other words, the aggregate average experience is one of *rejection* of the Kuznets hypothesis—a contrast to Cornia and Kiiski's result and our preliminary result reported in table 3.1. For example, the share of the first quintile for the world had declined from 6.7 to 5.9 percent for the developing world, or an implied elasticity of 0.87.

This important unitary elasticity or no-Kuznets-curve result has been interpreted differently by different authors—some legitimate interpretations, some not so. The correct explanation of a "flat" U-curve is that the data reveal that a "typical" country will experience no change in inequality. The unit of observation is a country-year; and if it is assumed that all the observations are drawn from the same "structural universe," there is no reason to worry that the above regression gives equal weights to a small country showing no change in inequality and to a large country showing a large change in inequality.

The *incorrect* interpretations start with the assumption that a regression of the bottom 20 percent containing all the world's countries says anything about absolute poverty. The titles of all four major papers on the subject (Roemer and Gugerty 1997; Timmer 1997; Gallup, Radelet, and Warner 1998; Dollar and Kraay 2000) contain the words "growth" and "the poor," even though the papers' texts contain the necessary disclaimers and statements about the differences between relative poverty (incomes of the first quintile) and absolute poverty (incomes below an absolute level of income).

It would be correct to assume that the regressions reflect changes in absolute poverty if the sample of countries chosen contained *only* countries with large populations of poor people in the base year. The later papers (Roemer and Gugerty 1997; Dollar and Kraay 2000) use *both* industrialized and developing-country data to rerun Ahluwalia's regressions. Though it must be admitted that it is good to have more data, their regressions no longer retain the connection with the incomes of poor people. The reason Ahluwalia chose the bottom 40 percent was because the poverty line was *defined* as the bottom 40 percent of developing economies. It is a case of the methodological trees being copied without paying due attention to the definitional forest.

Elasticity of Connection, 1960-2000

Figure 3.3 reports on the estimates of the "elasticity of connection" for the bottom quintile found by various studies. The model that had been developed by Ahluwalia and the HIID researchers was reestimated using data for 617 household surveys in nonindustrialized countries, and the unitary elasticity result appears to be grossly in error. For the period 1980-2000, the elasticity of connection for the first quintile is not 1; it is 0.80, with a robust standard error of 0.1.[13]

It is not the newly available data that lead to a rejection of the original robust conclusion of a unitary elasticity. Nor did the results reached before the mid-1980s contain an error (e.g., Ahluwalia 1976; Fields 1980; World Bank, *World Development Report 1990: Poverty and Development*). But studies after them do have an error. And the error is a simple one: the nonrecognition of the reality, and the structurally different experience, of Eastern European countries and countries that had been part of the USSR. Though Eastwood and Lipton (2001) (an excellent survey of the issues related to poverty, inequality, and growth) do not reestimate the Dollar-Kraay regressions, they broadly hint at the possibility that the presence of the Eastern European economies was biasing Dollar and Kraay's results strongly in favor of a unitary elasticity.[14]

In an unusual development (in the sense of historical patterns), the Eastern European economies simultaneously experienced *declining* equal-

---

13. The log-log model was estimated with fixed effects; incorporation of industrialized-country (nonpoor) data raises the elasticity to 0.83 with a standard error of 0.098.

14. Dollar and Kraay run several regressions and report one set of results, which incorporate regional dummies (2001, table 4, 39). Their basic regional dummy specification yields an average elasticity of 0.91 with a standard error of 0.09. Reproducing their results with their data but our specification and estimation method (fixed-effects model with robust standard errors, and instead of regional dummies all Eastern European countries excluded from the sample for the period 1980-2000), an elasticity of 0.84 with a standard error of 0.116 is obtained.

ity and *declining* incomes; this joint occurrence results in the elasticity of connection being close to 1.6 for the 1980-2000 period. During this period, a 1 percent decline in average incomes led to a 1.6 percent decline in the incomes of the bottom 20 percent!

This simple result for Eastern Europe demonstrates, without the use of fancy econometrics,[15] that Dollar and Kraay's conclusion—"incomes of the poor do not fall more than proportionately during economic crises"—is invalid. Note the elasticity for Eastern Europe: 1.6. Ordinarily, one would say that this economy was becoming most equal—a 1 percent increase in average incomes is resulting in a 1.6 percent increase in the incomes of poor people. But what is actually happening is a fast jump toward inequality—a 1 percent *decline* in *average* incomes is leading to a 1.6 percent *decline* in the mean incomes of poor people.

This large 1.6 elasticity has just the opposite consequence of the elasticity that would have been observed if the average income had risen, not fallen. In this instance, the incomes of poor people are falling considerably faster than the incomes of nonpoor people. Negative growth has been worse for poor than nonpoor people. Now, when this negative-negative elasticity of 1.6 (two negatives make a positive) is combined with a world excluding Eastern Europe (positive-positive) elasticity of 0.8, one obtains the controversial,[16] and wrong, finding of a unitary elasticity for the average country (a finding reached by Roemer and Gugerty 1997; Timmer 1997; Gallup, Radelet, and Warner 1998; and Dollar and Kraay 2000).

Using virtually identical data to those used by the HIID researchers and Dollar and Kraay, an elasticity that is significantly lower than unity is obtained. This "true" elasticity for all the world's countries, excluding those in Eastern Europe, is about 0.8, with a standard error of 0.10 (i.e., significantly less than 1). For the previous 20-year period (1960-80), the elasticity was 0.96, with a standard error of 0.12. The conventional wisdom—that inequality has essentially stayed constant for long periods—is incorrect. It was constant during the 1960-80 period, but it has clearly not been constant since then.

Country-Level Inequality

Five conclusions follow from this detailed analysis of country inequality. First, over long periods of time, inequality at the country level does not

---

15. Dollar and Kraay run several models, and use sophisticated econometrics, to justify their conclusions, something approvingly noted by others, e.g., Srinivasan (2001), who concludes in a review of several such studies that "in many ways, the most careful (econometrically) study is that of Dollar and Kraay" (20).

16. There was a lot of objection to Dollar and Kraay's finding that the poor shared equally in the growth process. If this objection occurred due to the conceptual error of not accounting for the fact that Eastern Europe contained the experience of declining incomes and worsening

display any significant change either way. Second, during the past few decades, some countries have registered sharp changes toward inequality; the notable instances are the United States, China, the United Kingdom, and those in Eastern Europe. (The change in the case of Eastern Europe is unprecedented.)

Third, there have been equally sharp movements toward equality in some countries (e.g., Sweden). Fourth, many countries have remained at the same level of inequality during the past decades, like India and Indonesia. Fifth, *all possible formulations of intercountry inequality suggest that inequality worsened during the 1980s and 1990s.* This last result contradicts most of the "no-change" results reported to date, but it is in accordance with Cornia and Kiiski's findings. Whether this increase in *intercountry* inequality leads to an increase in world *individual* inequality is the subject of chapter 11.

Toward Individual Inequality Estimates

If country data are aggregated (assume each country is an individual), and population weights are used, then a crude, first-cut profile of a world distribution could be obtained. With such a distribution, one would just be able to read off what happened to quintile shares, Ginis, or any other index of inequality in a given year. One would also be able to interpret the trends.

Korzeniewicz and Moran (1997) constructed a distribution for each country that uses a quintile as a unit of observation (i.e., the average income of each quintile is attributed to all residents in the quintile). In the case of a country with a population of 10 million, this method assumes that each segment of 2 million has the same income. For India, it means each 200-million segment; for China, each 250-million one.

Though useful, such an approach may yield more wrong than right results. Why? Because a lot is going on within each country, especially large countries. If a detailed distribution for each country is not available (as is most often the case), the next-best procedure is to parameterize the distribution. Schultz (1998) converts each country's distribution into a log-variance model; this yields a mean and a standard deviation, parameters that can yield an estimate of mean income at *any* level of aggregation.

The problem with this approach is that it is prone to large errors in the approximation. Schultz finds that PPP-measured inequality has been relatively stable throughout the past 20 years; indeed, such inequality has had a slight tendency to decline, a result echoed by Melchior, Telle, and

---

inequality, and therefore two negatives making a positive, then the objection was for the right reason. If the objection occurred because of a prior belief that this result "cannot" occur, then it was an objection for the wrong reason.

Wiig (2000).[17] There is no basis, therefore, for concluding that individual inequality has worsened during the globalization period.

Individual Inequality

The John Lennon song "Imagine" contains the fundamental idea behind the generation of these *world individual income inequality* estimates, or W3i for short. What happens if there is no country, only one world? What if we have world distributions, distributions that imply that individuals in the world are lined up according to their income and their calculated share of world income—in other words, a distribution that has no regard for sex, color, national origin, or individual prejudices?

The generation of both intercountry inequality (dubbed "international inequality" in Bourguignon and Morrisson 2001) and individual inequality require essentially the same data, that is, the population of each country, its per capita income in a common currency,[18] and its distribution of income. A summary of research on international inequality computations is as follows. The first level of aggregation is to assume nothing about the distribution and allocate the per capita income to each resident.

The next lower level of aggregation is to allocate each individual their mean quintile income (as was done by Korzeniewicz and Moran). The next lower level of aggregation is to allocate incomes according to each decile of the population and, depending on data availability, even finer gradations. This method would yield a reasonably close approximation to the desired goal of obtaining an index for global individual inequality; this was the procedure outlined by Berry, Bourguignon, and Morrisson (1981, 1983) in the early 1980s.

There can be some controversy over the selection and estimation of *average* income (it can be obtained either from surveys or from national

17. In two recent papers, Sala-i-Martin (2002a) constructs world distributions like those of Korzeniewicz and Moran (1997) (using country quintile income) and in a later paper (2002b) extends the methodology to map individual country quintile data onto a world distribution. Sala-i-Martin's results are not analyzed in any detail here because they came just after the draft was submitted to referees.

18. There is (almost) universal agreement that the currency of choice is purchasing power parity incomes; for reasons that are not clear, the United Nations *Human Development Report 1999* used constant US dollars as the "numeraire" and not surprisingly found that rich countries were getting richer while poor countries were found entering the gates of oblivion. This study was unique in other respects as well—it forced the United Nations to set up a committee to investigate the statistical methods used by its own staff; see Report of the Friends of the Chair of the Statistical Commission (2000). The investigation into the UN statistical methods seems to have had little impact. The latest UN *Human Development Report* (2002) follows the earlier tradition. It reaches the conclusion that world inequality has worsened, thus completely ignoring all available evidence suggesting the opposite.

accounts), so it is not so simple. And distribution data may not be available for every country for every year. So it is not so straightforward. But assumption, thy name is economist—and Berry and his colleagues made reasonable assumptions to arrive at an income distribution estimate for the world (124 countries) in 1970. Their assumptions involved both the generation of income distribution for countries for which such data are not available, as well as the growth in incomes of countries like China.

Berry and his colleagues eschewed the generation of a Lorenz curve for each country, a major intermediate step for the simple accounting procedure (see chapter 8). Instead, they aggregated the available distributional data—not by deciles or quintiles (as was done by Milanovic) but rather by "income brackets, so that none of them include a significant percentage of the world's population . . . and no income bracket was to include more than 2% of the world population in the low income range and 1% in the high income range" (Berry, Bourguignon, and Morrisson 1983, 333).

Using PPP income growth rates, Berry and his colleagues reported on the evolution of world inequality between 1950 and 1977. The assumption that individual country inequality did not change for 27 years (they use the same distribution for each country as was generated by them for 1970) may be a bit extreme but is nevertheless understandable, given the paucity of country distribution data at that time. Their result: a highly unequal Gini index of 66.2 for the world income distribution, and only a slightly lower inequality level of 65.2 for the distribution of consumption.[19]

What Berry and his colleagues did was exactly what one would do if confronted with the task of estimating the distribution for an individual economy. Collect the data for each economy for only three variables: population, average income, and the distribution of this income. Once these data are assembled, it is then a simple *accounting* procedure to estimate the Lorenz curve and such associated inequality measures as the Gini, Theil, log-variance, ratio of the incomes of the 10th to the 1st decile, and so on.

Much like the 1970s, the availability of newer survey data in the 1980s and 1990s, and the compilation of the World Bank and WIDER datasets, have allowed for a resurgence of individual inequality studies. The first to undertake such a study were Bourguignon and Morrisson (2001),[20] two of the authors of the original first study on W3i by Berry, Bourguignon, and Morrisson. They not only improved and updated the original study to 1992, but also provided the first set of estimates for several years going

---

19. The authors present estimates under alternative assumptions in the two papers, but the figures reported here can be considered "representative."

20. This is the date of the final draft; the first draft was dated June 1999.

back to 1820. Soon after, three other studies appeared (Milanovic 1999; Bhalla 2000d; Dikhanov and Ward 2000).[21]

Bourguignon and Morrisson's improved method still does not involve the estimation of a Lorenz curve; instead, they attempt to collect as much disaggregated data as possible—in particular, the average income of each decile of the population, as well as the mean income of the top two ventiles (90th-95th and 95th-100th percentiles). Because most of the published data exist only for quintiles, and at most deciles, they must have used some interpolation (i.e., some attempt must have been made to generate portions of the Lorenz curve).[22] They use data for 33 selected countries to approximate regional distributions. Clearly, much ambition was involved in constructing estimates back to 1820, but both the assumptions made, and the results obtained, seem compelling.

Milanovic (1999) assembled the survey data gathered at the World Bank and estimated inequality for 1988 and 1993. Sometimes these data were available in decile form, sometimes only in quintile form. For such large countries as India and China, Milanovic had data on both rural and urban areas, so the level of disaggregation achieved for these countries is twice as large as for others (i.e., if original data are available in decile form, then there are 20 units of observation for each country, or 20 units of data to estimate average income). Milanovic's estimate is a "pure" estimate of inequality; *no* interpolation is made of survey data to arrive at any portion of the Lorenz curve. On *average*, Milanovic probably achieved the same level of disaggregation as Bourguignon and Morrisson; that is, about 12 inequality data points per country-year.

To sum up the results of these studies: Bourguignon and Morrisson's results suggest that W3i worsened until 1980 and since then has remained relatively flat, at a Gini of 65.7. Milanovic shows a *huge* increase in inequality in the space of just 5 years, 1988 to 1993—from 62.5 to 65.9. Dikhanov and Ward reach the same conclusion as Milanovic; Bhalla reaches the conclusion that not only had W3i declined in the past 40 years, but it was at its most equal in the late 1990s (the latest estimates of this method are presented in chapter 11).

---

21. An earlier version of the SAP was used to generate world inequality and world poverty estimates in the paper presented in June 2000 at a seminar at the International Monetary Fund. The SAP method has undergone improvements, especially in the generation of a Lorenz curve from limited data. The present version can be considered the final version! The June 2000 method, however, had a slight tendency to overestimate world individual inequality, but this made little difference to the generation, and estimation, of world poverty levels.

22. Bourguignon and Morrisson (2001) do not use the expanded distribution set made available by Deininger and Squire (1996) and the World Institute for Development Economics Research (the database referred to above in note 9), but instead use an updated version of the data in Berry, Bourguignon, and Morrisson (1983). Of course, data from before 1950 are unique to the Bourguignon and Morrisson study.

Summing Up: The Facts as We Know Them

The trends in *country* inequalities documented above highlight one major conclusion: World inequality (as measured by the inequality of a "representative" average economy), after having stayed relatively constant and even improved until the late 1970s, significantly deteriorated in the post-1980s globalization period. If the world is disaggregated by regions, one obtains the same conclusion. The observation of trends in individual large countries yields the same conclusion. Observations over long periods of time lead to the same conclusion—though some dampening in the worsening-inequality result is obtained if the time period used is more than 8 years. The use of popular log-log regressions (regressing the log of quintile income on the log of average income) yields the same result—the average elasticity is 0.8, suggesting that the first quintile's share of the pie has declined over time (or inequality has increased).

Moving toward a lower level of aggregation—the individual rather than a country as a unit of analysis—yields a mixed result. Milanovic obtains the same result as that yielded by country inequalities, that is, a significant worsening in the globalization period. His results are an extension of the individual country results. Bourguignon and Morrisson report a mild increase in inequality (their last date of observation is 1992). In an earlier version of the findings reported here, Bhalla (2000d) suggests that the result for individual inequality is completely contrary to that for country inequality: Not only did individual inequality not worsen in the 1980s and 1990s, it actually improved, and did so significantly! The veracity of these findings is explored in detail in chapter 11.

4

Poverty as We Are Told It Is

Income growth, especially for developing countries, is a means to an end: survival, "basic needs" satisfied. The World Bank's slogan is not "go for growth" but "our dream is a world free of poverty." Industrialized societies can afford the luxury of going for growth. Their political concern is with the middle class; this change from concern for the poor to concern for the middle class is a change from developing-country status to industrialized-country status. All the formerly poor countries in the world are not there yet; hence, reduction of poverty must be the number one goal of policy for developing countries.

As many have pointed out, "poverty" is a multidimensional concept. It means not only a lack of income, but also a lack of the basic necessities for a decent life—equality of opportunity, health care, education, sanitation, and democratic and human rights. All this makes the job of research and policy difficult. Though all these goals should be achieved, is there an optimal sequence of policies? And is there any ranking of priorities; that is, does it make more sense to spend public money on reducing adult illiteracy so that, via the mother's health, infant mortality rates will decline more quickly? Does it make more sense to educate the female child, especially since research (and common sense) shows that a mother's education affects child welfare much more than does a father's—or even father's income?

These questions are meant to emphasize the fact that there are no shortcuts to knowledge, or to appropriate policy, in the dream of removing poverty. But policymakers do not have the luxury of nuances; decisions must be made now. Thus, shortcuts are mandatory for good policy formulation. Further, there is the practical knowledge that money income, though imperfect, is the best proxy for human welfare. This income measure of poverty will lead to type I errors (those defined as poor but who are not) and type II errors (those defined as nonpoor but who are actually poor). But cannot there be an index (e.g., life expectancy, infant mortality, adult illiteracy, schooling enrollments, access to clean water, sanitation, human rights, empowerment—the list is only limited by one's imagination) that does not also involve type I and type II errors?

So the search should be for an index that minimizes errors, and most have converged on a poverty index based on income. For three common-sense reasons, this choice is the right one. First, income allows one to purchase the goods needed to reduce poverty. Second, income is highly correlated with access to public goods that reduce poverty. Third, income is highly correlated with the ability to bribe, and therefore to buy "public" goods that—in most developing countries—are not free but are supposed to be free.

The rest of this book (except briefly in chapter 12) will concentrate on just one measure of poverty: the head count ratio (HCR). This measure is the choice of most academics, institutions, and politicians. It is catchy; it quantifies the proportion (hence the ratio in its name) of a population whose incomes are estimated to be below a certain absolute level of consumption. It is also likely that HCR works better than any other index in capturing poverty.

Having chosen index of poverty, it is a simple matter to compute HCR (computationally cumbersome, but simple conceptually). It is even simpler to count the number of poor people in the world (given by the multiple of HCR with population). There should really be no controversy on the methods used to generate either HCR or the number of poor people—especially once a poverty line has been chosen and accepted. Alas, that is not the reality. Without understatement, HCR has been used, misused, and abused more than any other index of poverty.

This chapter first discusses the origins of national and international poverty lines. The pioneering role of the World Bank in research and policy is acknowledged. The first international poverty line was defined to be an *income* level at purchasing power parity (PPP) of $200 per capita per year, at 1970 prices,[1] or $1.53 a day at 1985 PPP prices. The initial experiment with a nonincome poverty line (e.g., caloric intake) is discussed, and the convergence toward accepting a poverty line equal to $1 a day in consumption (at 1985 PPP prices)[2] is documented.

---

1. Ahluwalia, Carter, and Chenery (1979).

2. Ravallion, Datt, and van de Walle (1991).

Although it might appear that the poverty line got reduced by a third (from $1.53 to $1), it is shown that the associated changes in definition (income vs. consumption) and methods of estimation (national accounts vs. surveys) cause the two international poverty lines (offered 12 years apart) to be virtually identical! The chapter concludes by reporting estimates of HCR, and the number of poor people in the world, for selected years since 1960.

Defining and Measuring Absolute Poverty

No matter what the starting point, all roads, and policies, legitimately reach the goal of reducing poverty, especially when large islands of poverty coexist amid a sea of plenty. It is not surprising that academic studies, and policy concern, on poverty first arose in India in the early 1960s.[3] And there the first absolute poverty line was developed. Rath (1996), one of the pioneers (along with Dandekar[4]), describes what happened in those early years:

> A Working Group consisting of nine distinguished economists and social workers, set up by a Seminar on Planning, organized by the Indian Planning Commission, recommended in July 1962 that the national minimum per capita consumer expenditure in India should be Rs. 20 (at 1960-61 prices). . . . The Planning Commission noted that on the basis of available data on distribution of population according to per capita expenditure, nearly half the Indian population in 1960-61 was below this national minimum level of Rs. 20 per capita per month, and the Commission called them poor. But in the absence of any details about the basis of this national minimum the discussion did not proceed further. (Rath 1996, 76)

The minimum level of expenditure of the poor, the poverty line, was calculated on the basis of a "physical volume of commodities," and implicit in the document is the assumption that these commodities primarily relate to food. It was also noted (though not published until 1974; see Rath 1996, n. 1, 106) that because of higher prices, the urban poverty line

---

3. British sociologists, economists, and journalists have long journeyed into the realm of poverty definition, and in that important sense the Indian definition of poverty was by no means the first. Rowntree had defined an absolute poverty line as early as 1901; also see Townsend (1954) for an early attempt at the definition of a relative poverty line. Himmelfarb (1984) contains an excellent account of the origins of poverty discussion going back to the Scriptures (e.g., "Ye have the poor always with you"). She quotes Samuel Johnson, who very likely originated the first definition of the poverty line in 1770: "A decent provision for the poor is the true test of civilization. . . . The condition of the lower orders, the poor especially, was the true mark of national discrimination." It is likely, however, that the Indian definition of an absolute poverty line was the first such attempt in the postwar period.

4. V.M. Dandekar and N. Rath, "Poverty in India: Dimensions and Trends," *Economic and Political Weekly*, January 2-9, 1977, 25-46.

should be 25 percent higher, at Rs25 a month. This was the estimate of the Planning Commission. In their classic study, Dandekar and Rath defined the poor in terms of an average consumption of 2,250 calories per capita per day (not much different from the current "norm" of 2,100); this yielded a figure of Rs15 for rural areas and Rs22.50 for urban areas, both at 1960-61 prices.[5]

This definition became *the* poverty line for academic studies in India and around the world. In 1979, the Planning Commission of India set up another task force to measure the "exact" poverty line; by aggregating in terms of age and sex specific calorie consumption criteria, the task force came out with a recommendation of a higher poverty line—2,435 calories for rural areas and 2,095 calories for urban areas. Using the 1973-74 National Sample Survey as a base, the task force concluded that the monetary equivalent of these calories was Rs49.09 and Rs56.64 for rural and urban areas, respectively, per capita per month, at 1973-74 prices. Curiously, this higher caloric line is the same in terms of average purchasing power—Rs15.3 and Rs21, at 1960-61 prices, per capita per month.

These two values (Rs15.3 and Rs21), with an urbanization rate of 18 percent and a purchasing power parity (PPP) exchange rate of 1.96 (1985 base), yield an Indian poverty line of PPP (current) $8.27 a month in 1960. The PPP 1985 inflation deflator (i.e., equal to 100 in 1985) was 27.77 in 1960-61. Thus, the 1960-61 Indian poverty line (obviously as well as the equivalent 1973-74 line) was equal to PPP $29.80 a month, or $0.98 a day, at 1985 PPP prices. HCR, according to the $1-a-day poverty line in India in the 1960s, was about 45 percent (see Ahluwalia 1977[6]).

This 1960-61 Indian poverty line became, by adoption and definition, the "World Bank I" international poverty line (of Ahluwalia, Carter, Chenery 1979), as well as the "World Bank II" international (absolute) poverty line (of Ravallion, Datt, and van de Walle 1991). Few possibly recognize these international lines of different vintages as the original Indian poverty line.

Poverty in the United States

It is an intriguing coincidence that, at almost the same time as these developments in India, a War on Poverty was being launched in the richest country in the world, the United States. The execution of this war, led by US President Lyndon Johnson, required targeting the enemy: poor people. In what was to be the first in a series of papers, Orshansky (1965)

---

5. Dandekar and Rath, "Poverty in India." *Op. cit.*

6. Among several good studies on poverty that have been published over the years, this is a classic. It was able to correctly anticipate virtually all shades of the debate that would take place over the next 25 years.

developed the first US absolute poverty line, just a year or two before President Johnson's commitment. As Fisher (1997) described it:

> Orshansky knew from the Department of Agriculture's 1955 Household Food Consumption Survey (the latest available such survey at the time) that families of three or more persons spent about one-third of their after-tax money income on food in 1955. Accordingly, she calculated poverty thresholds for families of three or more persons by taking the dollar costs of the economy food plan for families of those sizes and multiplying the costs by a factor of three—the "multiplier." In effect, she took a hypothetical average family spending one third of its income on food, and assumed that it had to cut back on its expenditures sharply. She assumed that expenditures for food and non-food would be cut back at the same rate. When the food expenditures of the hypothetical family reached the cost of the economy food plan, she assumed that the amount the family would then be spending on non-food items would also be minimal but adequate. (6-7)

The proportion of the population found to be poor using Orshansky's poverty line was about 20 percent.[7] This level dropped rapidly, to about 12 percent, by 1968. But strangely, it has hovered at about this level for the past three decades.[8]

Thus, in about the early 1960s, in both the richest and poorest countries in the world, absolute poverty was a major concern. As perhaps befitted the different levels of development, the rich country had a poverty line approximately equal to the *income* of PPP $10.40 a day, at 1993 prices,[9] and the poor country had a *consumption* poverty line about one-seventh that of the rich one, $1.54 per capita per day in 1964. The rich country had approximately 20 percent poor people, and the poor country about 45 percent poor people. Per capita per day consumption in the United States was $26.65 in 1964, and Indians were considerably poorer at $2.40 a day.

If the US and Indian estimates of poverty are taken to be representative, then one approximation is that poverty levels are likely to be somewhere between 20 and 50 percent of the population in rich and poor countries, respectively. These two (Indian and US) poverty lines provide the "original poverty lines" estimate of the elasticity of the absolute poverty line with respect to consumption, about 0.59.[10] A simple regression of the

---

7. See Fisher (1996a, 1996b, 1997), Plotnick et al. (1998), and Burtless and Smeeding (2000) for discussions about measurement of poverty in the United States.

8. But see chapter 7 for possible explanations and resolution of the paradox of so much improvement in the living standards of the poor in the United States and no change in conventionally measured poverty levels.

9. This is derived on the basis of an income poverty line equal to $13,003 for a family of three, at 1998 prices (Burtless and Smeeding 2000, 4).

10. The US poverty line of $10.40 is converted into a consumption line of PPP $6.40 a day, using the ratio (0.62) of consumption to income observed in 1964.

51 poverty lines on per capita consumption (1993 PPP) for 1964 yields the following:

log (poverty line) = 0.18 + 0.63*(log per capita consumption, national accounts)

with the standard error on log (consumption) being 0.07 and R^2 equal to 0.61. For 1993, the regression result is:

log (poverty line) = 0.04 + 0.54*(log per capita consumption, national accounts)

The three elasticities—0.59, 0.63, and 0.54—are strikingly close; the 1993 estimate of elasticity is used in chapter 11 to advocate a new poverty line.

The World Bank Enters the Poverty Arena

In the early 1970s, the World Bank's study of absolute poverty received a major impetus—perhaps initiated by the World Bank president, Robert McNamara, at a speech in Nairobi in October 1973. Until then, the bank had been mostly a source for financing infrastructure projects in developing countries. By directing the bank's extensive resources toward the study of poverty, and by leveraging funds to study poverty in other institutions and countries, McNamara created a "natural monopoly" of intellectual leadership, in-house research, and funding for research outside the bank.

The availability of resources meant that front-line concern with poverty became de rigueur for all economies and development economists, regardless of their political or ideological orientation. There was now almost a universal concern with the development practitioner's "triad"—the search was on to find the relationship between poverty, inequality, and growth. And the search was on to find policies that would both remove poverty and result in higher growth—and create more equal economies.

Not long after McNamara's 1973 speech, the first of several World Bank studies on income inequality and poverty appeared. That study—which was written by economists at the World Bank, and had a title that revealed its ideological moorings, *Redistribution with Growth* (Chenery et al. 1974)— was launched not only as a new book but also as a new tool for development policy. The *Redistribution with Growth* model was only a departure in the issue it examined, but was *not* a departure from the existing philosophy of development, a philosophy almost universal at quasi-governmental organizations and at leading centers of learning in the United States and the United Kingdom.

This philosophy, or ideology, gave considerably more weight to the power of governments, and considerably more respect for their abilities, than was perhaps justified. (This was the mid-1970s, before globalization, before Margaret Thatcher, and before anyone knew that there was an alternative, let alone a Hayekian one.) The core McNamara model was one of loco parentis: The state and its instruments knew better. But the captains were asked to change the emphasis from import substitution for industry to "poverty alleviation policies" by the government.

Any similarity between the "new" and "old" development models, and between these models and the Marxian-socialist view of the world, was not coincidental. In the 1970s and 1980s, several of the recommended policies of international institutions (import substitution, central planning, a larger role of the state—not to mention computable general equilibrium models) were implemented. Less than a decade later, it was observed that most of these policies had failed.

How successful was the new *Redistribution with Growth* strategy? It depends on what poverty levels were at the beginning of the 1970s, on what poverty levels are today, whether these levels are correctly measured, and on whether the observed reduction in poverty can be attributed to direct policies of poverty alleviation or the indirect effects of economic growth—a debate equally in vogue in the mid-1970s when Bhagwati (1988) originated the discussion on direct and indirect effects of growth. For a discussion of these issues, see chapter 10.

First Absolute Poverty Line, Estimates, and Forecasts

This centralized international concern with poverty alleviation, and therefore its measurement, led to the search for an *absolute* poverty line. Note that both the United States and India were concerned with poverty, and policymakers in both countries came up with poverty lines appropriate for their respective economies. But if international monies had to be allocated for poverty reduction—regardless of caste, color, creed, sex, or nationality—then an objective standard of poverty was necessary. Should poor people in Malaysia obtain poverty reduction grants, or those in South Korea, or those in Brazil, or those in India? There was no objective way of evaluation other than to construct, and estimate, an absolute poverty line—a line not only absolute within an economy, but across countries and across time.

Given that only two poverty lines existed (those of India and the United States), it was not surprising that the first definition of an international poor-country poverty line should rely overwhelmingly on an Indian poverty line. In an important paper published in 1979, "Growth and Poverty in Developing Countries," Ahluwalia, Carter, and Chenery laid much of the groundwork for the poverty research that was to follow for the next two decades. Issues pertaining to definition, measurement, and forecasts (for 2000) were discussed in detail.

Regarding the poverty line, Ahluwalia and his colleagues explicitly rejected a calorie consumption approach and opted for a monetary poverty line; and lack of data on consumption survey data for several developing countries made them reluctantly opt for an income rather than a consumption poverty line. The poverty line chosen was $200 per capita per year (according to the International Comparison Programme, later to be named PPP), at 1970 prices. The authors tagged this poverty line to be the income of the 45th percentile of the Indian income distribution for 1975.

But Ahluwalia and his colleagues did not have an income distribution for India. The 45th percentile of the *consumption* distribution yields a level of PPP $1.25 per capita per day, at 1985 prices, and $1.67 a day, at 1993 prices. (The corresponding *income* levels for the 45th percentile are $1.79 [1985 base] and $2.39 [1993 base].) All of these levels are on the basis of national accounts data. In the early to mid-1970s, household surveys in India were capturing about 80 percent of national accounts consumption. Thus, the first international poverty line, the line of Ahluwalia and his colleagues, if *benchmarked on the basis of a lower level of mean survey consumption, yields a lower poverty line of $1 a day ($1.25 multiplied by 0.8), at 1985 PPP prices.*

The publication of this first *international* poverty line by Ahluwalia et al. set off a flurry of research on the dimensions of world and regional poverty.[11] In the context of what was to develop only a decade later (a "new" poverty line), the methodology used by researchers needs to be understood. The four-step method is not complicated at all. The first step involved the creation of an income distribution for all countries; this was done through the use of the consumption or income distribution for each country.[12]

The second step involved a consistency transformation (i.e., the survey *means* were transformed into the corresponding national accounts means by multiplying all values in the distribution by the ratio of incomes as revealed by the survey and national accounts).[13] The third step involved the use of PPP exchange rates rather than dollar exchange rates. The fourth step was a simple counting of the heads below the poverty line.

---

11. E.g., see Fields (1980, 1989); Berry, Bourguignon, and Morrisson (1981); and Yotopoulos (1989).

12. All distributions were transformed into an income distribution by Ahluwalia, Carter, and Chenery (1979). So if only a consumption distribution was available (e.g., India) this distribution was "converted" into an income distribution by dividing the mean by one minus the savings rate.

13. Ahluwalia, Carter, and Chenery (1979) realized that the appropriate match was with per capita personal incomes, but the choice was "dictated by the absence of data on the personal component of GNP." This absence is present today as well, for most developing countries.

The researchers arrived at two main findings. First, excluding China (for which data were not available), 38 percent of the world's population was living in poverty. Second, most poor people (three-fourths) resided in South Asia, Indonesia, and sub-Saharan Africa; the researchers estimated the poverty rate in the developing world at 50.9 percent in 1960, 38.0 percent in 1975, and a "base case projection" of 16.3 percent in 2000. These projections, again, exclude China for lack of data; also, the projection for 2000 is very close to the United Nations Millennium Declaration Goal of 15 percent poor people for 15 years *later* in 2015.

The Search for an *Absolute* Absolute Measure

No sooner had the Ahluwalia, Carter, and Chenery (1979) poverty line appeared in print than it was rejected. This very reasonable absolute poverty line was considered not absolute enough. Part of the reasoning might have been that the poverty line was dependent on PPP estimates, and these estimates were just that—estimates of the unknown purchasing power. The PPP project had only started in 1968, and it was highly unclear that an acceptable measure of incomes would be available anytime soon. And income estimates based on a dollar exchange rate were no good, because such exchange-rate-based conversions did not yield comparable values. Hence, the search for an absolute *non*-income-based poverty line was launched.

If no comparable measure of income was available, how could poverty levels based on incomes be generated? This was a case of "If there is no bamboo, there can be no flute." An intensive search for the bamboo was on. The absolute item of choice became the consumption of calories, and not the food that was used to consume these calories. (The developers of the original poverty line, Ahluwalia et al., had explicitly warned against the beguiling calorie trap, but their warnings were not heeded.) Food shares were dispensed with because it was felt that they were not volatile enough for a precise measure of absolute poverty. Engel ratios were not useful in distinguishing Mexican poor people from Korean poor people (both had food consumption Engel ratios at the height of the 1960s).

Caloric consumption seemed the most appropriate reference point (for comparing poverty). Food was a major component of the consumption basket of the poor, and survival instincts all pointed toward first removing hunger, before shelter or clothing. The reason that shelter and clothing were not considered relevant to the first stage of poverty removal was that most poverty was concentrated in tropical areas, where clothing and shelter were not as necessary as food for survival.

Perhaps coincidentally, the mid-1970s was also a time for a big push forward by nutritionists to understand why Americans were overweight, and so there might have been a coincidence of interests in zeroing in on

Table 4.1 Calorie intake in the United States, 1971-74

Group	Mean	Percentile 10th	Percentile 90th	Calorie requirement (KCal/day) FAO	Calorie requirement (KCal/day) United States	Percentage malnourished[a] FAO	Percentage malnourished[a] United States
All							
Males	2,393	1,257	3,733	3,000	2,535	67	46
Females	1,618	852	2,469	2,200	1,870	80	70
Males							
White	2,428	1,298	3,778				
Black	2,141	1,098	3,350				
Females							
White	1,626	866	2,470				
Black	1,551	766	2,439				

FAO = UN Food and Agriculture Organization

a. Percentage malnourished are those below the stated requirement level.

Source: US Health and Nutrition Expenditure Survey, 1974; as quoted in Bhalla (1980).

calories. In very little time, the conventional wisdom became that poor Indians consumed too few calories, and rich Americans too many. Even after shocking revelations to the contrary (see table 4.1), the paradigm of calories as a measure of poverty has still not disappeared from the horizon of some economists.

Considerable research on caloric consumption levels was published. The search for the Holy Grail of an absolute poverty measure was on, and several economists joined the pilgrimage.[14] The Rome-based UN Food and Agriculture Organization took the lead in publishing estimates of country consumption of food and calories.

Economists were quick to recognize that the caloric method of estimating poverty suffered from major conceptual problems. For example, how is the caloric measure accurate if on becoming richer, a person moves from potatoes to meat, from a cheap to a rich source of calories? One answer to this objection was that the poor people being compared were not Tanzanians and Americans, but rather Tanzanians and Indians; that is, people for whom meat was not even an option, let alone a luxury. Although this answer silenced the objectors, it laid the groundwork for several false estimates of poverty decades hence. What was observed was that consumers were continually making choices among food items (e.g., cereals or vegetables), and that therefore the error in equating calories with poverty was continuing.

---

14. See Reutlinger and Selowsky (1976). I myself was an eager participant in this search for the poverty grail; see Bhalla (1980).

It was not long, however, before serious doubts began to be raised about the reliability of *any* calorie-based measure of poverty. The likelihood of type II errors (people consuming few calories but otherwise rich) was large. Sukhatme (1977) documented that *intra*-individual variation in caloric consumption (people's varying metabolisms and physical activities lead to differences in their efficiency of digesting food) was large and swamped *inter*-individual variation. And a common caloric level for individuals was not really accurate since the sedentary lifestyle of an urbanite was not really comparable with the lifestyle of a person residing in the rural area.

Finally, careful measurements of caloric input data by the US Health and Nutrition Expenditure Survey for the period 1971-74 yielded the shocking result that, if Food and Agriculture Organization norms were used (3,000 calories for an adult male 25-34 years of age and 2,200 calories for an adult female in the same age range), then more than two-thirds of American males and 80 percent of American women were *malnourished* (see table 4.1).[15]

Rediscovering the $1-a-Day Poverty Line

The influence of the Indian poverty line, and the legitimacy it gained in being adopted by the World Bank, was considerable. Although the motivation may have been different, both Indian and US lines had an identical three-step methodology. First, decide, on whatever basis, a value for food consumption that is deemed to be a minimum. Second, for the group of people defined as poor, observe the share of nonfood consumption. Third, add average food consumption to average nonfood consumption and obtain the poverty line. The reference to calories was obligatory, but ultimately irrelevant.

Altimir (1981) set up poverty lines for the Economic Commission for Latin America and the Caribbean and used a vague nutritional basis to get at minimum food consumption (à la India) and then a multiplier of 2 to get at a minimum total consumption, à la the United States. (Recall that Orshansky used a multiplier of 3 for the United States.) Also, like Ahluwalia and his colleagues, Altimir preferred the national accounts means of income rather than survey means. He justified his procedure thus: "Estimating the incidence of poverty by applying independently valued poverty lines to income distributions that are subject to different degrees of income underestimation would not only result in exaggerating incidence but, even more important for our purposes, in *incomparable* estimates of poverty" (1996, 8; emphasis added).

---

15. Again, it does not take rocket science measurement techniques to observe that most Americans are weight challenged the wrong way.

Throughout the 1980s, new lines were set up for individual developing economies, and the poverty line developed by Ahluwalia and his colleagues was used to calculate global poverty. But the feeling seemed to persist that the international poverty line of PPP $200 was too arbitrary and too dependent on the poverty line of just one country, India. Hence, the search for an absolute line that was not overly dependent on one country's line—albeit one that included most of the world's poor people (along with those in China)—continued.

By the late 1980s, the poverty profession had come full circle. Calories were definitely out, but not food consumption (and rightly so). The search for an absolute poverty line ended with the second World Bank line, this time put forth by Ravallion, Datt, and van de Walle (1991). They had first published their estimate in *World Development Report 1990: Poverty and Development*. Since then, Ravallion has been associated (not unlike Ahluwalia before him) with several publications on the measurement of poverty. These two international poverty lines, and the methods used to develop them—more than just reflecting the work of the researchers who articulated them—bore the imprimatur of the World Bank. Hence, these lines are sometimes referred to as "World Bank I" and "World Bank II."

The World Bank II researchers correctly noted that the absolute poverty line in countries varied with the level of their per capita income; hence, the obvious choice for an absolute poverty line was the line in the *poorest* country. They also use a model relating the poverty line to per capita consumption, and from this model they derived the *predicted* poverty line for the poorest country:

> The lowest mean consumption amongst the 86 countries studied in the *World Development Report* is Somalia at $22 per person per month in 1985 PPP prices. At this point, equation (1) [the model] predicts a poverty line of $23, only slightly different from that of India. Thus, India's poverty line is very close to the poverty line we would predict for the poorest country, and as such, can be considered a reasonable lower bound to the range of admissible poverty lines for the developing world. (Ravallion, Datt, and van de Walle 1991, 348)

Ravallion and his colleagues note that whereas $23 is the lowest, the poverty lines for six of the poorest countries—Indonesia, Bangladesh, Nepal, Kenya, Tanzania, and Morocco—formed a cluster around $31 a month, and two other poverty lines—for the Philippines and Pakistan—were "close to this figure." Given the (memory) appeal of such a value, the $1-a-day line, at 1985 prices, soon became *the* absolute poverty line.

Recall that the Indian poverty line at 1985 prices was almost exactly equal to $1 per capita per day, rather than what Ravallion and his colleagues indicate that it is—a poverty line close to $23 a month, or $0.76 a day. This divergence mirage occurs because Ravallion and his colleagues choose (for unknown reasons) to use the *rural* poverty line when available.[16] If the

---

16. If the purpose was to develop a rural international poverty line, such a procedure might have been justified, though one might ask the purpose of such a line.

poverty line for all of India for the last survey year (1987-88) before the development of the World Bank II poverty line is chosen, then the Indian poverty line (at the national level) is observed to be $1.04 a day—almost (definitionally) identical to the $1-a-day line chosen by the World Bank I researchers and very close to the $1-a-day line popularized by the World Bank II researchers. In other words, the search for an alternative poverty line ended exactly where it had started, after more than 15 years of effort—30 years, if one includes the effort of India's Planning Commission in 1962.[17]

The fact that the two seemingly different poverty lines are identical should not really be a surprise. Ahluwalia and his colleagues make their poverty line *equal* to the Indian poverty line, by assumption; though Ravallion and his colleagues do not do this by assumption, they do it de facto. It is interesting that the World Bank II researchers do not compare any of their results with those of the World Bank I researchers (or with the national Indian poverty line). Indeed, the trend-setting study by Ahluwalia and his colleagues is not even referred to by the World Bank II researchers (or by *World Development Report 1990*)—nor are several other studies on the development of poverty lines in the world, including Altimir's work on Latin America.[18]

The methods used by the two sets of World Bank researchers could not have been more different. Whereas one set literally adopted an existing line, the other identified the line through a "model."[19] The first set of researchers believed they had constructed an absolute poverty line, but they were also explicit about its arbitrary nature, and the fact that it was the Indian poverty line. The second set developed an involved method, and they believed they had discovered a new poverty line. If questionable assumptions (e.g., for countries where both rural and urban poverty lines were available, like India, they chose the rural poverty line) had not been made, the equivalence would have been noted by the second set themselves.

The Poverty Line Reduced

During the past few years, data on PPP incomes and exchange rates, based on a new set of "base" 1993 prices, have become available for a

---

17. Or as T.S. Eliot wrote, "We shall not cease from exploration / And the end of all our exploring / Will be to arrive where we started / And know the place for the first time."

18. Some of the possible reasons for this occurrence (e.g., a research funding and research monopoly) are explored in Bhalla (2002b).

19. Although an actual model is presented (regressing the poverty line on per capita consumption), the results of the model are really not relevant—it is the cluster that decided, appropriately, what the poverty line should be.

large set of countries. These data are the outcome of the International Comparison Programme and have been released by the World Bank and made available to the international community via their prestigious data publication, *World Development Indicators*, and its associated CD-ROM.

There are two basic reasons why new PPP data are constructed: to involve additional countries (the 1993 data involved 110 countries vs. only 60 for the 1985 PPP series); and to incorporate the effects of changing relative prices, both within a country and for countries relative to international prices. (This is not unlike revisions that are undertaken with respect to national accounts within each country.)

The PPP data supplied by the World Bank consist essentially of one variable per country per year: the nominal PPP exchange rate. The division of variables, expressed in local currency, by this exchange rate yields PPP estimates at *current* international prices. For example, the 1998 GDP in local currency for India was reported as Rs17,600 billion, and the exchange rate (termed the "conversion factor") was given as 8.53. In PPP terms, therefore, the 1998 GDP for India, at then-current international prices, was Rs2,063 billion.

The conversion from current to constant international prices is done via the use of the numeraire; in this case, the GDP deflator for the United States.[20] Between 1985 and 1993, for example, the US deflator increased from 78.4 to 100. Thus, over these 8 years, international inflation was equal to 27.6 percent.[21] For each country, therefore, one would expect international inflation to be approximately 28 percent. Thus, given the $1-a-day poverty line in 1985, the equivalent poverty line at 1993 prices should be about 28 percent higher, or $1.28.

The first researchers to use the new PPP data were Chen and Ravallion (2000). They updated their earlier work on global poverty and produced a set of estimates for regional and global poverty for selected years from 1987 to 1998. They contended that the new, 1993-prices-based poverty line equal to $1 a day in purchasing power (at 1985 prices) was $1.08 a day. This is the third World Bank definition of an international poverty line (World Bank III). It was seen above that the first two international poverty lines were essentially equivalent; it remains to be determined whether this new poverty line is also the "same" in purchasing power terms.

Taken at face value, the equivalence of $1 a day at 1985 prices and $1.08 a day at 1993 prices suggests that the average *international inflation*

---

20. On the *World Development Indicators 1998* CD-ROM, both nominal and real PPP income levels are published for all the years and all the countries. This World Bank document uses the US GDP deflator to convert nominal PPP to real PPP for all the countries and all the years; I am following the same procedure here.

21. Note that even the United States has a PPP exchange rate that is not necessarily equal to 1; for the 1993 PPP series, this varied between $0.905 and $1.06.

between the 2 years was only 8 percent and not about 28 percent, as was just suggested. The two estimated rates of international inflation (Chen and Ravallion 2000 for the developing world, and US inflation) do not appear to be close enough to be due to either relative price changes or relative currency appreciation.

Was international inflation really as low as 8 percent, or less than 1 percent a year, during the period 1985-93? US consumer price inflation averaged three times this rate, and most industrialized countries were not far behind. It is not possible, therefore, that international PPP inflation was only 8 percent. It cannot be, and it was not. Given this easy calculation, what is interesting to note is that there was not a single comment,[22] let alone disagreement, when this "revisionist" view on world inflation was first presented. Part of this deficiency was also rectified later by Deaton, who stated:

> Given world—and U.S.—inflation between 1985 and 1993, it is somewhat surprising that the international poverty line should have increased by only 8 percent, from $1 to $1.08. But the updating was carried out by going back to the country poverty lines, and converting back to international dollars, so that the modest increase comes, not from a failure to allow for world inflation, but because the PPP international dollar has strengthened relative to the currencies of the poor countries whose poverty lines are incorporated into the international line. (2001a, 4)

The hypothesis that the international PPP dollar has appreciated was tested, and found wanting (see below). Then what explains Chen and Ravallion's error? What they appear to have missed is that there are *two* adjustments to inflation when conversion is made from a domestic currency to international prices. The first is a "depreciation" with respect to an international exchange rate; the second is international inflation itself. The latter is expected to be the *same* for different countries, and indeed is what is needed to convert incomes (or consumption) from one base to another.

Table 4.2 documents that this is indeed the case. Two sets of inflation data are presented for various regions of the world, as well as for the poorest eight countries that constituted the sample in both studies by Ravallion and his colleagues on the international poverty line, 1991 and 2000.[23] Although there is some minor variation around the residual PPP

---

22. This is not exactly true. I was one of the referees for *World Development Report 2000/2001: Attacking Poverty*, and had pointed out in June 2000 that international inflation was 27 percent. Later, in Bhalla (2000a), I stated: "The most recent publication of the World Bank, however, reports a *new* international poverty line of $1.08 per capita per day, 1993 prices . . . i.e., the new line of $1.08, 1993 prices, is equivalent to $0.82, 1985 prices. The reasoning behind this large 18 percent reduction in the absolute poverty line is not transparent, and debatable" (p. 1).

23. The two studies, again, are Ravallion, Datt, and van de Walle 1991 and Chen and Ravallion 2000. The 1991 study included two additional countries, Tanzania and Somalia; unfortunately, data for these two countries were not available for the 1993 base.

Table 4.2 What is the $1-a-day poverty line at 1993 prices: $1.08 (World Bank) or $1.30 (simple accounting procedure)?
(median percentage)

Region	Depreciation of PPP exchange rate, 1985-93	"Residual" PPP inflation, 1985-93[a]	Domestic inflation, 1985-93[b]	Domestic food inflation, 1985-93[c] (percent)
Asia	33.1	28.4	61.5	62.7
Sub-Saharan Africa	42.2	32.3	74.5	101.0
Latin America	116.2	15.2	131.4	182.6
Developing world	41.6	27.7	69.3	105.2
Developing world, excluding China and India	43.4	25.9	69.3	105.9
Eastern Europe	327.6	−3.6	324.0	566.4
Industrialized countries	−2.8	29.7	26.9	28.3
World	**37.5**	**24.0**	**61.5**	**88.7**
World, excluding Eastern Europe	**26.2**	**27.8**	**54.2**	**67.5**
Poorest eight countries				
India	41.0	30.6	71.6	74.7
Bangladesh	22.6	26.4	49.0	52.6
Indonesia	37.2	26.7	64.0	68.2
Kenya	42.2	34.7	76.9	
Morocco	13.2	29.2	42.3	47.7
Nepal	64.7	29.3	94.0	95.3
Pakistan	26.1	35.4	61.5	66.7
Philippines	44.5	25.2	69.7	63.0
Overall	**39.1**	**29.2**	**66.9**	**66.7**

PPP = purchasing power parity

a. Data are available for domestic inflation (measured by the GDP deflator) and exchange rate depreciation with respect to international prices. The PPP inflation for each region is derived from the above two estimates.

b. By definition, overall domestic inflation is equal to the depreciation of the PPP exchange rate plus international inflation.

c. Domestic food inflation figures (food consumer price index) are from World Bank, *World Development Indicators*.

Note: The $1-a-day, 1985-prices poverty line was based on the 10 poorest countries in 1985. This set included Tanzania and Somalia, two countries for which complete data are not available.

Sources: World Bank, *World Development Indicators*, CD-ROMs, 1998, 2001; Maddison (2001); Penn World Tables, various years.

inflation amount (residual because it is the difference between observed domestic inflation and assigned depreciation), it is comforting to note that the PPP method is exactly as advertised—international inflation is (approximately) the same for all countries. All the regions, as well as the poorest countries, show a median PPP inflation of about 30 percent.

What about the possibility that food, which is a major consumption item of poor people, had a different, and lower, inflation rate than nonfood items? This does not appear to be the case because, on average, food prices seem to have increased at a faster pace, by about 5 percent for all of the poorest developing countries—though they rose at the same rate as overall inflation for the selected poorest countries listed in table 4.2.

Another statistic that easily reveals that world inflation was indeed 30 percent during the eight years from 1985 to 1993 is to look at average world income in 1985 for 151 countries for which both 1985 and 1993 base data are available. The result: Average daily income at 1985 prices was $10.72; at 1993 prices, it was $13.99—a difference of 30.5 percent. Given international inflation of 30 percent between 1985 and 1993, the line of $1.08 is nothing but a *reduction* in the absolute poverty line by 17 percent. *The equivalent to $1 a day at 1985 prices is $1.30 a day at 1993 prices, and not $1.08 a day.*

The computation of the poverty line has a bearing on how many poor people there are in the world, and the aid effort needed to eliminate poverty. The higher the poverty line, the more poor people; the lower the line, the fewer, and the smaller the aid effort required. By reducing the poverty line, it would appear that the World Bank is understating the number of poor people in the world. That this is not the reality— indeed, that poverty is considerably lower than the World Bank estimate based on a reduced poverty line—is documented in chapter 9.

Poverty lines are expected to rise through time and with development— not to fall so radically (17 percent) during the 8 years (1985-93) when income per capita in the developing world increased by close to 30 percent. The level of the absolute line does not matter for the interpretation of trends, as long as the level is kept constant in real terms. If the level is changed, and it is stated that it has actually remained the same, the best that one can hope for is a vast amount of confusion—and possibly yet more input for "theories of development" that have little to do with the underlying reality.

Evolving World Bank Definitions of Poverty

Given the fortuitous coincidence of the equivalence of the *national-accounts, income-mean*-based World Bank I poverty line (PPP $200 per capita per year, at 1970 prices) and the *survey-consumption-mean*-based World Bank II poverty line (PPP $1 a day, at 1985 prices), the stage is set for a comparison of world poverty trends since 1960.

According to the Ahluwalia, Carter, and Chenery study (1979), poverty in the developing world (excluding China) declined by 13 percentage points during the 15 preglobalization years 1960-75. For this same period, the present study finds (using national accounts data and 1993 PPP prices; also for the developing world, excluding China) the decline to be only 7 percent. For the 13 years 1987-2000, this study finds that poverty declined by a slightly larger amount, 8 percentage points. Whether this decline was less or more than what should have been expected is something examined in detail in subsequent chapters. Per capita consumption during the period 1960-75 (again, excluding China) increased by 34 percent; from 1987 to 2000, per capita consumption only increased by a considerably lower 13 percent. The yield (the decline in HCR per unit of increase in income) was 0.21 during the period 1960-75, and it tripled, to 0.62, during the globalization period 1987-2000.

A priori, this yield suggests that growth during the recent period was fantastically propoor, and/or that inequality in the developing world (excluding China) improved considerably during the globalization period. This is the second major hint that analysts and commentators have missed about the golden age of the poor—the so-called globalization period from 1980 to 2000.

II

DISCUSSION OF KNOWLEDGE ON POVERTY, INEQUALITY, AND GROWTH AND ANALYSIS OF DATA AND METHODOLOGIES

5

Taking Stock of the Facts

A consistent picture emerges about poverty, inequality, and growth during the era of globalization. There was strong growth in the developing world during the period 1980-2000. During this period, the developing world started the process of catch-up and did so by clocking an extra 1.5 percent a year growth than was achieved by the industrialized world.

This good news about growth was counterbalanced by somewhat bad news on the inequality front. Intercountry inequality—the Kuznets curve stipulating worsening inequality in the developing world—was verified by several tests. The elasticity of the incomes of poor people (the bottom 20 percent) with respect to overall growth was observed to be only 0.8, a full 25 percent lower than the unity level required for the conclusion that "growth was good for the poor."

Moreover, instead of convergence in intercountry incomes, there appeared to be wide divergence—the rich countries almost doubled the relative gap with respect to the poorest countries. Fulfilling the fears of many, it was also observed that *individual* income inequality had worsened in the world, and most likely by a frighteningly high amount in the late 1980s and early 1990s. Thus the wishes of many, especially neoclassical economists, that the natural process of convergence would occur, and that intercountry inequality would decline, were belied.

Despite this inequality change, high growth might still have meant an improvement in the living standards of poor people. Mathematically, if mean growth is larger than mean worsening of inequality, vast proportions of poor people can still be better off. Unfortunately, this was not to be. It appears that the really significant reduction in poverty occurred in the 1960-75 period—13 percentage points, from 51 to 38 percent for the world excluding China (see Ahluwalia, Carter, and Chenery 1979). The much publicized globalization period saw only a minuscule decline—5 percentage points, from 28 to 23 percent,[1] from 1987 to 1999.

The second half of this chapter discusses the basis for these results and asks whether they are plausible. It is contended that rocket science is not needed to differentiate between the various research products, and conclusions, available in the marketplace. "Smell" tests, or "duck" tests, can suffice. Simple consistency and plausibility checks when applied to conventional wisdom suggest that not all is right with the received *perception* of what happened during the era of globalization. But first, let us look at the overall picture.

The Global Pie, 1960-2000

Although it is little realized, in recent decades the developing world (again, the world excluding industrialized countries and Eastern Europe) has sharply increased its share of world population and world output (table 5.1 and figure 5.1). The population of poor countries constituted 71.4 percent of global population in 1960; today, this share is 81.3 percent. The developing world's share of global income was 29.3 percent in 1960; in 2000, this share had increased to 42.4 percent. So while its population share increased by 13 percent (log change), its income share increased by (log) 37 percent. In other words, welfare gains in poor countries exceeded those in rich countries by approximately 24 percent, and did so especially during the period of globalization.

But these facts are precisely the ones causing the apparent angst: so much growth in poor countries, and all of it in the wrong hands. The bottom half of the population received precious few benefits of growth, as "revealed" by the minuscule decline in the official world head count ratio (HCR). Rich people in poor countries had become considerably richer, perhaps at the expense of poor people in poor countries. These are the conclusions of the received wisdom—which may not be entirely right.

Inequality Trends

In a widely quoted essay, Wade reaches the correct conclusion:

> Anybody interested in the wealth and poverty of nations must be interested in what is happening to the global distribution of income. A lot turns on the question.

1. This decline is now for the entire developing world, including China; figures are from the World Bank.

Table 5.1 Global regions' shares of income and population (percent)

Region[a]	Share of world population				Share of world income			
	1950	1960	1980	2000	1950	1960	1980	2000
Asia	53.0	49.7	52.5	53.5	12.6	12.1	12.2	25.9
China and India	41.1	36.5	37.7	37.6	8.4	7.9	6.5	16.8
Sub-Saharan Africa	6.6	7.4	8.6	10.9	3.2	3.2	3.0	2.5
Middle East and North Africa	3.8	4.4	5.1	6.2	3.0	3.5	5.1	4.7
Latin America	6.2	7.2	8.2	8.5	7.7	7.9	9.9	8.4
Developing world[b]	72.0	71.4	76.9	81.3	28.8	29.3	32.5	42.4
Developing world, excluding China and India	31.0	35.0	39.2	43.7	20.4	21.4	26.0	25.6
Eastern Europe	10.2	10.4	8.7	6.8	11.2	11.3	12.6	6.1
Nonindustrialized world[c]	79.7	79.2	83.0	86.0	37.5	38.1	42.8	47.6
Industrialized world	20.2	20.8	17.0	14.0	62.5	61.9	57.2	52.4
World	100.0	100.0	100.0	100.0	100.0	100.0	100.0	100.0
World, actual*	2,696.0	3,022.0	4,432.0	6,071.0	6.2	9.7	23.1	39.2

* = World population is in millions; per capita income is in PPP dollars per day (1993 prices).

a. For the classification of regions, see appendix C.

b. The developing world is the world excluding the industrialized world and Eastern Europe.

c. The nonindustrialized world is the world excluding the industrialized world.

Note: Nominal purchasing power parity (PPP) data, 1993 base, have been converted into constant PPP data, 1993 base, using the US GDP deflator, a practice followed in World Bank, *World Development Indicators*, 1998. World population figures are in millions; world income is in trillions of 1993 PPP dollars.

Sources: World Bank, *World Development Indicators*, CD-ROMs, 1998, 2001; Maddison (2001); Penn World Tables, various years.

Figure 5.1 Changing patterns of world income and population shares

World income shares

1960

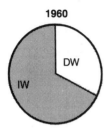

1980

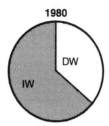

2000

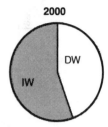

World population shares

1960

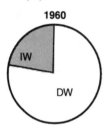

1980

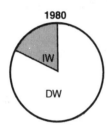

2000

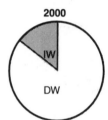

Ratio of per capita incomes: Developing countries to industrialized countries

1960

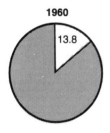

1980

2000

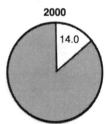

DW = developing world
IW = industrialized world

Note: The developing world is the world excluding the industrialized world and Eastern Europe. The data reflect those reported in table 5.1.

Sources: World Bank, *World Development Indicators*, CD-ROMs, 1988, 2001; Maddison (2001); Penn World Tables, various years.

If the world's income distribution has become more equal in the past few decades, this would be powerful evidence that globalization works to the benefit of all. . . . It would answer some of the fears of the anti-globalization protesters. And it would help to settle a crucial and long-standing disagreement in economic theory, between the orthodox view that economic growth naturally delivers "convergence" of rich and poor countries, and alternative theories which, for one reason or another, say the opposite.[2]

Inequality trends *appear* to be in line with the "fears of the antiglobalization protesters." The previous chapter documented the results on change in the distribution of country inequality according to various studies, and various indices of inequality. Several, sometimes conflicting, results emerged. The first was of no discernible change in country inequality during the past 20 years or so. This result was offered by the research of Deininger and Squire (1996); Li, Squire, and Zou (1998); three studies from the Harvard Institute for International Development (Roemer and Gugerty 1997; Timmer 1997; Gallup, Radelet, and Warner 1998); and Dollar and Kraay (2000). Ranged against this impressive set of evidence was Cornia and Kiiski's study (2001), which offered the opposite conclusion, that is, country inequality had definitely worsened.

Traditional tests of inequality change were conducted on the national household data collected—more than 1,000 surveys, larger than any collection to date. Several tests conducted on these data supported Cornia and Kiiski's findings. Further, it was found that the elasticity of income growth of the bottom 20 percent was significantly lower than unity (equal to 0.8) in the globalization period—and equal to unity in the preceding two decades: strong evidence that not only was inequality worsening, but that it had not always been the case. Thus, there was a large contemporaneous correlation between globalization and worsening country and intercountry inequality. Note, however, that according to the Kuznets curve, this increase in inequality was entirely to be expected; that is, things get worse on the inequality front, with growth, before things get better.

On individual income inequality—i.e., inequality measured with the individual, rather than the country, as the unit of analysis—the evidence was again mixed. Bourguignon and Morrisson (2001) suggested that individual inequality had stayed flat for the second half of the twentieth century; Milanovic (1999) found a large increase in world inequality during a short 5-year period, 1988 to 1993. An earlier version of the present study (Bhalla 2000d) found evidence that individual inequality had actually *improved* in the past 20 years; this study also documented that given the per capita growth rates of China (and, less important, India), world inequality *had* to have declined.

---

2. Robert Wade, "Winners and Losers," *The Economist*, April 28, 2001, 73-75; the quotation is on p. 73.

So two conclusions can be made about what happened to world inequality during the past 20 years. First, there is strong evidence to suggest that country inequality worsened. Second, there is mixed evidence regarding the pattern of individual inequality. This second, ambiguous result is converted into a "definite" finding in chapter 11. Although inequality between countries no doubt worsened, the globalization period was associated with a significant improvement in world inequality—a finding contrary to all the studies published to date, and especially contrary to the "celebrity" (or celebrated) finding of Milanovic (1999).

Poverty Trends

Given continuous and strong growth for 40 years (2.1 percent a year, 1960-80, and 3.1 percent a year, 1980-2000) and worsening inequality, what happened to absolute poverty? Theoretically, it could have gone up or down, depending on whether inequality change was larger, or smaller, than economic growth. Unlike inequality studies, all studies of global poverty have (to date) originated from one source: the World Bank. From 1987 to 1999 it appears that poverty fell by only 5 percentage points, from 28 to 23 percent. Given that these are the only estimates available, and that they emanate from a large institution whose function is to provide such numbers to the international research and policy community, it is not surprising that these results are used by everyone. So they are not only the conventional wisdom, they constitute the *only* wisdom.

Not Propoor Growth

These results have not gone unnoticed. The world community has taken note, seminars have been organized, policy huddles have convened, and research has been financed to generate theories and models of *alternative* development patterns—or efforts in keeping with the traditional model of growth but tweaking it to ensure that it yields propoor growth. This new growth industry has yielded several outputs (all of chapter 10 is dedicated to analyzing them), prominent among which is Thomas's appropriately titled study, *The Quality of Growth* (2000).

It is important to recognize the origins of such research, and the possible consequences for policy. Economists have been studying growth patterns and poverty reduction for decades. They were now suddenly made to question everything they had learned. They were told to go out and enhance productivity and growth in poor nations. They went and did that—after stumbling with *statist* policies during the 1960-80 period, fortunately the thinking changed, and they stumbled on the importance of economic freedom for generating growth.[3]

The pressures of globalization might have forced the thinking to change, but that is not so important. Helped by Margaret Thatcher, all governments could not all do right all the time; indeed, the road to the perpetuation of poverty hell had been lavishly paved with good intentions. But now the very organization that *was* the Washington Consensus was informing the world that the whole class, under its leadership, had failed—yet again. This result was credible given the source—the World Bank had more resources to study poverty than any other institution or any government in the world.

So the result economists had to accept was that while considerable growth had been achieved, while India and China, home to 75 percent of the world's poor people in 1980, had enjoyed per capita increases of the miracle variety—an average annual growth rate of 4.9 percent for 20 years—despite all this, poverty was stubbornly persisting at 25 to 29 percent. And in the South Asia region dominated by India, poverty levels had hardly budged from 40 to 45 percent.

Thus, a new look was needed, and this new look did come up with the answer. It documented the nature of nonpoor growth, blamed the lack of poverty reduction on high levels of inequality and worsening levels of such inequality, and suggested the means to engineer a Third Way—the "quality" of growth is what counts. And what also counts is the voice of poor people, and the need to empower them with something besides what they need most: money.

Is the Conventional Wisdom Correct?

But how do we know that the reality may *not* be what the World Bank is stating? How can these estimates of poverty be reproduced and checked for validity? How can we know that the lack of good-quality growth was responsible for the lack of any meaningful poverty decline? To date, there are no alternative estimates of world poverty.[4] But there are likely to be several in the coming years, with this book being the first such attempt.[5]

The emphasis throughout this book is on establishing the "facts." The assumption is that the "truth" is out there, waiting to be found. It is elusive, sometimes metaphysical, and often hard to define. But it is there.

---

3. See Bhalla (1997a) for an analysis of the joint roles of political and economic freedom in generating productivity growth.

4. Preliminary results on world inequality, and world poverty, were presented in Bhalla (2000d); the improved, updated estimates are presented in this book.

5. The second one is Asian Development Bank (2002).

As researchers, we can only try to *approximate* the underlying reality. The difference between various studies is in the rigor, and accuracy, with which they reach the unknown. Each individual has to be her own judge and executioner. One can be freely prejudiced and no (other) one will be the wiser, though some will end up intellectually poorer.

Ultimately, it boils down to what the numbers are, and what trends they reveal. Whether inequality has gone up or down is first an empirical question, and then a policy determinant. Unfortunately, gathering data on income distribution is an expensive, time-consuming exercise, and one subject to the possibility of large measurement errors. This means that interpretations of "trends" in inequality are difficult, and definitionally subject to large variation. And this means that claims of all kinds of results could go unquestioned. Inequality decreased—of course. Inequality increased—of course, and let me show you how.

The foundation of this book is the economic statistics that are routinely put out by most governments, as well as data emanating from official government surveys of household behavior, as well as data constructed by quasi-government authorities (e.g., purchasing power parity, or PPP, estimates), as well as data constructed by such analysts as Maddison (2001). If these data are *manifestly* wrong, then there is little anyone can say, on inequality, on poverty, or on globalization and its consequences. Note the emphasis on manifestly; obviously, all data come with excess baggage of error, for which analysts need to make "adjustments." But one should not get into the nihilist trap on "data errors."

Facts and Figures

The facts pertain to three important variables: poverty, inequality, and growth. There are numbers associated with each of these important policy concerns, and the numbers vary by author and study. So we are back to basics—basics of definition, measurement, and reexamination from the roots. Growth—measured how? By the growth in incomes. Measured in what currency (local currency, US dollars, or PPP exchange rates)? Poverty—measured how? If done so in the most common, and useful, manner (i.e., by computing HCR), then what poverty line is being used? Inequality—measured how? In terms of quintile shares, or the Gini index? The Gini on the basis of *country* inequality, or *individual* inequality? Though there is some obfuscation (actually quite a bit), the facts are not that difficult to establish.

But if the world is the unit of analysis, as in this book, then the assertion that facts are easy to ascertain is hugely incorrect. The difficulty is not so much conceptual (after all, a world with several countries is no different from a country with several states) but in the accessibility, and comparability, of data. The comparability of income is there, through the availability of exchange rates (in PPP or US dollars) for most of the postwar period and for most countries.

Income distribution data have also been available since the first such assembling in the mid-1970s. But a similar convergence on comparability has not been achieved with respect to these data. And the consistency checks reported in appendix B suggest that some of these data have huge errors.[6] Difficulty of access to the raw survey data[7] has often prevented consistency checks from being conducted by unofficial researchers. Technology and data dissemination reforms have now opened the world, and its data, to research.

The Importance of Data

Policymakers do not operate in a vacuum—statistics form an important feedback loop, because numbers determine government action (or inaction), which determines individual welfare, which feeds back into the loop and allows policymakers to attempt to micromanage and set corrective action. The process is Bayesian, and not unlike the corrective action followed to set the spacecraft right when it goes offtrack. To be sure, in the latter case much greater precision is achieved. This is why aeronautics is a science but policymaking and economics are arts. This is also why one sees fewer unemployed economists than unemployed scientists. And, of course, there is no unemployment among policy analysts as they cater to whatever spin their political masters desire.

This iterative process (with iterations often being dictated by fashions among Western economists) has been most prominent in developing countries, as they have attempted to steer a course for rapid growth and the alleviation of poverty. Many policies, often contradictory, have been pursued, but all have been well within the *tâtonnement* Bayesian process.

This book makes no apologies about being numbers oriented. When the polemics are over—or as Shakespeare put it ("Macbeth," Act I, Scene I):

When the hurly-burly's done,
When the battle's lost and won

—it is back to deciding what is the appropriate policy response.

---

6. These errors relate to a "basic" statistic like the Gini—the reported Gini for several distributions is significantly different from that computed by the simple accounting procedure (see figure 8.1).

7. Until very recently, governments have been hesitant to release household survey data to institutions and researchers, except to the World Bank. This policy has now changed, at least in India. Indeed, if there still were a lack of access to Indian survey data, large sections of this report, and especially the methodological innovations, would not have been possible.

Duck and Smell Tests to Differentiate

How should the different sets of estimates for poverty, inequality, growth, globalization, and so on be compared and evaluated? Throughout this book, consistency tests, "smell" tests, "duck" tests (if it does not walk like a duck, and does not talk like a duck, it cannot be a duck) are advocated, especially for such emotive, and sometimes intractable, subjects as income inequality and absolute poverty. The normal tendency is to take the raw "facts" at face value, and then to construct theories to fit the constructed facts. At a minimum, the construction needs to be vetted, its foundations tested, and its veracity established *before* theories are modeled.

What are duck and smell tests? They are tests that immediately tell you that something is wrong with the observed "reality." For example, if someone drives a BMW, and it is claimed that she is poor, then she fails the duck test; that is, she may walk like a duck, but she certainly does not run like a duck! Or, if it is claimed that world inequality changed by 5 percent in 5 years, or almost 4 standard deviations away from the norm, well, that fails the smell test. Or if poor Indians are spending a considerably larger fraction of their expenditures on fruits and vegetables, and on education and health, and yet have not crossed the poverty line, well, that fails the smell test as well.

Experts Debate

In late 1999, Milanovic published a study contending that on the basis of an exhaustive analysis of data on income distribution for more than 90 countries, the seemingly incontrovertible conclusion was that world individual inequality had significantly worsened in the late 1980s and early 1990s. It was an incontrovertible conclusion because the change observed—5.1 percent, or 3.4 Gini percentage points—was not small and hence explainable by data errors or noise.

Milanovic's study (1999), along with a companion study by Dikhanov and Ward (2000), formed the basis for a review essay by Wade published in the *Economist* in April 2001. Wade used these results to state that "world inequality increased from a Gini coefficient of 62.5 in 1988 to 66 in 1993. This is a faster rate of increase of inequality than that experienced within the United States and Britain during the 80s" (p. 74). He could have added, but did not, that such a large speed in an elephant-type variable (a *world* Gini), in such a short period of time, was most likely unprecedented in the history of the world.

This possibly was the first hint of a "duck." A large inequality change estimated by Milanovic in a world Gini is suggestive of social upheaval of a magnitude we have not witnessed, or imagined. But is a 5 percent increase in the Gini that large? It is very large, as based on the following facts. First, the world is a large place; at last count, it has more than 6 billion people. As the size of the economy increases (from Lithuania to the United States to China to South Asia, and so on) large changes in the Gini are that much more difficult to realize—indeed, an imperceptible change is a miracle. If ever the law of large numbers was supposed to operate, it is within the context of a Gini based on 6 billion people. Excess growth of someone at the 80th percentile level is balanced by deficient growth somewhere else.

The changes cancel out—hence, a very slow-moving world Gini is the expected reality, as thoroughly documented by Bourguignon and Morrisson (2001) for the world economy, for 1820 to 1992. Between 1820 and 1890, world Gini increased from 50 to 59; from 1890 to 1910, by 3.7 percent. From 1910 to 1950, after two world wars, the Great Depression, and 40 years, the Gini moved by half a percent *less* than that observed by Milanovic (1999) for 5 years. Between 1950 and 1992, 43 years, the Gini increased by 2.7 percent to 65.7 in 1992. Major upheavals like the Depression or world wars can cause changes in the Gini. But that is the point—one needs huge upheavals, and 5 years of globalization is possibly not in the same league, let alone the same ballpark.

Second, on the basis of annual estimates of the Gini for the past 51 years (see chapter 11), the standard deviation is observed to be 1.5 percent, or 1.04 percentage points; the largest move is between 69.3 (1973) and 65.1 (2000). Thus, the entire range of changes for the past 50 years is about equal to the world Gini change observed by Milanovic (1999), Dhiranov and Ward (2000), and Wade for the 5 globalization years, 1988 to 1993! During 50 years (1950-2000), the average 5-year change of the world Gini has been -0.35; the 5-year standard deviation is (log) 1.34 percent. So the change of 5 percent observed by Milanovic is almost 4 standard deviations away from the "norm"—a statistical impossibility.

Elasticity of the Gini with Growth

The third "smell" test is presented in figure 5.2. For purposes of this test, the relative incomes of those residing in the Western world, the rich countries, was progressively increased (i.e., the incomes in the nonindustrialized world were kept constant, and an across-the-board increase in the incomes of individuals in the nonindustrialized world was simulated). The x-axis is the "excess" growth in the West; the y-axis is the percentage change in the world Gini. The simulation shows that the move of the Gini from 62.5 (Milanovic's estimate for 1988) to 65.7 (estimate for 1993) would require the relative incomes of the Western world to increase by 27 percent, and that too in just 5 years. The estimated elasticity is 0.18.

Let us try and grasp this estimate—27 percent in 5 years is 4.8 percent each year. Given that average per capita growth in the West during this

Figure 5.2 Elasticity of world Gini with respect to "excess" growth in industrialized countries

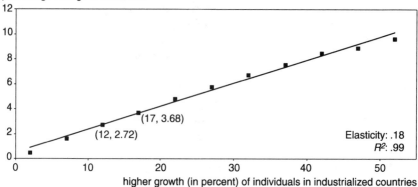

percentage change in world Gini

(17, 3.68)

(12, 2.72)

Elasticity: .18
R^2: .99

higher growth (in percent) of individuals in industrialized countries

Note: The world distribution for 1988 is "shocked" by income gains (x-axis) for the industrialized world; income levels for the nonindustrialized world are kept constant; see the text for the details.

Sources: Deininger and Squire (1996); World Income Inequality Database, available at http://www.wider.unu.edu/wiid; Asian Development Bank (2002); Milanovic and Yitzhaki (2001).

period was about 1 percent, for the Milanovic estimate to be true, it would imply that the incomes in the developing world were *declining* at about 4 percent a year. And this would be at a time when the poor world was recovering from the debt crisis, Chinese per capita incomes were rising at double-digit rates, and per capita Indian and Bangladeshi incomes were rising at more than 3 percent a year. Further, this was also a period when oil prices were rising. A priori, therefore, one would have expected the opposite to happen; that is, world inequality should have become more equal, though obviously not at the pace "estimated" in the other direction![8]

The net result is that the world Gini has an elasticity of 5 with respect to relative incomes in the West (i.e., for each 5 percent gain in these relative incomes, the world Gini changes by only 1 percent). A movement of "only" 5 percent may not appear very large. But that is an illusion. The important thing to note is that the world Gini is worse than an elephant; it moves very, very slowly, and certainly considerably slower than 1 percent a year on a sustained basis for 5 years. Surely, the large

---

8. Yet another simulation exercise is to increase the relative incomes of everyone in the top 20 percent of the population. When done for the base Gini for 1993, this resulted in an elasticity of 0.22 rather than the 0.18 noted above. This would require the relative incomes of the top 20 percent to increase by 25 percent to achieve the Milanovic inequality increase. Some idea of the Milanovic error is gleaned from the fact that the relative incomes of the top 20 percent in China showed a similar 25 percent increase (relative to the bottom 80 percent of China) but did so over 15 years, 1980 to 1995, and on almost one-sixth the population base!

Gini increase emphasized by Wade was a giveaway. Something must surely have been wrong with the data. But given the careful research done by Milanovic (1999), that was unlikely. Then something must be wrong with the method. Given the vetting involved with such a conclusion, and that a companion study (Dikhanov and Ward 2000) had also reached the same conclusion, that also was unlikely.

Perhaps because of these "background" factors, an "Economics Focus" article accompanying the article in the *Economist* also failed to catch the "smell." This article accepted the findings and opined (in typical two-handed fashion!): "Without longer runs of data it is hard to know whether this change is part of a well-established trend . . . or a short-term fluctuation." And even more interesting, not one of the four inequality experts who commented on Wade's essay (Richard Jolly, Ian Castles, Nancy Birdsall, and Gary Fields) seriously questioned, let alone challenged, the empirical validity of Milanovic's and Wade's conclusions. Jolly accepted the results in toto; Birdsall emphasized the probable link between high inequality and low growth as being the real issue deserving attention; and Fields suggested that inequality might have risen, but poverty might have fallen. Castles came closest to questioning the method and suggested that accounting for public goods might diminish the inequality result somewhat.[9]

The "duck" reality is that a simple methodological assumption yields the implausibly large inequality change observed by Milanovic, Dikhanov and Ward, and Wade. This assumption is one of relying exclusively on household survey means of consumption and income for wisdom on trends in average income in the economy. This method yields these kinds of results: Ethiopia substantially richer than India in 1993; and South Korea richer than the United Kingdom, Sweden, and Australia in 1993. A detailed examination of this method of assigning incomes or consumption to the mean of the population (as is done by the World Bank in constructing "official" estimates of world poverty) is done in chapter 7.

It is surprising that the result of large inequality changes was so readily accepted. Especially when one considers that before Milanovic's sensational findings, the first draft of Bourguignon and Morrisson's (2001) paper was available (June 1999); this showed that the world Gini had increased by 1.6 percent from 1950 to 1970, and then seen an additional 1 percent increase from 1970 to 1992, and no change from 1980 to 1992. What does the neglect of one plausible set of numbers, and the acceptance

---

9. In his other writings, Castles has been a serious critic of these and related findings [e.g., UN *Human Development Report 1999*]. Note also that Atkinson and Brandolini (1999) had warned as early as 1999 about some of the pitfalls in using secondary data sources for inequality computations. All of us are "forced" to use secondary data; the best one can do, which this study attempts, is to recognize, and accordingly adjust for, the pitfalls.

of a duck set, prove? The power of numbers, especially those contained in conclusions showing that not all is well with the capitalist world.

Poverty "Smell" Tests

The small decline in poverty during a period of high growth was another giveaway clue. The World Bank's poverty estimates are based on the same foundation as Milanovic's (1999) inequality study (i.e., they use the survey means to estimate average income, and do not use any information contained in national accounts estimates of the same). With this method, one observes that there was a 5.6-percentage-point decline in HCR over 12 years, 1987 to 1999.

This startling finding, from the most (and only) authoritative source on the subject, the World Bank, raises several questions. First, some incredulity—can it be that a 21 percent increase in average consumption in developing countries led to a minuscule decline of only 5.6 percentage points in HCR? Then, some additional questions—what related, or consequent, set of outcomes would have to occur if this conclusion were true? Would not social upheavals, besides those provided by the Seattle anti-globalization types, have been the order of the day in the developing world? And what about all the stories of stupendous growth coming out of China, home to a quarter of the world's poor people in 1987? Did none of this hugely advertised growth (supported by hard evidence of accumulating trade surpluses, the kind that would put Japan to shame) percolate to poor Chinese people? Even India, home also to a quarter of the world's poor people in 1987, had grown at an average annual per capita rate of 3.5 percent since 1980.

Together, China and India accounted for more than half the world's poor people. Their economies (collectively) annually grew at more than 5 percent per capita for 12 years—which means an *82 percent increase* through the power of compounding—and yet no dent was made in world poverty?[10] The World Bank itself acknowledged the puzzle and concluded that the question of "why countries with similar rates of economic growth can have very different rates of poverty reduction" needed to be studied.

World Bank researchers, and several outside analysts, failed to note that estimates of income (or expenditure) growth and poverty decline

---

10. It should be emphasized that no economist, and certainly not the World Bank, is making, or has made, the argument that growth does not lead to a decline in poverty. The debate, discussion, and disagreement are about the extent to which growth leads to poverty reduction—with the World Bank arguing, on the basis of its findings, that growth has led to a much smaller poverty decline than should have been "expected": "Even though past growth has often helped reduce poverty, some growth processes may do so more effectively than others. One potential role of government is then to foster a *pattern of growth* conducive to poverty alleviation" (Ravallion and Lipton 1993, 49; emphasis in original).

come in pairs. They are two sides of the same coin—a given amount of survey income growth yields a given amount of poverty decline. When national accounts data are used (as was done by the previous set of World Bank studies, led by Ahluwalia, Carter, and Chenery in 1979) then both income growth and poverty decline were based on survey data adjusted to national accounts. Thus, analysts have a choice: either use the survey data to generate results on *both* growth and poverty, or adjust the survey mean to national accounts and derive new estimates for both poverty decline and income growth. These are the only two logically consistent sets of estimates. The big mistake is to take consumption growth from national accounts, and poverty change from survey data.[11] It is just as wrong as taking Peter's income to estimate Paul's poverty.

This simple methodological correction means that one does not need pyrotechnics to explain the result that there was high growth and low poverty decline. The survey data used by Chen and Ravallion for the period 1987 to 1999 show an increase in consumption of approximately 11 percent for the developing world and a 5.6-percentage-point decline in poverty.[12] This joint occurrence of low growth and small decline in poverty does not make one jump to find explanations about the causes of this small decline in poverty; nor does it push one to explore the frontiers of "quality of growth" as an explanation for this small decline.

But the figures for growth that all researchers are accustomed to, and the ones talked about in seminars, conferences, books, academic articles, and so on, are not the figures on survey consumption growth (11 percent), and not even the figures on national accounts consumption (21 percent), but actually the figures on per capita GDP growth. And per capita GDP growth was 17 percentage points higher than survey consumption and was equal to 24 percent.

So what is happening is that researchers state (correctly) that per capita incomes increased by 24 percent; and they state (correctly) that poverty only declined by 5.6 percentage points. But researchers conclude (incorrectly) that growth led to very little poverty reduction. What is wrong is

---

11. The list of economists making this mistake is too long to document. The most recent to make this mistake is Nobel Prize winner and former Chief Economist of the World Bank Joseph Stiglitz. "A growing divide between the haves and have-nots has left increasing numbers in the Third World in dire poverty, living on less than a dollar a day. Despite repeated promises of poverty reduction made over the last decade of the 20th century, *the actual number living in poverty has actually increased by almost 100 million. This occurred at the same time that total world income actually increased by an average of 2.5 percent annually* (Stiglitz 2002, p. 5; emphasis added).

12. The Chen-Ravallion analysis is for the period 1987-98; World Bank (2002b) reports that the head count ratio for 1999 was 22.7 percent and the number of poor, 1,151 million. Data on survey-based consumption growth for 1998-99 are not reported by the World Bank authors. But Chen-Ravallion suggest that such growth was 0.90 percent a year or 10 percent between 1987 and 1998.

attributing Peter's increase in income of 24 percent (based on GDP per capita) to the reduction in Paul's poverty (5.6 percent), because Paul's "income" (survey-based consumption) only increased by 11 percent. What is correct is to compare the survey-based decline in poverty to the survey-based increase in mean consumption—i.e., 5.6 percent decline in HCR with an 11 percent increase in survey consumption (World Bank data).

If anything needs to be questioned, it is the estimate of low growth, low at least relative to what researchers have been led to believe by the national accounts data for poor countries. The World Bank's method fails the simplest of "smell" tests—the basic numbers on growth (from national accounts) and poverty decline (from surveys) are not consistent.

The above set of statistics points to a major "journalistic" error made by commentators, and unfortunately by economists as well. In any given developing economy, two *headline* numbers are closely watched by the public, and journalists. The first is growth in per capita GDP, measured obviously in (real) local currency terms. The second is the head count ratio of poverty, again according to local definitions. It is natural to look for a link between the two, but highly inaccurate. And it is especially inaccurate if incomes are measured according to national accounts and poverty according to household survey consumption.

Table 5.2 illustrates the tortuous link between the headline numbers. Although data for several regions are presented, the discussion below pertains only to the developing world. For each region of the world, six numbers are presented. The second column reports the observed growth in GDP per capita over 12 years, 1987-99. This is headline growth. The third column reports the growth that is really relevant for poverty calculations, namely, growth in consumption. A major stylized fact of development is that if the savings rate increased with economic growth, that is, over reasonable lengths of time (e.g., 12 years, 1987-99), consumption growth would significantly lag behind income growth.

The final column of the table reports the decline in poverty as measured via surveys and according to the poverty line of PPP $1.50, national accounts means. These numbers do not necessarily match those provided by the World Bank; hence, the poverty decline observed over the 12 years, 13 percent, is substantially more than the 5.6 percentage points advertised by the World Bank.[13]

The first correction to the headline comparison is provided by a match-up between consumption growth and poverty decline, rather than income growth and poverty decline. This comparison still suggests that growth was bad for poor people—rather than the decline of 13 percentage points occurring with a 24 percent increase in incomes, it actually occurred

---

13. The World Bank figures are for the nonindustrialized world; the data presented by this study are for the developing world; the difference is minor, because there are very few poor people in Eastern Europe according to the $1-a-day poverty line.

Table 5.2 Income growth and poverty change of global regions, 1987–99

Region	Change in per capita levels (percent)				Change in HCR (percentage points)[a]	
	Income, NA (GDP)	Consumption, NA	Consumption, survey	Average SDE	Forecast	Actual
East Asia	63.3	56.8	55.8	0.48	−26.8	−29.1
South Asia	35.3	34.3	15.3	0.71	−10.8	−12.8
China and India	67.4	60.4	51.5	0.61	−31.4	−27.9
Sub-Saharan Africa	−13.0	−11.1	−21.2	0.48	10.2	5.3
Middle East and North Africa	2.2	4.4	−0.7	0.19	0.1	4.3
Latin America	−0.7	−0.5	−23.1	0.20	4.6	4.9
Developing world	24.1	21.0	7.1	0.48	−3.4	−13.0
Developing world, excluding China and India	8.1	9.3	−7.4	0.36	2.7	0.4
Eastern Europe	−44.0	−28.4	−49.3	0.18	8.9	1.8
Nonindustrialized world	12.7	13.9	2.7	0.45	−1.2	−12.0
World	9.0	10.2	3.5	0.39	−1.4	−9.9

HCR = head count ratio
NA = national accounts
SDE = shape of the distribution elasticity

a. Purchasing power parity $1.50 poverty line, national accounts means.

Sources: World Bank, World Development Indicators, CD-ROMs, 1998, 2001; Maddison (2001); Penn World Tables, various years; Deininger-Squire (1996); World Income Inequality Database, available at http://www.wider.unu.edu/wiid; Asian Development Bank (2002); Milanovic and Yitzhaki (2001).

with less growth of 21 percent in consumption.[14] This is an improvement, but still not good. An inaccurate comparison is still being made; essentially, Peter's income is wrongly being attributed to Paul. The poverty decline has *not* been calculated on the basis of national accounts consumption, but rather on the basis of measured *survey* consumption. Was the growth in survey consumption equal to the growth in national accounts consumption? It would be, if surveys maintained the same level of "capture" over time; as is discussed in chapter 7, this assumption was particularly untrue during the 1990s.

The fourth column of table 5.2 reports the growth in survey consumption. This is observed to be strikingly lower than income growth, and lower by 17 percentage points. Now the comparison appears reasonable— 7 percent growth in average consumption and a 13-percentage-point decline in HCR. The residual feeling that the decline in poverty is not commensurate with measured consumption growth is because the headline numbers are 24 percent growth, corrected to 21 percent consumption growth, and a 13 (or 5)-percentage-point decline in poverty.

In a study of Malaysia (World Bank 1991),[15] and subsequently in several other papers (e.g., Bhalla 2000a, 2000b), the point was made that the position of the poverty line relative to the consumption distribution has a very important bearing on any calculations of growth neutrality or pro-poor growth. A legitimate question is that given the survey growth of 7 percent observed for developing countries for 1987 to 1999, what *should* be the expected decline in poverty? This expected decline is obviously subject to some ceteris paribus conditions; namely, that the distribution of consumption stays constant, and given a *particular* poverty line. In other words, growth-neutrality calculations are not independent of the level of the poverty line, a mistake made all too often by most research to date.

The net effect of the "location of poverty line" considerations is summarized via the estimate of the "shape of the distribution elasticity" (SDE),

14. As was discussed in chapter 2, local currency growth rates are on average higher than the corresponding PPP growth figures; hence, the growth, and poverty decline, is understated by the PPP calculations. In other words, the calculated PPP-based poverty decline is a lower bound to what actually occurred.

15. This World Bank report on Malaysia was published in January 1991 but the work had been completed substantially earlier. It states: "Choice of a poverty line dictates the initial level of absolute poverty, which has an important bearing on subsequent achievements. . . . Since poverty is defined in terms of a simple head-count measure (incomes above or below a fixed income) the decline is dependent on the defined poverty line. . . . If there are many people slightly below the poverty line initially, then a relatively small amount of growth can have a large effect on reducing poverty" (p. 82). The bank's *World Development Report 1990: Poverty and Development* reached a very similar conclusion: "For any given increase in the incomes of the poor, the reduction in poverty depends on where the poor are in relation to the poverty line. If they are concentrated just below the line, the increase in their incomes will have a bigger effect on poverty than if they are spread more evenly" (p. 47).

a concept developed in detail in chapter 8. The fifth column of table 5.2 reports the average SDE observed for each region for the chosen sample period and the $1-a-day poverty line. In the developing world, for example, this averaged 0.48. Thus, the 7.1 percent (survey) growth observed in developing countries *should* have led to a decline in HCR of approximately 0.48*7.1, or 3.4 percentage points. The actual decline is 13 percentage points, or about 10 percentage points more than would be dictated by no change in the distribution assumption!

The only reason this extra-large decline could have occurred is if the distribution of consumption *improved* within the developing world. The first two quintiles for developing countries show an increase in the share, from 11.2 percent (1987) to 12.8 percent (in 1999). This is an increase of (log) 13.4 percent. Because equality increases are symmetric and equivalent to increases in consumption, this equality increase, on its own steam, would have led to approximately a 13.4*.48, or 6.4-percentage-point, decline. This almost explains the entire extra decline observed. The reason it does not explain all of the extra decline (of 10 percent) is because we have taken the average share of the first two quintiles; the share of the poor population might have increased even more than 13.4 percent.

The above "smell test" simply informs researchers to be consistent; it does not tell them which estimate, survey or mean, is closer to the *unknown* true mean. Some indirect methods can be used to assess *that* important question. The World Bank figures on absolute poverty suggest that in 1987, there was approximately the same percentage of poor people in South Asia and in sub-Saharan Africa—about 45 percent. As has been emphasized by John Williamson,[16] formerly chief economist for South Asia at the World Bank, the result that both South Asia and sub-Saharan Africa have the same HCR is unlikely, given the "intuition" that though somewhat poorer, South Asia boasts a much more equal distribution. World Bank statistics bear him out—in 1987, South Asia's mean consumption was 20 percent lower than Africa's; but the share in consumption of the bottom 40 percent (poor people) was 36 percent higher. Together, the two statistics show that poverty in South Asia should be significantly lower than in sub-Saharan Africa.

The Need for Alternative Studies

The World Bank's research results on the small decline in poverty, questionable as they are, had a major impact on research and policy, as they should. The World Bank is a major source of research funds, and the major (and only) supplier of development finance for several poor economies. It is a tribute to the way academia and policy analysts work that in virtually

---

16. Comments to the author in private communication, June 2000.

no time the media, and the world, were discussing the reasons for the failure of capitalism and markets. The World Bank itself, as part of its millennium poverty study, *World Development Report 2000/2001: Attacking Poverty*, claimed that all was not well and that poor people needed a voice, and empowerment, two factors that traditional "market development" had not given them:

> [This report] proposes a strategy for attacking poverty in three ways: promoting opportunity, facilitating empowerment, and enhancing security. . . . Overall economic growth is crucial for generating opportunity. So is the pattern or quality of growth. . . . *There is no hierarchy of importance.* The elements are deeply complementary. Each part of the strategy affects underlying causes of poverty addressed by the other two. For example, promoting opportunity through assets and market access increases the independence of poor people and thus empowers them by strengthening their bargaining position relative to state and society. (pp. 6-7; emphasis added)

Although *World Development Report 2000/2001* recognizes growth as important, it clearly states that growth has not done its expected job, especially during 1987 to 1999. Thus, growth is perceived as only one equal partner among three, and not even the first among equals. It is just as important to have growth as to achieve such intractables as empowerment—that is the message.

It is an open question as to what studies, and conclusions, would have been undertaken if the World Bank's estimates of growth without poverty decline had been scrutinized when they were first made public in late 1999.[17] The question of why, when the data were so starkly out of line, the World Bank itself had not seriously questioned these numbers, and nor had most of the academic community, is a subject examined in Bhalla (2002b).

For now, the reader has been warned that statistics are not just damned lies, they can be worse. At the same time, they affect lives, poor lives. For researchers and policy analysts, there are lessons: Beware of pitfalls, and also look for a modicum of plausibility and a minimum of consistency—the passing of the "smell" test. Think also about the one important contribution economics makes to the science of inquiry: the concept of the counterfactual. What are the implications if World Bank poverty trends are right—and what are the implications if these estimates are grossly in error? The same reasoning, and yardstick, should, of course, also be applied to any alternative estimates, including the simple accounting procedure estimates contained in this book.

---

17. At a conference in mid-January 2000, I presented alternate estimates of Indian poverty; these estimates were for an HCR in the mid-twenties for 1987 and the mid-teens for 1998, rather than the 40-percent-plus figure reported by the World Bank for both the years (Bhalla 2000a).

A Web site called http://www.jumptheshark.com catalogues the major turning points for various individuals and institutions. The turning point is almost always downhill—the point at which the institution, individual, or television show started losing popularity, fame, credibility, and so on. The results offered here, and in the following chapters, suggest that the World Bank jumped the shark once it "went to town" with the finding that despite record growth, poverty levels declined little in the developing world for 12 long years, from 1987 to 1999.

6

Recounting Poor People

This chapter is about the numbers of poor people in the world, and how such numbers have changed during the past 40 years, and especially the past 20. Why this exercise, one might justifiably ask. National governments bring out annual reports on the subject of who poor people are, how many of them there are, where they are located, and so on. The World Bank, which is dedicated to precisely the goal of removing poverty, brings out annual reports on the subject, and has produced three important volumes (*World Development Report* in 1980, 1990, and 2000) and hundreds of related documents. Of what importance could an additional report be, especially one emanating from the research confines of not only not a financial institution, but a mere researcher? If the results are broadly the same, what will be the value added? If the results are radically different, who will believe them? Precisely my sentiments.

But what if precisely the same methods as the World Bank's were used, along with the same published data, the same definitions, and the same techniques? What if the recount then showed vastly different and fewer numbers of poor people?

The recount suggests that the poverty numbers are very different. The differences can theoretically arise out of differences in exchange rates, growth rates of consumption, and "survey capture"; that is, the proportion of consumption (or income) that the survey captures of national accounts (known as NA; see the next chapter for a detailed discussion). With this important caveat, I obtain the following results: The World Bank's figure for the number of poor people in 1999 is 1.15 billion or 22.7 percent of the population; my replication of the World Bank's method and data yields 19.1 percent; and my own survey capture data yield 12.8 percent.[1] Using a different and higher poverty line ($1.50) and NA means deflated by 15 percent to account for underestimation and undercoverage of rich people in household surveys, I obtain the "final estimate" of 688 million in 1999 and 650 million (13.1 percent of the population) in 2000.

Whether 1.15 billion (or 620 million or 650 million), we should care that the number of poor is a very large number. We should also care because we are told that the number has stayed broadly constant for the past 15 years, and especially the 15 years of the famed globalization period, the period when two poor nations, China and India, ostensibly showed remarkable progress in winning *their* wars on poverty. We should care because, besides the important goal of monitoring, the numbers of poor people affect the capacity of nonpoor people to help them. If the number is too large, then resources have to be spread thinly. If the number is small, then resources can be targeted more finely. The mean daily income of poor people was estimated to be about $0.79 in 2000. This means that the average poor person needs $0.29 extra a day to push her above the poverty line of $1.08 per day.

Thus, simple mathematics tells us that we can today live in a world free of poverty. If there are 455 million poor people (adjusted NA data with the $1.08 poverty line), it will cost the international aid-giving community only $48 billion annually to eliminate poverty as we know it; if there are 620 million poor people (survey means), the amount needed is $65 billion—and in 2000, aid flows were roughly $60 billion.[2] We know where poor people are (mostly in sub-Saharan Africa and parts of Asia), so targeting is not a problem. If 1.15 billion people are poor, then the annual aid effort involved to eliminate poverty (on a flow basis) is $121 billion a year—somewhat less manageable, and perhaps why the aid agencies have asked the industrialized world to shell out an extra $50-60 billion to end poverty.

If the number of poor people is actually 650 million, then the head count ratio (HCR) is 13.1 percent, given that the developing world's population was 4.93 billion in 2000. This HCR is put in perspective by noting that the goal of the international institutions, as expressed via the UN Millennium Declaration, is for the percentage of poor people in the world in 2015 to be half the number prevailing in the early 1990s—i.e., half of 30 percent, or 15 percent. Thus, toward that goal, 15 years *hence*, and *already achieved today*, resources are being raised to fight the nonexistent

---

1. Part of the difference between the World Bank estimate (22.7 percent) and mine (12.8 percent) is due to the use of consumption PPP versus official PPP estimates; and part may be due to different estimates of the survey capture ratio for different countries.

2. The purchasing power parity (PPP) dollar is almost the same as the US dollar for the industrialized world. There has been inflation of about 20 percent since 1993; so all PPP 1993 numbers can be multiplied by 1.2 to arrive at estimates of current US dollars.

poverty of tomorrow. Some might say it does not get more Kafkaesque than this.

This is only part of the different results reached. But now the reader is asked for patience with the brickwork. Documenting what ultimately is a simple counting number is an involved exercise, made considerably more complicated when the new numbers, from an individual researcher, fly directly in the face of so much received wisdom (from an authoritative source like the World Bank). It has been made more difficult by the sure knowledge that provision of the usual bounty of evidence would not suffice—there can be no ambiguity about the *new* numbers.

Definitions and Methods

How do we know the consumption levels of the poor? Via national household *surveys* of consumption. What if these surveys are not conducted annually, as they most often are not? In that all too common instance, NA data are used to "update" the mean consumption figures in the nonsurvey years. How is the update done? By imputing the NA real consumption growth to the observed real survey mean of consumption in the previous survey year. This is the method used by Chen and Ravallion (2001) and in the first such methodological study, by Ravallion, Datt, and van de Walle (1991).

Are the data on distributions obtained for the present study different from those available at the World Bank? No. The NA data are also the same (indeed, obtained from the World Bank's *World Development Indicators* CD-ROM, and supplemented for 2000 with the IMF financial statistics CD-ROM). Are the methods the same? Yes.[3] Then how is it possible that radically different conclusions have been reached, on both the level of absolute poverty today, and its trend since 1985?

Using Different PPP Exchange Rates

Per capita income and consumption data (surveys or NA) are available in nominal units of the local currency for each country and for each year. These data are converted into purchasing power parity (PPP) figures using an exchange rate of local currency to PPP.[4] How the PPP exchange

3. As argued in other chapters, the data used in this study are possibly the most extensive to date, and the methods used for generating detailed distributions from limited data are somewhat more advanced. But none of the conclusions about considerably reduced poverty hinge on either new data or advanced methods.

4. The PPP exchange rates can be very different from US dollar exchange rates. For example, in 1999, the PPP exchange rate for India was Rs8.65 per PPP dollar, compared with an exchange rate of Rs43.1 per US dollar. The corresponding figures for China were 1.81 and 8.28.

rate is itself derived is not usually discussed, because it is considered either too involved a question, or not a question per se. It is involved because the PPP method has been developed by hundreds of researchers during the past 30 years. It is not considered a question because researchers take these data in the same manner they take for granted industrial production data, inflation data, or GDP data.

No one—not the official source of poverty figures, or any institution, or any outside researcher—is questioning the PPP estimates. This is not because everyone believes that these figures are accurate; it is only because no one has the capacity, or the resources, to come up with a "better" estimate of the PPP exchange rate. It is also recognized that PPP methods will improve with economic progress, and keep on improving for decades to come.

The estimates of the PPP exchange rate, and the corresponding *current* per capita income in PPP dollars, at 1993 prices, are available on the *World Development Indicators* CD-ROM. In 1987, for example, the per capita annual PPP income for Indonesia is reported as 2,354, for Ethiopia 717, and for India 1,665. That is, India is twice as rich as Ethiopia, and Indonesia is 50 percent richer than India—figures that pass the "smell" test.

If the data used by the present study and by Chen and Ravallion are the same, and if we are both using the same method (reliance on survey means), then we both should be obtaining identical results on income distribution, HCR, and so on. But we are not—indeed, the difference is as much as 10 percent of the developing world's population. This study gets 13 percent as HCR for 1999, with survey means of consumption; Chen and Ravallion obtain 23 percent. What is causing this large wedge?

It appears that this large difference is being caused by the fact that I am using the published annual PPP exchange rates but the World Bank is using a separate exchange rate series, called the "consumption" PPP exchange rate. This PPP "consumption" exchange rate series was until recently *internal* to the World Bank, and even now it is available for only one year, 1993, and that only on the Web.[5] The World Bank's flagship data publication, *World Development Indicators*, has yet to publish this internal series.

According to the *World Development Indicators 2001*, the published PPP exchange rate is "based on price and *expenditure* surveys conducted by the International Comparison Programme (ICP) and represent[s] the conversion factors applied to equalize price levels across countries" (p. 293; emphasis added). Given that the exchange rates are based on expenditures, what is the additional derivation needed to determine a consumption PPP exchange rate? Does the published PPP exchange rate not pertain to

---

5. The World Bank estimates of poverty using the 1993 consumption exchange rates have been in circulation for the past 3 years, but only now these deflators been made publicly available via the Web, http://www.worldbank.org/research/povmonitor.

Table 6.1 Differences in income and consumption purchasing power parity (PPP) exchange rates, 1993

Region	PPP exchange rate[a]		Gap (percent)[b]
	Official	Consumption	
East Asia	167.3	164.6	1.6
South Asia	6.5	7.8	−18.3
Sub-Saharan Africa	98.5	93.5	5.2
Middle East and North Africa	1,302.4	1,305.2	−0.2
Central Asia	2.9	2.8	1.1
Latin America	54.4	54.2	0.3
Eastern Europe	12.7	15.8	−21.9
Industrialized world	137.8	145.0	−5.1
Developing world	**176.6**	**175.4**	**0.7**
World	**159.7**	**160.1**	**−0.3**

a. The official PPP exchange rate is available for each year on the *World Development Indicators* CD-ROM; the "consumption" PPP exchange rate is available only for 1993, and only at the Web site given below.

b. The gap is the (log) percent difference between the official PPP exchange rate and the new "consumption" exchange rates. A negative sign for the gap means that the mean income is understated by the consumption PPP method relative to the official PPP estimate.

Sources: World Bank, *World Development Indicators*, CD-ROM; World Bank Web site: http:// www.worldbank.org/research/povmonitor/.

consumption? And is consumption not close to three-fourths of income for most poor countries?

Differences between World Bank Consumption and Official PPPs

In other words, it really should not matter whether one uses the published PPP rates or the "consumption" PPP exchange rates. And it does not— except for some key, heavily populated poor countries. Table 6.1 reports the population-weighted means for the two exchange rates for different regions of the world, and the gap between them; the gap signifies the amount by which the "consumption" PPP exchange rate is understating purchasing power relative to the official PPP exchange rate. For the world as a whole, and even for the developing world in the aggregate, there is virtually no difference between the two. Given that the PPP exchange rate is commonly accepted, and widely disseminated, this is an additional reason for ignoring the "consumption" exchange rate (which has the additional disadvantage of being available for only 1993).

Unfortunately, the new World Bank estimates of poverty are based on these recently disseminated "consumption" PPPs. Eastern Europe has the highest underestimate, −21.9 percent, but this does not matter for poverty calculations around the $1.08 poverty line. For the largest poor region, in terms of the percentage of the world's poor, South Asia, the "consumption" PPP estimate is a huge 18.3 percent *lower* than the official PPP estimate. For sub-Saharan Africa, purchasing power is boosted upward by 5.2 percent by the World Bank consumption estimate. Aggregating these two results, one finds that sub-Saharan Africa is "richer" than South Asia by 23.5 percent—purely on account of using "consumption" PPP estimates rather than official PPP estimates.

Relative to official PPP estimates, the use of the consumption PPP data overstates poverty for India and understates it for Africa. For South Asia, the overstatement is in the neighborhood of 250 million extra poor people. For sub-Saharan Africa, the error is an understatement of poverty, but the magnitude is small, about 15 million. So for just these two regions, the use of consumption PPP estimates increases the world poverty estimates by 235 million.

What assumption reduces the average South Asian's purchasing power by 18 percent? Perhaps this new "consumption" exchange rate is closer to the "truth"; perhaps not. Unfortunately, there has been no vetting of this important issue, and there could not have been, because the consumption exchange rates have just been released on the Web, and only for a period 9 years ago, 1993.

Even if the consumption exchange rate is considered "better," how does one use it? How are the 1993 exchange rate values converted into values for other years? What happens if countries begin to open up (as all of South Asia has done during the past decade)? The use of the new consumption exchange rate series raises several new questions without answering any old questions. And it causes havoc with poverty figures calculated using official PPP exchange rates.

Before we move on, into the realm of PPP transformations, let us note one simple logical relationship about surveys, national accounts, and poverty lines—that is, there is a one-for-one correspondence between *an undercount in the surveys and a lowering of the poverty line, or between an overcount in the NA and a raising of the poverty line*. This was emphasized above in the discussion on the evolution of international poverty lines. It deserves a reiteration.

The point is that it really does not matter (within bounds) whether one believes that survey data are correct or NA data are correct—as long as one is consistent. If surveys are deemed correct, and it is believed that they correctly capture 86.5 percent of NA data (the unrecorded goes for the underestimation by rich people, and noncoverage of rich people, prisons, and nongovernmental organizations), and if it is believed that a survey-based poverty line of $1.30 is the appropriate poverty line, then if NA data are to be used, the poverty line for NA data should be 1.30 divided by 0.865, or $1.50.

As was noted above, there is a problem with the use of the consumption exchange rate for South Asia. The severity of this problem is indicated by the following analysis for India for just 1 year, 1993-94. Assume that the true unknown nominal consumption level is equal to X, and the known poverty line is PPP $1.30. The consumption mean can either be approximated by the NA estimate for the same year (Rs547 per capita per month) or approximated by a household (National Sample Survey, 1993-94) mean for the same year (Rs328 per capita per month). Note that the survey mean is only 60 percent of the NA mean.

For 1993, the published PPP exchange rate for India is Rs5.95 (i.e., it took Rs5.95 to buy one current international dollar). The survey mean of Rs328 per capita per month[6] translates into PPP $54.60 (income data). Curiously, the World Bank Web site does not publish the survey mean for the 1993-94 Indian survey; nor does it publish the mean for the 1998 Indian household survey.[7] But it does publish a mean for the 1992 survey, $41.56, which translates into a consumption of $42.84 in 1993-94 at 1993 PPP prices.[8] Given the consumption exchange rate of Rs7.016 for 1993 (obtained from the World Bank Web site), this translates into a consumption level (in current and constant 1993 rupees) of Rs300.6 per capita per month for 1993. This "derived" survey mean of Rs301 for India for 1993-94 is Rs27 lower than the *actual* mean of Rs328!

Thus, there are two "gaps" involved in a calculation of mean consumption for India for 1993. First is the gap in the estimate of survey mean consumption in current 1993 rupees. The official figure for mean consumption is Rs328; the derived World Bank estimate for the survey mean (Rs300) is a full (log) 9 percent lower.[9] There should really be a zero gap, because in both instances the survey estimate of the mean is being reported. The second gap occurs because of the difference between the consumption and official PPP exchange rates—Rs7.016 versus Rs5.95, a (log) gap of 16.5 percent. The two gaps—9 percent for a lower survey mean and 16 percent due to different PPP estimates—together amount to 25 percent lower average consumption; and this artificially lower

---

6. The official survey data are published separately for rural and urban India. The published mean for rural India is Rs281.4, and that for urban India is Rs458 per capita per month, with an urbanization rate of 26.3 percent.

7. Thus it appears that all the available national survey data are not being used to arrive at the survey means used for calculations of poverty. This insertion of "private judgments" is another reason to prefer national accounts data to survey data (see the next chapter).

8. Ravallion, Datt, and van de Walle (1991) and Chen and Ravallion (2001) suggest using growth in national accounts when survey data are not available; between 1992 and 1993, there was 3 percent per capita consumption growth in India.

9. This inexplicable gap persists over time; for 1997, the last date for which Indian survey data are posted on the World Bank Web site, the estimated gap in Indian survey consumption is 7.9 percent.

consumption means that poverty is artificially boosted in India by at least 15-20 percent for any given poverty line!

The World Bank's stated purchasing power of an Indian in 1993 is Rs300, and not Rs328 as yielded by surveys, and not Rs547 as yielded by NA. If the survey means are deemed accurate, then a $1.08 poverty line has been transformed into a $1.18 poverty line via the use of incorrect survey means, and a $1.39 poverty line via the use of consumption PPP estimates rather than official PPP estimates! Note that for most parts of the world, the poverty line is $1.08, because there are no differences between official survey means and World Bank survey means, and no differences between consumption and official PPP estimates (except in South Asia and Eastern Europe).

Now, if the NA data are deemed "correct," and if the NA data closely match the survey data in one country and not in another (as in China, where the survey/national accounts [S/NA] ratio in 1999 was 82.1 percent, in contrast to the Indian S/NA ratio of 55.7 percent in the same year), then for China the World Bank poverty line is $1.32 (1.08 divided by 0.82) while for India the World Bank poverty line is $2.50 (1.39 divided by 0.557).

No—there is no typo there. The World Bank poverty line for India in 1999 was not $1.08 a day but $2.50, and for China it was only $1.39. It does not take much to calculate that for China the poverty level (independent of level of income or income distribution concerns) will be substantially below India's; as a guess, this roughly translates into a difference of 30 percentage points in the head count ratio! Given India's population of 1 billion, that is an error of about 300 million.

Perhaps it is the case that the "error" for India is balanced somewhere else. As is shown above (in table 6.1), that is not the case. All countries in South Asia are afflicted by the underestimation of consumption, and overestimation of poverty and disease. But for most other countries of the world, including the populated countries of East Asia, the World Bank consumption PPP does not deviate much from the official PPP; for example, the consumption PPP exchange rate for China for 1993 is 1.42, as is the official PPP exchange rate. It is interesting to observe that in all their global poverty publications, the only country for which the World Bank publishes separate poverty estimates is China. Perhaps if the same policy had been followed for all the regions (singling out the largest country in each region), the problem caused by differing PPP estimates would have been identified earlier, and rectified.

This deciphering of the basis for the official poverty estimates helps unravel some mysteries. Table 6.2 highlights the virtual confusion. National accounts data for 1993 suggest that the average South Asian is about (log) 7 percent richer than the average African. Surveys, by capturing less and less of the NA in South Asia, and more and more of the NA in Africa, reduce this 7 percent gap in favor of the South Asians to a 24 percent gap in

Table 6.2 Which data do you believe? Per capita consumption, 1993

Region	National accounts	Survey, official PPP exchange rates	Survey, World Bank "consumption" PPP exchange rates
South Asia	3.0	2.10	1.48
Sub-Saharan Africa	2.8	2.66	2.40

PPP = purchasing power parity

Sources: World Bank, *World Development Indicators*, CD-ROM; World Bank Web site: http://www.worldbank.org/research/povmonitor/.

favor of the Africans! The use of the World Bank's new "consumption" PPP exchange rates exaggerates this relative African richness to 48 percent, or about twice the amount suggested by survey data and official PPP estimates.

Thus in 1993, NA data suggest that the average South Asian income was $3 a day compared with $2.80 for Africa. The use of survey data, and "consumption" PPP data, leads us to believe that the average daily consumption of a South Asian was $1.50, and that of an African was about $2.40 or (log) 54 percent more!

So far we have discussed only average means and said nothing about the distribution. The share of the bottom 40 percent is higher in South Asia by about (log) 46 percent (21.4 percent consumption share vs. 13.5 percent consumption share). Thus, the 54 percent mean disadvantage is transformed via a better distribution pattern into only an 8 percent disadvantage for the Asian first quintile. This implies that the head count ratio in South Asia and sub-Saharan Africa should be approximately the same (within 4 or 5 percentage points) in 1993; that is, we have identified the source of Williamson's concern and dilemma about the poverty ratios being equal in the two regions.

All Indians Were Dead in 1950, or 1960

Sometime in the early 1980s, the World Bank published a book on the Romanian economy. The analysis in this book showed that Romania had enjoyed East Asian growth rates during the preceding 20 years or so. Going backwards, these growth rates implied an unrealistically low level of per capita income in 1960, which prompted a *Wall Street Journal* editorial to state, "In 1960 all Romanians were dead."

As every analyst and forecaster has discovered, sometimes, even with the best of intentions and the best of methods, a particular analysis can go seriously wrong. And potholes can be discovered in any empirical exercise. My intention here is not to be clever and show that a curious result can be obtained by using World Bank consumption estimates for India for 1997 (the last such estimate available). It is to show how by most likely getting India wrong, and South Asia wrong, and not counterbalancing this error by an equivalent and opposite error elsewhere, the World Bank estimates of world poverty are serious overestimates of true poverty in the world today.

A necessary and explicitly stated part of the World Bank method is to use NA growth rates when surveys are not conducted. These NA growth rates for income suggest an average annual growth of 2.0 percent per capita for income, from 1950 to 1997.[10] Projecting the World Bank's new "consumption" PPP and survey means estimate of $45 a month or $1.48 a day backward to 1950, one obtains a consumption level of 11.4 cents per day; this is the implied World Bank consumption PPP *mean* for India for 1950. For 1960, the average is somewhat higher, at 18 cents a day. To reiterate, these are estimates of the mean consumption of the entire population, not the poor population, at constant 1993 prices. History (at least since 1950) has yet to record such low levels for any economy. The lowest consumption level (NA data) for any country in 1950 was 44 cents a day for China. For 1960, the lowest average consumption level was in Tanzania, at 60 cents a day.

The World Bank's (imputed) figures for India for 1950 are a *fourth* of the lowest level observed; that is, a very poor average Chinese consumed four times as much as an Indian; a very poor average Tanzanian consumed more than three times as much as the even poorer average Indian. Because these consumption levels are for the average, and considerably lower than anything recorded in history, then all Indians must have been dead in 1960, or 1950.

What this smell test suggests is that either the "forecast" for 1950 is wrong, or the present consumption levels à la Chen and Ravallion and the World Bank, are too low. If the latter is true, then the head count ratio for South Asia, and other parts of the world, is too high. If so, the number of poor people in the world is considerably lower than the official figures of 1.15 billion or 1.20 billion. And a considerably lower number is several hundred million; as discussed above, for 1999, the error is about 500 million; that is, the official figure for world poverty, according to the $1.08 poverty line, is almost *double* the estimate we obtain using survey means but official PPP estimates.

But $1.08 is not the appropriate poverty line; $1.30 is, and as discussed in the next chapter, if NA means are used, one should adjust such means downward by a factor (1.3 divided by 1.5) or raise the poverty line by

---

10. The latest Economic Survey for India reports per capita income for 1950-51 to be Rs3,687, and Rs9,242 for 1997-98, both at 1993-94 prices. These two figures imply a growth rate of 2 percent a year. (National accounts data for consumption for 1950 were not available.)

the same factor. For example, the $1.08 poverty line gets transformed into a $1.25 poverty line, and the "correct" poverty line of $1.30 is raised to $1.50. The poverty levels according to the correct poverty lines are higher at 13.1 percent of the developing world's population in 2000, or close to 650 million—still high, but still half of the official estimate.

7

Surveys and National Accounts: Can a Choice Be Made?

When the first international poverty line was developed by Ahluwalia, Carter, and Chenery (1979), the method used by scholars and international agencies was to adjust the "noisy" survey mean to the considerably less noisy national accounts mean. With the advent of the second international line, the method also changed. Henceforth, no adjustments were made to survey means, at least none that were "official." As we have seen in the previous chapters, some adjustments have been made to survey data anyway. Which raises the obvious question: Is there a method that will use survey data and will adjust it to national accounts in a transparent and objective manner? Toward the end of this chapter, such a method is offered.

Given that a distribution of incomes is available, one question remains: What is the mean level of income in a country in any given year? There are two choices—either use the survey mean as the estimate, or use a national accounts (NA) mean. The natural tendency is to use the NA estimate, not least because such estimates are available every year, unlike the survey estimates, which appear on the scene every once in a while. Long before household surveys, there were statistical authorities in every country churning out "national accounts" estimates. We take it for granted, but generating data on industrial production, agricultural growth, average computer prices, software exports, and so on is part of the work of the national accounts system (NAS) department in *each* country. And NASes contain estimates of mean household income and mean consumption.[1]

---

1. Not strictly since the definition of private final consumption expenditure (an NAS figure) is different from household consumption, and household income has to be approximated

And when the survey does appear, it is used to "update" and verify national accounts estimates for individual items of expenditure or income. Thus, the close correspondence between the two for many countries is not a function of the accuracy of the survey—it is a matter of definition, i.e., the survey estimates of expenditure, for individual items and/or the aggregate, are often taken as the estimate for the system of national accounts.

Thus, survey and national accounts are not competing estimates for mean expenditures—at least they were not in the old days. Today, statistical systems in most countries have become considerably more developed (at least in comparison with the practice 30 years ago), and consumer surveys (income or expenditure) are now one among several competing estimates.[2] Now what should be done?

What Is the Problem?

That surveys and national accounts yield different means is neither surprising (their coverage is different, the prices they use can be different, etc.) nor a problem. In the 1960s in India (where all debates on poverty seem to have originated—as a wag said, in India they discuss poverty, in East Asia they remove it), there was intense discussion about the divergence of the survey mean from the national accounts mean. Does this sound familiar? Yes, except the divergence was a few percentage points in the late 1960s; in the last national survey (1999-2000), the survey estimate of mean consumption was only 55 percent of national accounts consumption.

So the problem is threefold. Less important, how much deviation is there between a survey mean and NA mean at *a point in time*?[3] More important, most often critically, the problem is the trend in the ratio over time—i.e., the degree of underreporting increasing or decreasing over time in percentage terms. (Note that with growth, the absolute underreporting will obviously go up over time and is not of much interest.)

Even this is not much of a problem if the "error" is random. But what if the error is *both* not random *and* has a *downward* trend (i.e., the surveys

---

by per capita GDP. The NAS contains estimates of consumption of nonhousehold institutions in the economy—e.g., prisons and nongovernmental organizations. These differences are well recognized and can easily be removed to obtain a comparable NAS estimate of *household* consumption.

2. Not, obviously, for all countries. Several (e.g., China, Kazakhstan, Laos, and Vietnam) still use the survey mean as the mean for national accounts, often with a deflation factor of 3 to 12 percent to account for differences in coverage.

3. Throughout this discussion, the concern is with deviation after controlling for differences in definition and coverage.

are systematically capturing less and less of the true value of consumption)? Then there are genuine problems, and unless these problems are confronted, there are likely to be several possibly unintended consequences of a methodology that relies exclusively on the information contained in the surveys and that is purist in not correcting the survey data through the use of other (e.g., national accounts) data. This was observed to be the case with Milanovic's estimate of global inequality, an estimate that had excess baggage in the form of the average Korean being richer than the average Swede in 1993 (rather than being 40 percent poorer, as suggested by the NA), or the average citizen of the Central African Republic having the same income as the average Indian (rather than being 40 percent poorer).

The problem occurs because the survey means are now capturing less and less of the national accounts mean, and a different pattern is observed for different countries. The examination of the causes of this decline is beyond the scope of this book, though research is under way. A reasonable hypothesis is that new products are being missed, a conjecture put forward by Minhas and his colleagues (Minhas et al. 1986):

> These surveys do not seem to capture a large number of new and emerging products, particularly in the field of consumer electronics, plastics, toilet goods and chemical detergents. In the absence of itemwise details of inputs as well as outputs in the unorganised sector, the CSO [i.e., national accounts] fails to make a number of needed adjustments. It is, therefore, necessary that the surveys of the unorganised sector are made more comprehensive in their scope and coverage in order to provide more reliable data in the future.

Another possibility is that the opportunity cost of time has gone up, even among the poor. Interview fatigue sets in, and/or the survey respondent has better things to do. Either way, the questions later on in the questionnaire will be answered less accurately.

Perhaps due to these genuine concerns, analysts and governments have almost always preferred to use *survey* distributions and *national accounts* means. India set the example by using this method, and it was not surprising that the world followed. Then a curious thing happened. The World Bank came out with a new poverty line and a new, exclusively survey-based method of measuring poverty (World Bank, *World Development Report 1990: Poverty and Development*; Ravallion, Datt, and van de Walle 1991). For the first time, the Government of India, and Indian academics, were followers rather than leaders in the poverty debate. An Expert Group constituted by the Government of India (hereafter, EGGOI) also changed its long-standing policy of using national accounts means to match survey means (Government of India 1993).

In line with the new World Bank practice, the new Government of India recommendation was to use only survey data.[4] As noted by both Bhalla

---

4. There is some evidence to suggest that the originator of the first poverty line, and of the first method of estimating absolute poverty, the Planning Commission of the Government of India, meekly gave up its leadership role by uncritically accepting the recommendations

(2000b) and Deaton (2001a), no convincing explanation was given, or even an attempt made, by the Government of India report to explain the change in its long-standing policy of poverty measurement. "This [adjustment of survey means to national accounts means] is how the official poverty counts used to be done in India, and no very convincing reason was ever given for the change following the recommendations of the government of India" (Deaton 2001a, 135).

Nor was any explanation given by Ravallion, Datt, and van de Walle for the mega-paradigm shift. Neither EGGOI nor Ravallion and his colleagues provided any evidence of why, or how, the survey method was able to overcome its known disadvantages, particularly the decline in the ratio of survey to national accounts. One possible explanation for the changeover could have been the knowledge that in the most statistically advanced country in the world, the United States, the exclusive use of survey data for generating poverty estimates was the norm. So the adoption of the new method might have had no more an intellectual basis than to copy the US "best practice." Although this (copying the United States) might be the recommended behavior for firms producing computers, it is unclear that this behavior is recommended for generating poverty estimates in poor countries, and in poorer statistical climes.

The political economy of the World Bank (and Indian) move to higher poverty estimates should not be underemphasized. The Government of India provides grants to states (and presumably the World Bank also grants monies for poverty reduction) on the basis of the estimates of poverty in the states or countries. If the average consumption is adjusted downward, and in a continuous fashion, more and more poverty will be shown than that which actually exists—and more and more money received by cash-starved state administrations (or governments). This is one governance, and moral hazard, problem that was actually encouraged by the sloppy change to survey means as a basis for measuring poverty.

There Is a Problem Even in the United States

Even in the statistically advanced United States, there is a survey problem. The survey-based method is showing no decline in poverty in the United States for 30 years; per capita income in the United States has increased by 67 percent since 1968, and yet the proportion of people who are poor has stayed the same, at around 12-14 percent—that is, the mean income of the bottom 15 percent has remained the same in absolute terms!

Along with survey capture (see Triplett 1997 for an extended discussion), there are other problems with the US method of measuring poverty:

of the World Bank to change the methodology to an exclusive survey-based method. See Bhalla (2000b, 2000d) for details.

an income measure is used rather than the preferred consumption measure; further, state transfer income is not counted as income. (Note that this problem (of transfers vs. income) would not arise in the case of consumption.)

But the largest problem, most likely, is the increasing divergence between survey and national accounts in the measurement of per capita income; about 55 percent in 1968 and 40 percent today—an increase in undercapturing of about 40 percent. If this undercapture ratio is assumed to be the same as in the 1960s, then even by the survey method, poverty in the United States would be half that which is reported (i.e., about 6 percent). Like India, the continuing politics of the United States's economic war on its own "poverty" should not be underemphasized, or underrated.

In Defense of Surveys

A decade after the introduction of the new method, Ravallion[5] attempted to add up the advantages of both the new and old methods of generating means for poverty measurement. He concluded in favor of the new, exclusive survey method, a conclusion in which he is not alone.[6] Broadly, he emphasized the following four major problems with the NAS. First (though this is not taken so seriously by Ravallion himself), "households are the residual claimants in the NAS."

Some items in national accounts are obtained as a residual, and some items use a fixed "blowup" multiplier to get to the total. For example, in India, in the fruits and vegetables category, the national accounts authorities may obtain information on only two or three fruits and two or three vegetables and come up with a number for the consumption of *all* fruits and *all* vegetables. The reason this is not a serious deficiency is because if tastes remain relatively constant, which they mostly do, then knowledge about local price and income elasticities and the observed change in consumption of apples, oranges, and bananas can tell one a fair amount about the *change* in consumption of grapes and peaches. And similarly, knowledge about the change in consumption of tomatoes and cabbages can inform one quite a bit about the changes in consumption of lima beans and broccoli.

---

5. Martin Ravallion, "Should Poverty Measures Be Anchored to the National Accounts?" *Economic and Political Weekly*, August 26-September 2, 2000, 3245-52.

6. Sundaram and Tendulkar state that the "the issue of accepting the NAS estimate of PFCE as more correct and reliable than the NSS estimate is far from settled" and seem to concur with Ravallion's conclusions: he "offers some cogent arguments against anchoring poverty measures to NAS" (K. Sundaram and Suresh Tendulkar, "NAS-NSS Estimates of Private Consumption for Poverty Estimation: A Disaggregated Comparison for 1993-94," *Economic and Political Weekly*, January 13, 2001, 119).

Second, Ravallion argued that the NAS includes institutional consumption, whereas household surveys do not, and this can result in a severe bias, particularly in democracies (like India) where campaign spending is important! To quote him:

> The difference between the NAS and NSS [National Sample Survey] consumption numbers reflects in part measurement errors in the former and the fact that the spending of the (apparently growing) non-profit sector cannot be separated from household consumption when accounting for domestic absorption of measured output in the NAS. . . .
>
> So replacing the NSS mean with consumption per capita from the NAS when measuring poverty would imply that campaign spending by politicians trying to get elected would automatically reduce measured poverty even if none of the money goes to the poor. And every rupee spent by an NGO [nongovernmental organization] would reduce measured poverty, even if none of the money went to the poor. . . . [Further,] it seems plausible that there has been substantial growth in spending by nonprofit enterprises.[7]

The NGO objection seems somewhat unrealistic because it would imply the share of expenditures of NGOs going up, and going up particularly in food consumption, a not so income-elastic or NGO-type consumption good. In the United States (see Slesnick 1998), the share of nonprofit organizations as a fraction of expenditures rose from 4.7 percent in 1959 to 12.1 percent in 1993. That is an increase of 7.4 percentage points over 34 years, and in a society where such growth has been the fastest. Even then, the increase is *2 percent* per decade.

The third major problem with the NAS, according to Ravallion, is that rich people are missed more by surveys than the poor, so matching survey means to NAS would falsely raise the incomes of the poor:

> It does not take much for the NSS to underestimate consumption. All it takes is for well-off sampled households to systematically refuse to participate in the survey, and be replaced by more compliant but less well-off ones, or for interview respondents to forget, or prefer not to reveal, items of consumption in the survey schedule.[8]

The fourth problem is that *included* rich people understate their incomes more than the included poor:

> At an aggregate level, the claimed underestimation of consumption in the NSS would appear to rise as income increases. So it is quite possible—and certainly no less plausible than the distribution-neutrality assumption—that the underestimation of consumption growth is largely for the non-poor. . . . The more consistent

---

7. Martin Ravallion, "Should Poverty Measures Be Anchored to the National Accounts?" *Economic and Political Weekly*, August 26-September 2, 2000.

8. Ibid.

Table 7.1 Ratio of surveys to national accounts: Disturbing trends

	Income surveys		Consumption surveys	
Region	1987	1998	1987	1998
East Asia	55.6	46.4	82.4	80.8
South Asia	74.9	61.8	73.1	55.7
Sub-Saharan Africa	69.0	63.1	125.1	114.9
Middle East and North Africa	64.0	43.6	85.6	81.1
Latin America	74.3	60.7	74.8	61.8
Eastern Europe	191.9	53.7	76.5	67.5
Industrialized world	49.0	48.3	64.1	63.2
Developing world	**65.1**	**54.4**	**85.4**	**76.5**
World	**73.0**	**53.4**	**80.6**	**73.6**

Note: The figures represent the ratio of the survey mean income (or consumption) with respect to the national accounts GDP per capita (or private final expenditure per capita).

Sources: Deininger and Squire (1996); World Income Inequality Database, available at http://www.wider.unu.edu/wiid; Asian Development Bank (2002); Milanovic and Yitzhaki (2001).

interpretation *would seem to be that the rate of underestimation (error as a share of consumption) rises as consumption rises, implying that inequality is underestimated.*[9] (emphasis added)

Unlike the first two assumptions, the last two objections to the use of NAS data are potentially important; potentially because it is all dependent on the magnitudes involved. Below, an attempt is made to estimate these magnitudes on the basis of data from the Indian household survey for 1993-94.

What Happened to the Survey/National Accounts Ratio?

Table 7.1 shows the pattern of the ratio of survey mean consumption to national accounts mean consumption. This ratio is designated as S/NA and is reported for the various regions of the world for 1987 and 1998. For the developing world, income surveys were capturing a very low fraction of national accounts in 1987—65.1 percent—and this ratio declined by an additional 18 percent from 1987 to 1998. This means that a poor person would have had to have increased her income by 17 percent in real terms over 11 years, or 1.6 percent a year, to be at exactly the same level she was in 1998 as she was in 1987. Above, we had emphasized the equivalence between changing income and changing poverty lines. *Because the surveys are now capturing less and less, it means that the poverty line is continuously being increased.* For the average income survey country,

---

9. Ibid.

Table 7.2 Elasticity of survey means to national accounts means

Time period	Income surveys	Expenditure surveys
Before or during 1990		
Number of observations	561	123
Number of countries	103	38
R^2	0.92	0.82
Elasticity	**0.89**	**0.94**
	(.026)	(.042)
After 1990		
Number of observations	201	177
Number of countries	85	75
R^2	0.87	0.64
Elasticity	**0.92**	**0.74**
	(.036)	(.064)

Note: A simple log-log model—(log) survey mean and (log) national accounts mean (GDP per capita or private final expenditure per capita)—is used to estimate the elasticity between the survey means and national accounts means. Figures in brackets are robust standard errors.

Sources: Deininger and Squire (1996); World Income Inequality Database, available at http://www.wider.unu.edu/wiid; Asian Development Bank (2002); Milanovic and Yitzhaki (2001).

the poverty bar got raised from $1.30 in 1987 to $1.55 in 1998, all in real 1993 prices.

The situation with a consumption survey country (like India or Vietnam) is equally bad. The average S/NA ratio for developing countries declined from 85.4 to 76.5 percent, or 10 percent. This means that the per capita consumption of the poor would have to have increased by 10 percent for the poor to be thought of as having the same consumption as before. Regardless of which part of the developing world one lived in, the poverty line (e.g., $1.08) got raised to $1.19 in the space of just 11 years. The implication for the head count ratio is that, on the basis of survey measurement errors alone, poverty is likely to have been underestimated in the world in 1998 (or 2000) by about 8 to 10 percentage points; that is, real, unobserved "true" world poverty—according to official data, World Bank methods, "consumption" purchasing power parity (PPP) exchange rates, and a low but constant S/NA ratio—is about 14-16 percent, rather than the stated 23-24 percent.

Table 7.2 reports on a simple log-log regression of survey means to national account means for consumption and income survey data and for two time periods, surveys before 1990 (mostly in the 1980s), and surveys from 1991 to 2000. The elasticity for income surveys does not change much—it was 0.89 in the 1980s and 0.92 in the 1990s. For both these periods, the elasticity was significantly less than unity.[10] For *expenditure*

---

10. Most surveys in industrial economies are income surveys, and as shown in table 7.1, the S/NA ratio in these economies is staying fixed at about 50 percent; hence, an unweighted regression shows a constant, rather than a declining, ratio.

distributions, during the 1990s elasticity collapsed from a level of 0.94 and not different from 1 to a level of 0.74 and significantly less than unity (with a standard error of 0.06).

The decline of the S/NA ratio in the 1990s is transparent. At the end of the 1980s, its elasticity was close to unity. Then came the adoption of the World Bank method of measuring poverty by survey means, and the elasticity promptly collapsed!

Summarizing, the three results on S/NA suggest the following. First, income surveys capture a lot less of the corresponding national accounts estimate than do consumption surveys. Second, there is no trend in the underreporting for income surveys in industrialized economies, but a declining trend for developing ones. Third, there appears to be a strong downward trend in the capture ratio for consumption surveys. As it happens, poverty estimates are mostly based on these (consumption) surveys.

That this downward trend in S/NA for consumption is near universal is also suggested by Triplett's (1997) analysis of data for the most statistically sophisticated country, the United States. He finds that the NAS estimates of per capita expenditures have grown at about 1 percent a year faster than survey estimates for the period 1984-94. He also finds that the underestimation of food was about the same as that of durable goods—both at about 0.7 percent a year. Durables less motor vehicles are an item with the largest amount of underestimation—1.7 percent a year.

The US data provide a perspective on developing-country (e.g., India) underestimation problems. The magnitudes involved are radically different—rather than a 1 percent difference a year, the difference is more than 3 times that; that is, the survey and NA data in India have diverged by more than an average of 3 percent a year since the early 1980s.

Unintended Consequences of Moving to Survey Means

The simple changeover to a survey-based method of measuring means was to have several unintended consequences. With the all-important ratio moving haphazardly and unpredictably, several level calculations literally went haywire. Some of the more problematical of these calculations are reported in table 7.3, which contains per capita income and consumption levels, circa 1993, for both the survey and national accounts, and for both consumption (referred to as World Bank) and official PPP exchange rates (referred to as simple accounting procedure, or SAP). The data for World Bank survey income are taken from Milanovic and Yitzhaki (2001) (referred to as WB1); the data for World Bank survey consumption are obtained from the World Bank Web site (referred to as WB2). All data are in per capita annual terms, PPP 1993 prices.

Only a few countries are listed in the table, but a cursory perusal suggests that there are several anomalies, and several problems, if survey

Table 7.3 Estimates of income and consumption per capita, circa 1993 (1993 purchasing power parity dollars)

Economy and survey type	Income			Consumption		
		Survey			Survey	
	NA[a]	SAP[b]	WB1[c]	NA[a]	SAP[b]	WB2[d]
Income survey						
China	2,073	931	1,122	937	891	817
Guyana	3,077	3,269	2,889	1,930	1,409	
Brazil	6,053	5,208	3,473	3,637	3,129	2,279
Czech Republic	10,986	4,757	4,678	5,486	2,544	2,475
South Korea	11,391	9,822	9,666	6,139	3,702	
Singapore	16,797	6,036	7,431	7,535	6,112	
United Kingdom	17,994	10,524	9,440	11,626	8,894	
Australia	19256	8,602	9,087	11,341	6,626	
Hong Kong	20,310	10,711	12,935	11,638	9,640	
Japan	22,375	12,244	11,668	13,118	9,389	
Switzerland	24,942	14,992	14,068	14,943	11,749	
Sweden	18,633	10,213	9,451	9,884	7,086	
United States	26,026	11,139	12,321	17,594	9,849	
Expenditure survey						
Tanzania	463	267	1,037	394	779	879
Ethiopia	523	302	738	438	856	508
Uganda	861	667	622	767	859	678
Rwanda	905	700		807	691	462
Central African Republic	997	575	512	829	456	492
Kenya	1,009	582	1,147	600	959	1,052
Nepal	1,026	1,053	643	798	822	623
Bangladesh	1,162	1,057	706	954	758	554
Senegal	1,205	933	510	960	714	726
Ghana	1,603	925	1,664	1,265	1,441	1,201
India	1,608	1,161	524	1,104	679	514
Pakistan	1,615	1,286	798	1,212	1,010	618
Nicaragua	2,233	1,564	4,338	2,094	3,584	654
Indonesia	2,496	1,430	884	1,461	748	822
Jamaica	3,563	2,589	1,674	2,204	1,602	1,421
Algeria	4,487	2,915	2,455	2,458	2,752	1,820
Thailand	5,136	2,874	2,001	2,765	2,071	1,670

NA = national accounts, PPP = purchasing power parity, SAP = simple accounting procedure, WB = World Bank

a. NA figures represent nominal PPP data deflated by the international PPP deflator (equal to the US GDP deflator).

b. SAP survey data are the NA data multiplied by the survey capture ratio, i.e., the ratio of survey mean incomes (or consumption) to the corresponding NA means.

c. WB1 income data represent nominal PPP data deflated by deflators presented in Milanovic and Yitzhaki (2001).

d. WB2 consumption data represent nominal PPP data deflated by the "consumption PPP" exchange rates on the World Bank Web site.

Note: In many cases, survey data are not available for the year 1993. In such cases, the table presents either the closest earlier year for which data are available, or, where earlier data are not available, data for the earliest later year. E.g., if the latest survey took place in 1991, the 1993 figures reflect these values.

Sources: Deininger and Squire (1996); World Income Inequality Database, available at http://www.wider.unu.edu/wiid; Asian Development Bank (2002); World Bank, *World Development Indicators*, CD-ROM; WB1: Milanovic and Yitzhaki (2001); WB2: http://www.worldbank.org/research/povmonitor/.

data are used (regardless of whether such data are provided by SAP, WB1, or WB2). If the widely accepted national accounts figures are taken as a base (what is being discussed here is just the means, not the distribution of income or consumption), then the problems are too glaring to ignore. Starting with the income surveys, China is observed to be a third as rich as Guyana, when NAS indicates that it was about 50 percent richer. South Korea is observed to be 30 percent richer than Singapore (a country that for a few months in 1995 had the same per capita income as the United States), when NAS states that Singapore is almost 50 percent richer.

The problems are possibly worse with the consumption surveys, especially given the diversity in the capturing of national accounts. India is shown to be just as poor as the Central African Republic, and about 30 percent poorer than Ethiopia. War-ravaged Nicaragua is almost twice as rich as Algeria. Note that what the table compares is not relatively intractable data, such as the mean incomes of a particular percentile or quintile. What is being compared is the most robust of all variables—a mean, a summary statistic that should cancel out many errors at smaller levels of aggregation.

All methods, and estimates, have to pass a "smell test" to survive false empiricism.[11] The example of Koreans being relatively richer beyond their own wildest imagination is one such smell test; Indians being considerably poorer than Ethiopians is another. There are several articles giving reasons for the extraordinary finding that growth has accelerated and poverty not come down. There are versions about "quality of growth"; about regional variations; about the need for new policies; about globalization having failed; and about the need for nonmarket instruments. The intellectual support for these ideas is derived from data that suggest that India is manifestly poorer than Senegal, that the average Korean was richer than the average Swede in 1993, and so on.

Do National Accounts Estimates Have Problems?

Although the emphasis above has been on problems with survey estimates of mean consumption, and therefore on survey-based estimates of absolute poverty, it is obvious that national accounts data also suffer from problems. The reason not much emphasis has been placed on errors in NAS is because of the expectation that the law of large numbers operates; the NAS collects data from different sources, reconciles different estimates,

---

11. Milton Friedman is rumored to have brought down the house, and a famous theoretician, with the argument that the theoretician's conclusions were not consistent with the operations of a Mom and Pop corner store.

and (with input from survey experts and economists) continues to update procedures.[12]

That some of these procedures result in guesstimates that are off the mark is obvious. The assumptions about blowup factors can be wrong, as can the assumptions about cross-elasticities. These can, and do, result in the NA mean being off the "true" mark by a few percent or so for any given year; in the case of surveys, for some countries, the error *compounds* at the rate of 1 to 2 percent a year.

This is one interpretation, and conclusion—that is, both surveys and national accounts have level errors, and trend errors are unlikely to occur in NAS because of the law of large numbers and a greater chance of errors canceling out. In particular, it is *unlikely* that ratio errors (e.g., mean NAS consumption as a ratio of the unobserved mean "true" consumption) are a trend in national accounts.

The problem is not with uncertainty about the distribution of survey expenditures (a difficult exercise) but with the *mean* of these expenditures. National accounts offer a different estimate of the mean, but a priori, it is difficult to say which source is to be preferred. The choice between the two involves a judgment that one source is more accurate. How is that to be determined? It can, if consumption (or income) data are available from a *third* source, and knowledge and assumption that the third source is more "accurate." This may seem like an impossible task—but actually, it is more tractable than it seems.

Choosing between Surveys and National Accounts

Two solutions to the problem of choosing between survey and national accounts are provided. The first presents details on what to do if the question is to compare the relative, and absolute, accuracies of the two sources. This is an exercise that needs to be conducted for each individual survey or set of surveys.[13] The second solution pertains to what is to be done with poverty measurement when such a detailed exercise is not possible. The recommended procedure is to raise the poverty line by an amount that will compensate for the known problems in survey data

---

12. In India, the survey-based estimates used to be continually higher than NAS for foodgrain consumption. With improvements in NAS methodology and data collection and verification, the ratio has now reversed and is as predicted (see Minhas 1988).

13. Bhalla and Glewwe (1985, 1986) offer such a method with tests for Sri Lanka; Bhalla (2000b) extends this analysis to Indian data for 1993. A Government of India Planning Commission research project is presently under way to examine the issues about poverty measurement raised by the results contained in the NSS surveys, especially since the early 1980s; see Bhalla (2002c).

(e.g., undercoverage of the rich, and a presumed greater underreporting by the rich).

It is possible to use a third source to reconcile survey and national account estimates. Using Sri Lankan survey data for 1969-70 and 1980-81, Bhalla and Glewwe (1985, 1986) offer an Engel curve method of choosing between the survey and expenditure means. Bhalla and Glewwe construct *survey* price-indices;[14] look for consistency checks within the household survey data (prices and quantities of individual consumption items); and compare the estimates of survey data on prices and quantities with national accounts data, as well as with data on production, imports, food distribution, and so on. In other words, the attempt is to identify an additional third source for the same (broad) units of information.

This comparison allows a first cut at determining which source is more accurate. The second cut involves estimating demand for broad categories of consumption, with simple assumptions about price and income elasticities. Even if these elasticities are not known, simulations can be done to converge on the likely set of elasticities. (The broad Engel pattern is known: food, after a minimum level, has an elasticity below 1; within food, items like edible oils, sugar, and meat have higher elasticities than potatoes, cereals, etc.) These computations yield the likely predicted change in total consumption expenditures, which can then be compared with the change in the survey and NAS means.

The result: The survey data were more accurate than the national accounts data! Probing deeper, it turned out that the government of Sri Lanka was holding back increases in its inflation measure, apparently to defer obligatory cost-of-living increases for union and government employees. Thus, the price deflator was being understated, resulting in a larger than "actual" increase in real consumption.

Using this same method with Indian data, Bhalla (2000b, 2002c) shows that—on the basis of external data on the availability of cereals, edible oils, and sugar, and some prior income and own-price elasticities—the real growth in per capita consumption between 1983 and 1999 was 48.4 percent, or 2.5 percent a year. The annual inflation rate during these years averaged 8.3 percent. Thus, in nominal terms, total expenditures increased at an annual rate of 10.8 percent. The survey-based estimates register only 9.8 percent growth a year. National accounts indicate that the increase was 11.4 percent a year. The Engel curve estimate (10.8 percent a year) lies in between (and closer to national accounts than the survey estimate of 9.8 percent per annum); but given that, by construction and definition, the Engel curve estimate is a *lower* bound to the "true" estimate, it implies

---

14. That just using these internal (survey) prices can cause a huge difference to poverty estimates for India has been documented by Dubey and Gangopadhyay (1998) for the 1987 and 1993 surveys, by Deaton and Tarozzi (1999) for the same surveys, and by Deaton (2001b) for the 1987, 1993, and 1999 surveys.

that the NAS is more right than the survey. (Data on wage growth confirm this interpretation—see table 7.3.)

By How Much Do Rich People Understate Expenditures?

We now look at an example from Indian household data for 1993-94. The Engel curve computations do not solve the problem of identifying whether the rich understate their expenditures to a greater extent than poor people. A method to do just that is outlined in Bhalla (2001a), a paper, not coincidentally, prepared for the 50th anniversary of the National Sample Surveys in India. This paper follows in the tradition of several studies in the 1970s and 1980s that searched for the elasticity of underreporting in income surveys.[15] This paper also improves upon the computations contained in the work of Sundaram and Tendulkar,[16] and consequently it reaches somewhat different conclusions about the accuracy of survey data for deductions on poverty levels, or decline, in India.

Note that the issue is not the validation, or comparison, of the consumption or income means; rather, the issue is who is underreporting (or overreporting) and by how much. The detailed analysis is reported for India below. Although the example is for only one country, and one year (1993-94), it is illustrative. It is unlikely that the same result will not hold for other countries. Validation for other countries requires access to both household surveys and detailed access to expenditure accounts in the national accounts, something beyond the scope of this book.

The following methodology suggests that, to some degree of accuracy, the different underestimation levels can be identified. Assume that the *individual* item (e.g., cereals, pulses, vegetables, fruits, dry fruits, consumer durables, or education) expenditures as tabulated by the national accounts are correct. The aggregate mean expenditure as computed by the NA was shown to be correct earlier. An assumption is necessary in order to proceed to the second part of the analysis—how much is underestimated by whom. With this assumption, an average multiplier can be obtained—this average is the ratio of the adjusted sum of individual and item-specific expenditures, to the sum of expenditures in the survey data. If this itemwise multiplier is used, then in the aggregate, the adjusted survey means will match the NAS means, for *each individual item and for the total.* Is any additional assumption being made with this method? Yes, that relative

---

15. See Bergsman (1980) (and references contained there) for an analysis of underreporting in Latin America, Renaud (1976) for a discussion of South Korea, and Bhalla and Vashishtha (1988) for an analysis of the NCAER income distribution survey of 1976.

16. K. Sundaram and Suresh Tendulkar, "NAS-NSS Estimates of Private Consumption for Poverty Estimation: A Disaggregated Comparison for 1993-94," *Economic and Political Weekly*, January 13, 2001.

prices and aggregate expenditure (and tastes) determine the revealed survey consumption level of each household!

Figure 7.1 reports the item-specific multipliers. Foodgrains reflect an understatement of about 10 percent, but more highly valued food products (milk and milk products, fruits, and vegetables) show considerably higher underestimation—here the ratio is as low as 53 (i.e., the surveys are able to capture only about *half* of national accounts consumption). As expected, durables are also vastly understated, but the highest understatement is for clothing and footwear, for which the surveys capture only 40 percent of NAS consumption.

Figure 7.2 aggregates individuals according to their per capita expenditures, and reports the resulting average multiplier for each decile. This multiplier is the inverse of the S/NA ratio. It shows by how much the survey estimate has to be multiplied to "match" the national accounts estimate. The results are striking, and given the data in the previous table, not that surprising. Even for the poorest decile, the underestimation is on the order of 30 percent. The multiplier is progressively higher for richer households, but the variation for the first eight deciles is in the narrow range of 30 to 46 percent. The average multiplier for the first five deciles is 1.35; that for the top half is 1.46. The average for the entire population is 1.41.

The relative constancy of the average decile multiplier may seem counterintuitive for it is a priori reasonable to expect that most of the missing consumption would be accounted for by the rich. It is! The adjustments *preserve* the original pattern of distribution; because the top 20 percent of the population have about 45 percent of the expenditures, they have a claim to 45 percent of the *missing* expenditures. Further, note the large multiplier for food items—1.43 percent, compared with 1.69 for nonfood items. Food items have a low income elasticity—and there is a physical limit to how much extra food the rich can consume, even if the rich eat only caviar. Hence, a "constant" multiplier is not only plausible but also likely.

So the "benefits" of the underestimation of food items accrue "disproportionately" to the nonrich, and likewise the benefits of the underestimation of nonfood items (e.g., durables) accrue "disproportionately" to the rich. Many poor households do not report any expenditures for durables or report a very small share; consequently, they get zero or very little "benefit" from the large amount of missing expenditures on durables.

The traditional method of matching survey data with national accounts was to assume a uniform multiplier—in this example, 1.41. If such an assumption is made, then the error made with regard to the first five deciles is that their consumption would be overstated by 4.4 percent (1.41 divided by 1.35) and that for the top half by 3.5 percent. The fact that so little error is caused by matching surveys with national accounts is

Figure 7.1 Example of mismatch, survey and national accounts, India, 1993-94

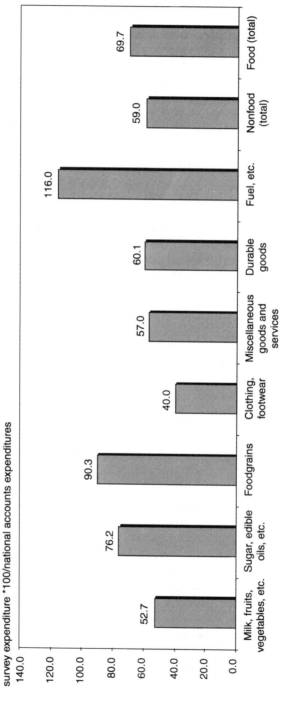

survey expenditure *100/national accounts expenditures

Note: For each item, a match is obtained between the survey expenditure per capita and national accounts estimate. This item multiplier is then imputed to all households. The numbers above each bar reflect the proportion of expenditure captured by the survey; e.g., for foodgrains, the surveys are capturing 90.3 percent of the expenditure as stated by the national accounts; for clothing, 40.0 percent, etc.

Source: Bhalla (2001a).

Figure 7.2 National accounts adjustment multipliers for different deciles, India, 1993-94

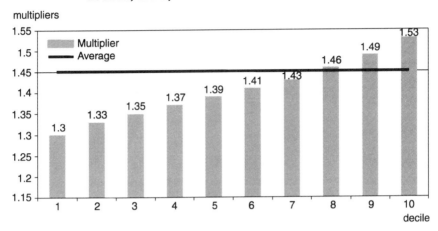

Note: Households are ordered according to the raw unadjusted per capita expenditure. The numbers reflect the average multiplier for each decile; e.g., to match national accounts at the aggregate level, the expenditures of the first decile have to be multiplied by 1.3, those of the 10th decile by 1.53, etc.

Source: Bhalla (2001a).

reassuring support for the originators of this method—the Government of India; followed by the World Bank via Ahluwalia, Carter, and Chenery (1979); followed by most development economists before the quiet "survey is all" revolution of the 1990s.

Estimating Undercoverage of Rich People

We now look at another example from Indian household data for 1993-94. One problem remains: The noncoverage of certain mostly rich households is not solved by the calculation of the item multipliers. There is no objective, "untouched-by-human-hands" way to adjust for these missing people and their large expenditures. These people are "missing" from the surveys because they do not get onto the interviewer schedules or because interviewers get scared away by electric gates or guards at the entrances to their mansions. But some bounds to the magnitude of their consumption can be offered, and bounds are easier for consumption than for income. It is likely that such households constitute less than 2 percent of the population. Such a percentage would mean more than 20 million individuals in India and China and 2.5 million in the United States— clearly significant proportions!

The average median consumption share of the top percentile in developing countries for the past 20 years is 7.5 percent; the average median share for the 99th percentile is 3.6 percent. Thus, a very safe assumption is that 10 percent of NAS consumption does not accrue to the surveyed population at all—i.e., if mean NAS consumption is 100, only 90 percent is consumed and 10 percent is missing and allocated entirely to the missed households—which could include, in addition to rich individuals, institutional NGOs, prisons, and hospital personnel missed by consumer surveys.

The SAP $1.50 Poverty Line

Above, it was mentioned that there were two genuine problems with the use of national accounts means as proxies for survey means. First, again, the richer surveyed households might understate their consumption to a greater degree (in proportional terms). Second, a "large" proportion of rich households are never surveyed by surveys. These two factors are apparently the reason for the decision to eschew national accounts in favor of surveys.

The above two sets of figures on the multiplier and the missed-out consumption allow one to calculate absolute poverty using distribution data from surveys and mean data from national accounts—a marriage of convenience, if not a perfect marriage. Note that an understatement of survey expenditures can be incorporated, for calculations of the poverty ratio using national accounts, via an overstatement of the poverty line. Recall that in the case of the line of Ahluwalia, Carter, and Chenery, the poverty line based on national accounts was $1.25 per capita per day, at 1985 prices, compared to a poverty line of $1 a day using survey means—i.e., the NA poverty line has to be raised by approximately the amount of consumption that the surveys are missing out.

Analogously, knowledge about undercoverage, and understatement, can yield an equivalent national accounts poverty line—a poverty line that will consistently imply the same understatement over time. The above calculations suggest that the multiplier is lower for the bottom half of the population by 4.4 percent. If NAS is being used, then the poverty line should be *raised* by this amount. Similarly, to account for the missed income of 10 percent consumed by the missed-out rich households, the poverty line needs to be raised by an additional 10 percent.

SAP uses national accounts means of consumption, with the above two important adjustments. If a baseline poverty line of $1.30 is chosen, then the fact that the surveys miss the top 2 percent of households (with consumption equal to 10 percent of the total) is factored by moving the poverty line to the quantity (1.30 divided by 0.9), or $1.44. Analogously, if the top half of the population understates its expenditures by 3.5 percent *more* than the bottom half, then this can be incorporated into the calculations by dividing the poverty line by (1 minus 0.035), or 0.965, which yields a poverty line of (1.44 divided by 0.965), or 1.497; rounding up, one obtains a poverty line of $1.50 a day.

To summarize, the above calculations imply four points. First, the base poverty line is defined as $1 a day, at 1985 prices, or as $1.30 a day at 1993 prices. Second, survey means are deficient or are likely to be measured with considerable error. Third, simple matching of survey means with national account means is incorrect, because such a procedure assumes that the poor understate their expenditures by the same amount as the rich. Fourth, such a procedure is also incorrect because it attributes to the poor the consumption expenditures of rich households not covered in surveys.

Using the 1993-94 Indian consumption expenditure survey as a benchmark, it is observed that *the errors inherent in using NAS means are corrected by increasing the poverty line by approximately 15 percent, from $1.30 per capita per day to $1.50 per capita per day.* Thus, whenever national accounts data are used for calculating poverty, the survey poverty line is inflated by a factor equal to the quantity (1.50 divided by 1.30), or 15.4 percent. Whenever an NA definition of a poverty line is used (e.g., PPP $2 a day), then the equivalent survey poverty line is obtained by deflating the NA line by 15.4 percent. Within this adjustment framework, alternative calculations based on surveys and NA can be compared, and contrasted—and poverty can be calculated for the $1.30-a-day (surveys) or $1.50-a-day (national accounts) poverty lines and done so for the period 1950-2000.

"Smell" Tests for Indian Poverty Estimates

The largest divergence between surveys and national accounts, for expenditure surveys, and the largest downward trend of this divergence, has been for India (survey expenditures only accounted for 55 percent in the year 1999-2000). It is the case that one of the largest deviations between official and "consumption" PPP exchange rates is also for India. It is also true that of the world's 1.2 billion poor people estimated by the World Bank for 1999, about 350 to 400 million reside in India.

It was also noted that there was *no* divergence between World Bank consumption and official PPP exchange rates for China, and that the survey estimate of mean consumption for China has been above 80 percent and closer to 90 percent for most of the years in the past two decades. *So the real test of which estimate of the scale of global poverty (1.15 billion or 650 million people) is right may have to do with which method gets the estimate of the number of poor people right for India.*

Using Engel curve methodology, and the Indian poverty line (equal to PPP $1.25 per capita per day at 1993 prices), Bhalla (2000b) had estimated absolute poverty in India to be about 15 percent. At that time, the most recent official estimate of poverty in India was 42 percent (National Sample Survey of January-June 1998). The World Bank poverty figures for South Asia had hinted (because, unlike China, no explicit estimate was published) that poverty in India was about 45 percent, on the basis of a 16 percent *lower* $1.08 poverty line.

Estimating Poverty in India in 1999

Figure 7.3 lists the various estimates of poverty in India for 1999-2000. Conveniently, the population for that year was 1 billion; so the number of poor divided by 10 also yields the head count ratio.

According to the national accounts data (and, therefore, a poverty line equal to $1.50, not $1.30, to account for the undercoverage of rich people and understatement by them), poverty in India was only 5 percent in 1999. Although this might appear unduly low, it may not be, especially if one considers the fact that the household surveys are missing about *half* of total NA consumption.

An Estimate of Poverty Based on Household Employment and Expenditure Surveys

There is one estimator of total consumption in India, which meets all the exacting demands of a survey-based estimate.[17] Apart from consumer expenditure surveys on which official poverty estimates are based, the National Sample Survey Organization has also been conducting a "wages and unemployment" survey. This survey, conducted every 5 years, asks for wage and employment information from respondents. The survey data on the wages of casual workers in rural areas (the lowest-paid workers in the country) can be used to estimate the lower bound to average consumption, and therefore the upper bound to poverty, in 1999. These data suggest a very different story of India's development than that indicated by the NSS *consumption* data (which are gathered by the same organization, but using a different survey interviewing different sets of households).

Nominal wages (median) of the most unskilled rural workers, termed "casual workers" in the survey schedule, increased at an average annual rate of 11.4 percent for 16 years, from 1983 to 1999 (with women showing a higher average growth of 11.9 percent in comparison with 11.2 for men). This increase in rural casual worker wages is both substantially above the increase in nominal consumption of the consumption survey (an annualized rate of 9.8 percent a year) and almost identical to the increase in

---

17. This section is based on Bhalla (2002a, 2002c).

Figure 7.3 Alternative estimates of the number of poor people in India, 1999 (millions)

number of poor people (millions)

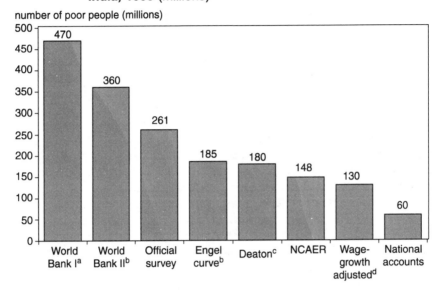

NCAER = National Council of Applied Economic Research

a. The World Bank I and World Bank II estimates are derived from data posted on the bank's Web site. The World Bank I estimate uses the international poverty line of $1.08 per day per capita (1993 prices), whereas the World Bank II estimate is based on the official Indian poverty line, $1.25 per day per capita in 1999.

b. The Engel curve estimate uses production, exports, import data for food grains, sugar, and edible oils, and derived estimates of consumption to obtain the growth in real consumption, 1983-99. See the text and Bhalla (2002a) for details.

c. Deaton (2001c) uses internal price indices for 1987-88, 1993-94, and 1999-2000 to get at estimates of "true" inflation.

d. The wage-growth adjusted estimate uses estimates of wage growth for casual workers in agriculture for 1983-99 and imputes this change to the consumption growth in the economy, 1983-99. See the text and Bhalla (2002a) for details.

Note: All the above estimates (except two) are based on National Sample Survey (NSS) data for India. The exceptions are the NCAER estimate, which is based on the NCAER Household Survey for 1998-99 (see Bery and Shukla 2002 for the details); and the national accounts estimate, which uses a poverty line that is approximately 20 percent higher to account for undercoverage of rich people, understatement by rich households, etc.

Sources: NSS 1999-2000 Consumer Expenditure Survey; Deaton (2001b); Bery and Shukla (2002); World Bank: http://www.worldbank.org/research/povmonitor.

per capita consumption revealed by the national accounts (11.6 percent a year). There are several different consumption deflators, but all converge to an annualized inflation rate of about 8.3 percent a year.

Thus, real wages of casual workers in the rural areas of India almost certainly increased by almost the same amount as per capita consumption, according to NAS—about 3.1 percent a year. Unemployment during these years stayed constant, at between 4 and 6 percent—and it is a bit hard to argue that unemployment levels showed a rising trend when real wages showed a trend increase of more than 3 percent a year in the most competitive labor market in the country. This increase in real wages therefore translated into an increase in real incomes, and therefore into an increase in real consumption. Some of it could obviously have gone into savings, but what is being discussed here are the wages of the poorest people, so this "leakage" into savings is unlikely to be large.

What level of poverty in 1999 is suggested by the growth in rural wages from 1983 to 1999? The survey data for 1999 cannot be used for the forecast, because the survey in 1999, apart from facing methodological contamination in the form of 7- versus 30-day recall for food consumption, also faces contamination in the form of the survey capturing about 25 percent less of national accounts than the 75 percent captured by the 1983 survey.[18] If the distribution of consumption did not change between 1983 and 1999 (and all indications are that it did not change by much; the share of the first quintile is reported by NSS as 8.3 percent in 1983 and 8.7 percent in 1999), then the 1983 consumption survey, and the real growth in rural wages from 1983 to 1999, can be used to project poverty in India in 1999.

Thus, if rural real wages grew at 3.1 percent for 16 years, the average real consumption in rural India in 1999 would be 64 percent higher. The poverty ratio according to the Indian poverty line for this higher level of consumption in rural India is 13 percent in 1999. If it is now assumed that wages of the urban poor in India grew at the same rate as those of the rural poor, then, coincidentally, the same figure for urban poverty (13 percent) is obtained. Thus, a conservative upper bound for poverty in India according to survey data is 13 percent in 1999. The Indian poverty line is equal to PPP $1.25 a day, so this estimate is also representative of poverty in India according to the international poverty line of $1.30 a day.

In the above calculation there are no PPP transformations involved, no national accounts, no changing ratio of surveys with respect to national accounts. The data used are household survey data for 1983; the assumption employed is that consumption expenditure of the poor increases one-for-one with growth in wages of casual workers in rural areas, mostly in

---

18. This implies, of course, that the incomes of the poor would have to rise by 25 percent in real terms between 1983 and 1999 before any decline in the poverty ratio is observed.

agriculture. The result: the head count ratio is 13 percentage points lower than (or half of) the official head count ratio of 26 percent as computed by the 1999 consumer expenditure survey.

Other Estimates of Poverty in India, 1999

Using a different survey (the NCAER MISH survey of households), Bery and Shukla (2002) estimate poverty to be 14.8 percent in 1999. Using internal (survey) price deflators for the survey years 1987-88, 1993-94, and 1999-2000, and ignoring methodological problems created by survey design,[19] Deaton (2001b) finds that the head count ratio in India in 1999 was 18 percent. The Engel curve method (discussed above) yields an almost identical figure for 1999: 18.5 percent.

What Was the Real Head Count Ratio of Poverty in India in 1999?

The official figure for poverty in India in 1999 was 26.1 percent. This is a much lower figure than the vastly higher official figure of 42 percent that was reported on the basis of the year earlier 1998 consumer expenditure survey. The largest figures for poverty in India are those of the World Bank. Two estimates are shown in figure 7.3. One of them, World Bank I, is an estimate based on not the Indian poverty line of $1.25 a day (as are all the other estimates reported in the figure) but a 13 percent lower poverty line of $1.08 a day. According to this estimate, there are 360 million poor people in India.

But according to the Indian poverty line of $1.25, there are 470 million poor people in India (World Bank II). Using the same household survey data, the Indian poverty line, and consumption PPP conversions, the World Bank II estimate of poverty in India, at 47 percent, is nearly double the official government of India estimate of 26 percent. Even with the lower poverty line (World Bank I), the estimate is 40 percent higher. And this lower estimate is almost three times the estimate of poverty suggested by a combination of household expenditure and employment survey data for India.

The answer to the question—how much poverty in India in 1999 based on the Indian poverty line of PPP $1.25 a day—is that it is substantially less than most people have calculated and is close to 13 percent.

---

19. The 1999-2000 National Sample Survey asked the respondents for their estimate of food consumption during the past week, as well as the past month. There is some (theoretical) question that by asking both questions, the survey estimates for 30 days might be biased.

Figure 7.4 Per capita consumption in the developing world

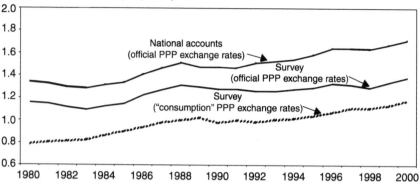

log of consumption per capita per day

PPP = purchasing power parity

Note: When survey consumption data are not available, the standard practice, which is adopted here, is to extrapolate data using data on growth in national accounts consumption means. Official PPP exchange rates are obtained from World Bank, *World Development Indicators*; "consumption" PPP exchange rates are World Bank estimates posted on the bank's Web site given below.

Sources: Deininger and Squire (1996); World Income Inequality Database, available at www.wider.unu.edu/wiid; Asian Development Bank (2002); *World Development Indicators*, CD-ROM; http://www.worldbank.org/research/povmonitor/.

Should Surveys or National Accounts Be Used? Or Both?

The World Bank's reason for not adjusting survey means with national accounts means is that the latter are plagued with measurement problems. Which is true. However, the choice of which estimate is finally chosen should be decided according to which method minimizes errors, especially errors in *trends*, because that is an important variable of interest. And it is likely that not adjusting survey means introduces a larger error into the trends than adjusting the survey means by national accounts data. The advantage of using NAS data is that the errors present, and there are many, are systematic in nature; the random component of errors is larger in survey data. And it is the latter that likely dominates any trend estimate, as is most likely what happened with Milanovic's worsening inequality conclusion for the 5 years 1988 to 1993, and the World Bank estimate of only a marginal poverty decline in the world for 1987 to 1999.

Figure 7.4 shows what has been happening to mean consumption for the past 20 years. Three consumption trends are reported: for national accounts, for surveys with easily available and official PPP exchange rates, and for surveys with recently released (and that also only for one year,

1993) consumption PPP exchange rates.[20] There are two gaps, and both have widened during the past decade. The first gap, between surveys and national accounts, is widely recognized; the second gap, that created by official (and unofficial?) "consumption" PPP exchange rates, has so far not been documented. The reasons, and problems, arising out of the first gap, as extensively discussed above, are many and well known. Little is known about the reasons for or origin of the second gap.

The widening gap or gaps in mean consumption have a mirror image in the finding of more, much more, than the "unobserved" true extent of poverty. Between 1987 and 1999, the gap between the lowest estimate (consumption PPP) and national accounts estimate (official PPP) has widened by about 4 percent. That is not much; it is the level difference that is huge. This difference is about 48 (log) percent. In terms of the head count ratio ($1.30 poverty line for surveys and $1.50 poverty line for national accounts), it is a difference between developing-world poverty of 14.2 percent in 1999 (my estimate) versus a head count ratio of 23 percent (official World Bank estimate).[21]

The important point to note is not that national accounts data are better or that survey data are better. Both are extremely useful, and necessary, for most purposes. Further, estimates of distribution can only be provided by household surveys. Sometimes, even mean income estimates are more accurate in survey data, especially when political realities suggest that official consumption deflators may have been "adjusted" (e.g., Sri Lanka during the 1970s).

The burden on analysts is to look at the respective data, before leaping to the conclusions. In an excellent review of methods of measuring poverty, Deaton (2001a) also endorses this use of an all-data approach: "It would seem more logical to use some average of NAS [national accounts system] and survey data to correct the expenditure survey when available, or to make some adjustment to the NAS estimate of the consumption ratio in the case when it is not" (p. 22). Atkinson and Brandolini (1999) also suggest that surveys may be problematic: "There are problems of misreporting (of household data), or of failure to tailor questions asked to the chosen definition. These may, as with tax information, mean that there is need for the adjustment of raw data to exogenous information, such as national accounts" (p. 17).

---

20. As is suggested by Chen and Ravallion (2000), local inflation, along with the 1993 conversion factor, is used to compute PPP consumption in 1993 prices for years other than 1993. As was discussed above, even for 1993, the World Bank estimates, at least for India, could not be entirely reproduced. Another problem with the method of using local inflation to obtain "real" PPP consumption is that it assumes that each country remains fixed at its 1993 openness level—clearly a nontenable assumption, especially for the past decade.

21. Note that our estimate is for a poverty line of $1.50, adjusted national accounts data; the World Bank estimate is for a poverty line of $1.08, survey data.

However, what is unclear is the method of combining survey and national accounts data; an average may not be representative, or do justice to the relative accuracy (comparative advantage) of each individual source. What happens if one of them—NSS data—is "clearly" in error, an issue explored in great detail in Bhalla (2000b). What happens when one of them—NAS—is clearly in error, as was the case with Sri Lanka (Bhalla and Glewwe 1985). But the spirit of Deaton's comment is correct: Make maximum and intelligent use of all the data that are available, both from surveys and national accounts.

One objective answer to what should be done is to use national accounts data but to deflate the mean consumption obtained from such data by a factor that accounts for the "problems" contained in the mean NA estimate. This factor can be different for different countries, and could be reviewed by the statistical authorities in the respective countries once every decade or so.

One adjustment suggested by the analysis given here is to deflate such expenditures by approximately 15 percent (or multiplication by the quantity 1.3 divided by 1.5, or 0.867, to be precise). In other words, it is assumed that 15 percent of NA consumption does not accrue to the poor at all. This seems a very reasonable assumption. Once this ratio is estimated, trends in mean consumption can be estimated over time; the distribution of these expenditures is provided by the surveys. This combination (analogous to the practice followed in official poverty estimates in India until the EGGOI report) is likely to yield far more accurate estimates of country and world poverty than are yielded by the current practice of estimating poverty on the basis of household surveys alone.

8

Other Methodological Considerations

This chapter discusses several necessary methodological issues that have to be dealt with before a proper analysis of global inequality and poverty can be undertaken. All that is needed is that, in addition to basic data on population, per capita income, and consumption, there are data on the distribution of expenditures (or income). These distributions need to be available for the different years in which the surveys were undertaken, and they need to be at a sufficiently low level of aggregation—quintile shares would not do, nor would decile shares. What might just seem right are percentile shares (i.e., mean expenditures for each 1/100th of the population in each economy for which there are survey data). This chapter is about the method developed to achieve this goal, and the accuracy of the method.

The Individual versus Countries

Concern about inequality, or convergence, or almost any economic phenomenon, is really concern about individuals, not countries. A country is an artificial concept, as has been found out by many societies that have been partitioned, with the USSR being just the latest example. Aggregation has its advantages, both conceptually and individually. But the reason economists have used the country as a unit of analysis to study essentially individual issues (e.g., inequality) is largely because of the *convenience* of data availability. Data are generally not available at an individual level.

For studies of globalization, of inequality, of poverty, and of convergence, *individual*-level data are the most meaningful. For example, when one looks at poverty, a poor person in Bangladesh has more in common with a poor person in Nigeria than with a poor person in the United States. The discussion is generally about the poverty of individuals, not the poverty of nations. The same is true for concerns about globalization; the protests against globalization most likely have more to do with how particular sets of individuals (in different countries) have lost out, rather than particular sets of countries.[1] Analogously, with inequality, surely it matters more how the bottom 20 percent of the *world* has fared with respect to income growth, rather than the bottom 20 percent in China or the United States.

In the analysis of world income inequality, two methods have been prominent: the computationally easy one of inequality, in which a country is the unit of analysis; and the cumbersome yet correct construction of inequality, in which the individual is the unit of analysis. In the former case, each individual in an economy is attributed the mean income for the *entire* country; in the latter case, each individual in the world has her own unique income.

However, the "easy" assumption of every person having the same income as the per capita income can be shown to be particularly wrong in the case of global individual inequality. The deduction, from trends in country inequality, that global inequality has worsened is not logical.[2] *Most* patterns of intercountry inequality change are consistent both with improving inequality and with worsening inequality. It all depends where in the overall distribution the change is taking place—if poor economies are getting richer faster than rich economies (and there is no significant overlap in distributions), then world individual income inequality estimates (W3i) will have a tendency toward improvement.

Economists have always recognized these simple facts, but a lack of data has prevented analysis from being done in terms of "groups of individuals." A country has been considered a reasonable shorthand approximation to "similar groups of individuals," and indeed has provided important insights. So the error has not been large; indeed, most of the time, there may not have been any empirical error at all (i.e., the results obtained from an analysis of nations may have yielded exactly the result that an analysis of individual-level data would have provided, if such data had been available).

Most of the existing statements on worsening income inequality are based on an analysis of income distributions at a *country* level. Relatively fewer studies exist on world individual inequality—and the ones that do

---

1. Obviously, issues such as defense and imperialism are national, not individual, matters; but they are not of concern here.

2. That journalists would make this connection is understandable; that economists would do so is somewhat surprising.

present a mixed picture of trends in the past 20 years. Both the construction of W3i, and the differences of simple accounting procedure (SAP) W3i from other existing estimates, are the subject of this chapter.

Simple Accounting Procedure for Generating W3i

Data are obviously necessary for an analysis of what has happened to poverty and inequality. Hence, the exhaustive exercise of assembling the data available on populations, income, and consumption for all countries and all the years after 1950 was undertaken. The next step was to assemble the distributions of income and consumption that were available. These distributions were available in quintile form; that is, shares of income or consumption for each 20 percent of the population. Normally, this compilation would be both necessary and sufficient for analysis. However, as has been mentioned several times, a new method of estimating both poverty and inequality has appeared on the scene.

This method uses estimates of survey means, not national account means. So data on survey means were needed. Conveniently, for a large number of household surveys in developing countries, the World Bank posts the means in purchasing power parity (PPP) 1993 prices. But it was observed that these means could not be reproduced using published PPP exchange rates. This meant that one had to go to sources alternative to the World Bank for these data.

The assembly of data on survey means was an involved, but doable, exercise. Analysts for Latin America have long been publishing the ratio of survey to national accounts for the income surveys in those countries. My own analysis of household surveys for India, Malaysia, and Sri Lanka yielded the survey means for several surveys in these countries. Data for the United States were the easiest to obtain—several publications, Web sites, and so on, are available. Milanovic has posted on the Web the survey means, in local currency, for the countries that he used in his analysis of world inequality for 1988 and 1993, including an update for Eastern European economies in the mid-1990s. And a large Asian Development Bank project on poverty in Asia, titled "RETA 5917—Building a Poverty Database," yielded estimates of survey means of more than 50 surveys in Asian countries for the period 1980-2000.[3]

This, then, is a brief description of which data are necessary, and which have been collected. Though several questions can be answered, the most important pertaining to levels and trends in individual inequality, and levels and trends in absolute poverty, cannot be answered with these

---

3. See Asian Development Bank (2002).

data. Why? Because the distributions are not available at a more disaggregated level than quintiles; the best that is possible is decile data, and even that for only a few countries and also too aggregated for such countries as China, where 125 million people (10 percent) are being attributed the *same* level of average decile income.

What is required is a *percentile* distribution for each country-year distribution. This method would attribute the same income to only 12.5 million people in China, to each 2.8 million people in the United States, and to each 600,000 people in the United Kingdom. Though it may be "required," the larger concern is one of accuracy. Because any such percentile distribution will have to be derived from data on quintile distributions, the interpolation is from knowing the mean income of 5 20-percentile sets to 100 1-percent sets. And if such a derivation is done, how accurate can it be? The accuracy of such a constructed Lorenz curve is an important issue— if the underlying data of global inequality distributions are not accurate, the compilation might be misleading, or even wrong; hence, appendix B is devoted to it.

Toward this end, the SAP method of estimating Lorenz curve distributions was developed, a procedure that yields 100 percentiles,[4] and therefore means, for 100 different and equal (in size) sets of individuals for each distribution year. The difference between the global inequality distributions developed by Berry, Bourguignon, and Morrisson in 1983, Bourguignon and Morrisson in 2001, Milanovic in October 1999, and the SAP global inequality distributions developed by me (the first estimate was in June 2000; Bhalla 2000d) is that the other three do not construct such detailed distributions of income.[5] Bourguignon and Morrisson's method has an average of 11 means per distribution, and Milanovic's combination of rural and urban data for some countries yields an average of about 12 different "means" per country-year.

The Lorenz curve method provides an estimate of mean income for each and every percentile *within* a country. Aggregating to obtain the global income distribution is now straightforward. The individual country and world populations for each year are known. Thus, the population of each percentile in each country is also known (e.g., India, with 1 billion people, has 10 million in each percentile, whereas Uganda, with 20 million,

---

4. The developed method allows even greater fine-tuning; e.g., a 200- or 400-point distribution. However, the gains from further disaggregation are probably not that great. Such increased precision is unlikely to change the mean income at each percentile level.

5. In a recent paper, Sala-i-Martin (2002b) also constructs a world income distribution based on quintile data but exaggerates when he contends that "to our knowledge, this is the first attempt to construct a world income distribution by aggregating individual country distribution" (p. 2). That credit should rightfully go to the pioneering work of Berry, Bourguignon, and Morrisson (1983) and Bourguignon and Morrisson (2001), both of which, remarkably, are cited and discussed by Sala-i-Martin.

has 200,000 in each percentile), as well as the population in each world percentile (e.g., if the world has 6 billion people, then each percentile has 60 million people).

If the data are ranked according to average percentile income, regardless from which country the data are gathered, then the global distribution is easily formed; that is, each world percentile has an estimate of the number of people and an estimate of the mean income (a weighted average of all the country observations within each percentile). This *is* the world Lorenz curve as estimated by SAP.

The Kakwani Method of Estimating a Lorenz Curve

If the Lorenz curve can be parameterized (i.e., given a mathematical formulation), then the study of the determinants of inequality can "begin." Unfortunately, there are an infinity of "patterns" of distribution, so where can one start? The Lorenz curves can cross, in which case it is a priori ambiguous which distribution is more unequal. In a pioneering study, Kakwani (1980) discusses methods of approximating the Lorenz curve and methods of estimating the same from the limited data (share in income of different income groups and/or shares of individual quintiles).

His preferred formulation, and one used by SAP, is the following:

$$L(p) = p - a^*[p^\alpha]^*[(1 - p)^\beta] \tag{8.1}$$

where p represents the bottom p percent of the population, and $L(p)$ is the corresponding share in income. Taking logs and rearranging terms, one obtains a form fit for regression:

$$\log [p - L(p)] = \log a + \alpha^*\log (p) + \beta^*\log(1 - p) \tag{8.2}$$

The parameters obtained from the equation 8.2 can be used to generate the estimated incomes of each percentile of the population. Often, only four independent observations are available for each distribution (the quintile shares—the fifth quintile is derived from the other four and equal to 1 minus the sum of the other four); thus three parameters (a, α, and β) are estimated from four observations, leaving only 1 degree of freedom.

The basic equation results are then *filtered* by SAP to satisfy the theoretical boundary constraints (i.e., the sum of the estimated shares of each quintile is actually equal to the *observed* shares, and the share of each percentile is equal to or larger than the share of the previous percentile). The filtering is done through an iterative procedure, whereby at the end of the first round, the shares of each individual percentile in the first quintile get estimated and fixed, then the next quintile, then the next, and so on. (The only somewhat "arbitrary" and somewhat "flexible" percentiles are the first and the last, and this flexibility shows up in the errors; see below.)

The filtering and consistency tests are the *additions* to the basic structure of the Kakwani method. To reiterate, the "base" calculation is made using Kakwani's method; this base prediction is then filtered again and again to obtain the best estimates. The only issue now left is one of accuracy; that is, are the SAP percentile distributions accurate? Can a method that generates percentile distributions from knowledge of five quintile shares be reasonably precise within any reasonable degree of confidence?

Is SAP Accurate?

Is SAP accurate? Yes. The SAP method was able to correctly estimate incomes at the percentile level of aggregation for several household distributions for which unit-level data were available (several distributions for India, 1983–99; for states of India, 1983–99; and for Malaysia, 1973–89). All in all, more than 250 "country"-level distributions were tested. Using Indian household data (see table B.1 in appendix B), it is shown that SAP-estimated percentile levels are within 1 percent of the *actual* (derived from unit-level data) levels for most of the 100 percentiles, except the bottom 1 percent and the top 1 percent. The mean error for the entire distribution as proxied by the Gini coefficient was only 0.4 percent, with the largest such error being 3.7 percent.

Figure 8.1 reports on an SAP reconstruction of household income data for the United States for survey years 1967 to 1998. These unit-level data were not available, but published data on quintiles, selected percentiles, and the Gini were available. The constructed and original Ginis are within a whisker of each other for all the years; further, the SAP method is correctly able to identify the levels of different ratios. For example, the ratio of the mean income of the 90th-percentile household to the 20th-percentile household is reported as 9.22 for 1967 and 10.44 for 1998; the SAP reconstruction suggests that the two ratios are 8.96 and 10.80, respectively.

Using SAP to Identify Errors in Published Ginis

The tests above suggest that the SAP method is accurate both at the aggregate Gini level (very, very accurate) and at the individual percentile level (very accurate). And if the distributions for an individual country-year are accurate, then it is simple accounting that gets one to (accurate) global estimates of individual inequality and poverty. Some additional,

Figure 8.1 How good is the SAP method? Evidence from the United States, 1967-98

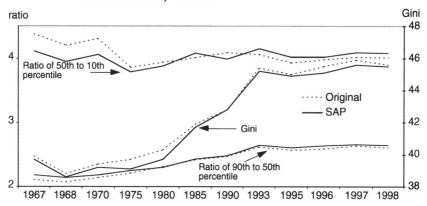

Note: The solid line reflects published data; the dashed line represents the approximation obtained for each percentile by the simple accounting procedure (SAP) method; see the text and appendices A and B for details. The SAP method converts quintile-level data into percentile-level data.

Sources: US Census Bureau, *Current Population Survey,* selected March supplements; http://www.census.gov/hhes/www/incineq.html.

albeit indirect, tests also suggest that the SAP method is reliable—so much so that it can help identify errors in published Ginis!

The Gini estimated by SAP is on the basis of the constructed percentile distribution, a distribution that is consistent with the published quintile shares. But some of the published Ginis do not "match" the accompanying published quintile data. What apparently is occurring is that the published quintile shares are for a different distribution than published Ginis; for example, the quintile shares might refer to a household distribution, whereas the Gini refers to a transformed per capita distribution. Atkinson and Brandolini (1999) correctly observe that even the "accepted" quality Ginis contained in the popular Deininger and Squire (1996) dataset are subject to large errors; they document a large number of cases for which the reported Ginis do not accurately reflect the underlying data. Thus, if the foundation is suspect, how credible is the edifice? The SAP cleaning operation was able to identify several such examples of mismatch, and figures 8.2 and 8.3 document some of the most egregious ones.

The figures contain eight pairs of country distributions; the pairs were chosen according to the original published Ginis, and chosen for suggesting that the published distributions are the same, at least according to the Gini. Also plotted in the figures is the cumulative distribution, so that

Figure 8.2 Ginis compared: Original source and simple accounting procedure (SAP), selected countries

Cumulative income distribution

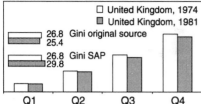

Cumulative income distribution

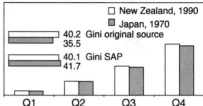

Cumulative income distribution

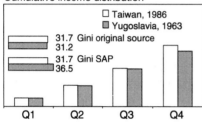

Cumulative income distribution

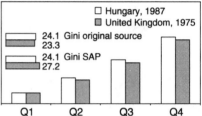

Q = quintile; Q1 = first quintile, etc.

Note: The SAP method converts quintile-level data into percentile-level data and computes the reported Ginis. Q1 (bottom 20 percent) through Q4 (bottom 80 percent) represent the cumulative quintile shares as published; the two Ginis reported are those published and those computed by SAP, along with the quintile shares.

A relatively high Gini value should approximately correspond to relatively lower cumulative income shares at each quintile level, comparing any two countries, or comparing across time for the same country. However, note that, in most cases, relatively higher (original) Ginis correspond to relatively higher income shares for the poorer quintiles. The SAP method yields results that conform far better to the former, expected pattern. For instance, comparing the United Kingdom for 1974 with the United Kingdom for 1981, we find both the (original) Gini and cumulative income shares to be higher in 1974 than in 1981. SAP Gini estimates, though, indicate the reverse, with a relatively higher Gini value in 1981, which corresponds directly to relatively lower cumulative income shares in that year. This, and other comparisons, verifies the accuracy of the SAP method.

There should, in theory, be no difference between the two Ginis; the difference exists because the published Ginis do not accurately reflect the underlying data, possibly because the quintile shares refer to one distribution (e.g., data ordered by households), whereas the published Gini reflects another distribution (e.g., households ordered by per capita expenditure). See also Atkinson and Brandolini (1999).

Sources: Deininger and Squire (1996); World Income Inequality Database, available at http://www.wider.unu.edu/wiid; Asian Development Bank (2002); World Bank, World Development Indicators, CD-ROMs.

Figure 8.3 Ginis compared, original source and simple accounting procedure (SAP), other selected countries

Cumulative income distribution

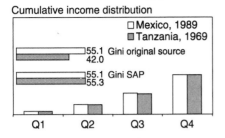

Mexico, 1989
Tanzania, 1969

55.1 Gini original source
42.0

55.1 Gini SAP
55.3

Q1   Q2   Q3   Q4

Cumulative income distribution

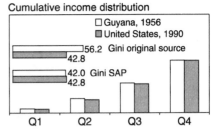

Guyana, 1956
United States, 1990

56.2 Gini original source
42.8

42.0 Gini SAP
42.8

Q1   Q2   Q3   Q4

Cumulative income distribution

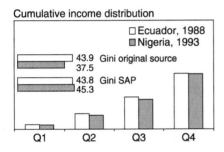

Ecuador, 1988
Nigeria, 1993

43.9 Gini original source
37.5

43.8 Gini SAP
45.3

Q1   Q2   Q3   Q4

Cumulative income distribution

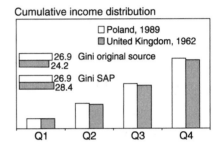

Poland, 1989
United Kingdom, 1962

26.9 Gini original source
24.2

26.9 Gini SAP
28.4

Q1   Q2   Q3   Q4

Q = quintile; Q1 = first quintile, etc.

Note: The SAP method converts quintile-level data into percentile-level data and computes the reported Ginis. Q1 (bottom 20 percent) through Q4 (bottom 80 percent) represent the cumulative quintile shares as published; the two Ginis reported are those published and those computed by SAP, along with the quintile shares.

A relatively high Gini value should approximately correspond to relatively lower cumulative income shares at each quintile level, comparing any two countries, or comparing across time for the same country. However, note that, in most cases, relatively higher (original) Ginis correspond to relatively higher income shares for the poorer quintiles. The SAP method yields results that conform far better to the former, expected pattern. For instance, comparing Mexico for 1989 with Tanzania (1969), we find both the (original) Gini and cumulative income shares to be higher for Mexico. SAP Gini estimates, though, indicate the reverse, with a relatively higher Gini value for Tanzania, which corresponds directly to relatively lower cumulative income shares in that year. This, and other comparisons, verifies the accuracy of the SAP method.

There should, in theory, be no difference between the two Ginis; the difference exists because the published Ginis do not accurately reflect the underlying data, possibly because the quintile shares refer to one distribution (e.g., data ordered by households), whereas the published Gini reflects another distribution (e.g., households ordered by per capita expenditure). See also Atkinson and Brandolini (1999).

Sources: Deininger and Squire (1996); World Income Inequality Database, available at http://www.wider.unu.edu/wiid; Asian Development Bank (2002); World Bank, World Development Indicators, CD-ROMs.

an "eye-inspection" can easily identify whether, and which, distribution is more unequal. The unshaded distribution is always the more equal distribution according to the Lorenz curve (quintile shares), the shaded distribution always the more unequal distribution. Because cumulative distributions are plotted, the unshaded bars should cumulatively be above the shaded bars. Because they are (and were chosen on that basis), the Gini based on the unshaded distribution should be *lower* than that based on the shaded distribution. If it is not, then the reported published Gini is inconsistent with respect to the reported quintile distribution.

Figure 8.3 documents the reality that the Mexican 1989 and the Tanzanian 1969 distributions are both highly unequal (Gini approximately equal to 55). It is not the case that socialist Tanzania had a relatively equal distribution of 42, as was suggested by the original data.

A surprising entrant among the error distributions is that of Nigeria for 1993 (figure 8.3). This distribution is reported in *all* the sources of data (Deininger and Squire 1996; World Institute for Development Economics Research, World Income Inequality Database; *World Development Indicators*; Dollar and Kraay 2000; etc.). This might be more an indication of how errors get transmitted than of anything being wrong with the original data! In any case, the reported Gini is 37.5, with the share of the bottom 40 percent reported as 12.9 percent, and the share of the bottom 80 percent as 50.7 percent. The SAP Gini for this distribution is 45.3, almost 20 percent higher than the official Gini.

Can the "official" estimate be that much in error? The "twin" distribution for Ecuador for 1988 shows that the answer is yes. The *Lorenz curve for Ecuador dominates that for Nigeria for every point on the quintile distribution* (i.e., it is more equal); and the SAP Gini of 43.8 is lower than the SAP Gini for Nigeria (45.3). However, the official estimate for Ecuador is higher by 17 percent! In this instance, it is unambiguously the case that the SAP Gini is correct and that the official reported Gini, and one contained in the various datasets, is in error. The same conclusion holds for all the top 10 errors reported in figures 8.2 and 8.3, and others not reported here.

This reliability of the SAP method is the final step before presentation of the results. If the method can pinpoint errors in published data, it cannot be too far off from being accurate. The next step is a matter of mere accounting, or counting; that is, given distributions for different regions, at a percentile level, it is a simple matter to compute the distributions and the inequality measures.

NEW RESULTS ON POVERTY, INEQUALITY, AND GROWTH, BASED ON SIMPLE ACCOUNTING PROCEDURE METHODS

9

Poverty as It Is—and Forecasts for 2015

The method of constructing percentile distributions can be used to assess trends in global and regional poverty, and it can be used not only for a given poverty line but for any poverty line. Further, the mean incomes of the poor can be computed, and the poverty gap derived. Knowledge of the poverty gap is critical for assessing questions about how much in transfers, or aid, is needed to alleviate poverty.

There has been a large *decline* in poverty during the past 20 years; this decline is based on a method that uses a constant poverty line—equal to a purchasing power parity (PPP) income of $1.50 per capita per day, at 1993 prices—and thus a line that is adjusted upward by 15 percent from the traditional $1-a-day line, equal to PPP $1.30 at 1993 prices. This upward adjustment is meant to compensate for the fact that the national accounts consumption means may contain an upward bias due to possible under-coverage of rich people and understatement by them in the household surveys that are used to obtain distributions of expenditure.

Some contend (e.g., Reddy and Pogge 2002) that use of PPP data under-states true "poverty" as measured by accurate local currency deflators and local currency baskets of consumption by poor people. Though theo-retically this possibility exists, as is documented above (chapter 2), empiri-cally it is the case that among poor countries especially, the use of PPP conversions is *overstating* the level and *understating* the decline in global poverty during the past 20 years.

Thus, a conservative, upper-bound estimate of global poverty at the turn of the century is 10.5 percent of the world's population, or 13.1 percent of the population of the developing world. In absolute numbers, the number of poor people in 2000 was 650 million, down by 800 million since 1980 (when the total was 1.48 billion) and down by 525 million since 1987. Because absolute poverty is ultimately a relative concept, such low levels of absolute poverty suggest that the time has come to *raise* the international poverty line. Using the relationship between levels of consumption and nationally defined poverty lines, a new poverty line is offered—rounding off, it is $2 a day, at 1993 prices. It is also worth noting that the *mean* poverty line in the world today (based on local currency lines and converted to PPP using official PPP conversion factors) is also close to PPP $2 a day.

How Much Poverty Is There in the World?

The $1.08 poverty line does not really belong as a line, given that it was forced on the international community due to deficiencies in both the survey mean method and the "consumption" PPP exchange rates in accurately reflecting levels and trends of consumption poverty. Chapter 7 documented how the $1.50 poverty line at 1993 prices captured the consistency of the national accounts, as well as the virtues of survey-based methods of estimating poverty. At one level, a $1.50 poverty line is equal to a $1.30 poverty line adjusted upward by 15 percent to account for undercoverage of rich people in surveys and the fact that they understate their incomes by a higher amount than do nonrich people. At another level, a $1.50 poverty line is equal to a $1.30 survey line with the survey capture of national accounts being kept fixed at 86.7 percent (the ratio of 1.3 and 1.5). No matter what assumption is used, the $1.50 poverty line has the virtue of consistency and constancy.

Table 9.1 reports on estimates of the head count ratio for the developing world according to different methods (survey vs. national accounts means) and the corresponding equivalent poverty lines. All the data given in this table were computed according to official PPP exchange rates, as published in the World Bank's *World Development Indicators*. The two preferred methods (survey data and the $1.30 line, or national accounts and the $1.50 line) are shown in bold. Note that these two methods yield virtually the same poverty ratio for all the years until 1980! But for 2000, the survey $1.30 line yields a poverty estimate of 18.2 percent; the old "matching-but-now-no-more" national accounts data yield a 5-percentage-point (or almost 30 percent) lower number of 13.1 percent.

The estimate most preferred for the present study is obviously the $1.50 poverty line, using national accounts (and official PPP exchange rates!). This method yields a figure of 650 million poor people in 2000, about 500 million fewer than suggested by "official" World Bank figures.

Table 9.1 Poverty over the years

Measure	1950	1960	1970	1980	1990	2000
Head count ratio (percent)						
Survey mean						
$1.08 poverty line	58.2	46.4	40.2	38.0	20.0	11.4
$1.30 poverty line	**65.8**	**55.4**	**49.3**	**46.5**	**29.0**	**18.2**
$1.73 poverty line	75.7	68.0	62.4	59.2	45.1	32.2
Country poverty line	75.4	70.4	65.9	62.6	50.2	37.3
National accounts mean[a]						
$1.25 poverty line	55.8	43.9	37.9	35.0	17.7	9.1
$1.50 poverty line	**63.2**	**52.5**	**46.4**	**43.5**	**25.4**	**13.1**
$2.00 poverty line	73.8	65.2	59.9	56.3	40.4	23.3
Country poverty line X 1.15	73.5	68.1	63.2	60.1	45.5	28.0
Number of poor people (millions)[b]						
Survey mean						
$1.08 poverty line	1,127	1,000	1,095	1,293	831	559
$1.30 poverty line	**1,275**	**1,193**	**1,342**	**1,581**	**1,208**	**899**
$1.73 poverty line	1,466	1,466	1,700	2,016	1,879	1,588
Country poverty line	1,461	1,517	1,794	2,130	2,091	1,840
National accounts mean[a]						
$1.25 poverty line	1,081	947	1,031	1,192	738	449
$1.50 poverty line	**1,223**	**1,131**	**1,262**	**1,479**	**1,056**	**647**
$2.00 poverty line	1,429	1,406	1,631	1,917	1,680	1,147
Country poverty line X 1.15	1,423	1,468	1,719	2,045	1,894	1,377

a. The national accounts poverty lines are all higher by a factor of (1.5/1.3) to account for the possibility that survey data undercount rich people and that they understate their consumption by a greater proportion. See the text for the derivation of the magnitude of this adjustment factor (equal to 1.5/1.3).

b. Poverty figures are for people in the developing world. Figures for the number of poor are computed by multiplying the estimated head count ratio by national populations.

Note: In many cases, income distribution data may not be available for decade-end years. In such cases, the table presents either the closest earlier year for which data are available, or, where earlier data are not available, data for the earliest later year. For example, if the latest survey took place in 1995, the 2000 figures reflect these values; if the first survey took place in 1975, the 1960 figures reflect those values.

Sources: Deininger and Squire (1996); World Income Inequality Database, available at www.wider.unu.edu/wiid; Asian Development Bank (2002); World Bank, *World Development Indicators,* CD-ROM.

Where Did Poverty Decline from 1960 to 2000?

It is tempting to conclude that declining poverty in the world is really about declines in China and India. Even if this were true, it would be an encouraging outcome if concern is with the world's poor people rather than with country-specific poor people. Many populous countries in the world have reduced poverty—Brazil and Mexico in Latin America; Egypt in the Middle East and North Africa; and China, India, Indonesia, Pakistan, and Vietnam in Asia. It is true that the 1980-2000 globalization period bypassed poor people in Latin America and sub-Saharan Africa; but these continents did not register any growth in the 1980-2000 period either. Most poor people, however, reside or resided in South Asia and China; they have seen a significant increase in their incomes during the past 20 years, and a significant decline in poverty. As is shown below, this decline was of a miraculous nature: unprecedented in its scale, and unlikely to ever happen again on the same scale.

Table 9.2 documents the evolution of declines in poverty since 1960. The period 1960-80 is marked by an increase in the number of poor people in all regions of the world, except Latin America and the Middle East. The next two decades represent the "Asian Drama"—a transformation in many countries that not only halted the increase in the absolute number of poor people (which was going up because of population growth alone) but reversed it significantly. Asia saw more than a billion people rise out of poverty in just 20 years—a miracle.

The Evolution of World Poverty, 1820-2000

The SAP dataset allows for the estimation of poverty according to any given poverty line, and with any given combination of methods—surveys and national accounts, consumption and official PPP exchange rates. Bourguignon and Morrisson (2001) report estimates of world poverty from 1820-1950 according to the poverty line of $1 a day, at 1985 prices. For 1950, they report that the number of poor people is 55 percent; using national accounts data, I obtain a lower figure, 47.2 percent. For 1992, the poverty ratio reported by Bourguignon and Morrisson is 23.7 percent; I obtain a lower number, 19.2 percent. One possible reason for this divergence is that Bourguignon and Morrisson attempt to "link" their national accounts method with the survey-based estimates of poverty produced by the World Bank in the 1990s; another reason could be in the PPP estimates used by them for China; and yet another reason could be a difference in the methods (the ones used in the present study being more complete).

Figure 9.1 reports estimates of poverty from 1820 to 2000; the estimates from 1820 to 1929 are from Bourguignon and Morrisson (and use the line of $1 a day, at 1985 prices, and national accounts data). The estimates for 1950-2000 are my estimates based on $1.50 a day, 1993 prices, and national accounts data. To be consistent with the earlier study, poverty ratios are reported in terms of the world's population, not in terms of the population of the developing world.

Table 9.2 Where did poverty decline?

Region and country	Population, 2000 (millions)	Change in number of poor people ($1.50-a-day poverty line)		
		1960-80	1980-2000	1960-2000
East Asia				
China	1,265	206.8	−727.0	−520.2
Indonesia	210	8.1	−67.4	−59.3
Thailand	61	−5.9	−7.4	−13.3
Vietnam	78	16.5	−24.9	−8.4
Total	**1,894**	**226.2**	**−841.0**	**−614.8**
South Asia				
Bangladesh	131	9.7	2.1	11.8
India	1,011	92.4	−207.2	−114.8
Pakistan	137	−7.9	−16.0	−23.8
Total	**1,355**	**101.2**	**−205.0**	**−103.8**
Sub-Saharan Africa				
Ethiopia	65	9.7	23.3	33.0
Kenya	30	4.9	5.6	10.5
Nigeria	129	11.3	50.9	62.2
Tanzania	35	6.6	12.4	18.9
Uganda	22	4.06	−1.76	2.31
Lesotho	2	−0.25	0.10	−0.15
Mauritania	3	−0.22	0.11	−0.11
Total	**661**	**70.6**	**173.8**	**244.4**
Middle East and North Africa				
Egypt	64	−11.8	−1.2	−13.0
Total	**374**	**−22.2**	**19.4**	**−2.8**
Latin America				
Brazil	172	−14.1	8.9	−5.2
Mexico	97	−6.8	0.0	−6.8
Total	**518**	**−21.8**	**14.0**	**−7.8**
All less-developed countries	**4,928**	**348.2**	**−831.6**	**−483.4**

Note: The poverty line used is $1.50 a day, national accounts means, 1993 prices. This is roughly equal to the popular $1-a-day, 1985-prices poverty line, when such a line is used with survey data. The $1.50-a-day poverty line incorporates within it the tendency for the rich to understate their expenditures to a greater degree than poor people, as well as the tendency for the rich to not be fully covered by surveys.

Sources: Deininger and Squire (1996); World Income Inequality Database, available at http://www.wider.unu.edu/wiid; Asian Development Bank (2002); World Bank, *World Development Indicators*, CD-ROM.

Figure 9.1 World poverty, 1820-2000

Head count ratio for extreme poverty (percent)
($1.50 a day, 1993 PPP prices)[a]

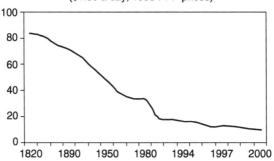

Number of poor people (in millions)[b]

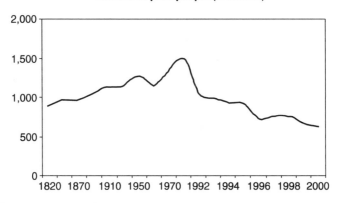

a. The poverty line used is $1.50 a day, national accounts means, at 1993 prices. This is roughly equal to the popular $1-a-day, 1985-prices poverty line, when such a line is used with survey data. The $1.50-a-day poverty line incorporates within it the tendency for the rich to understate their expenditures to a greater degree than poor people, as well as the tendency for the rich to not be fully covered by surveys.

b. Figures for the number of poor are computed by multiplying the estimated head count ratio by the world population.

Sources: Deininger and Squire (1996); World Income Inequality Database, available at http:// www.wider.unu.edu/wiid; Asian Development Bank (2002); World Bank, *World Development Indicators*, CD-ROM. For years prior to 1950, data were taken from Bourguignon and Morrisson (2001).

Table 9.3 Poverty reduction yield of growth

Time period[a]	Income		Head count ratio		
	Change	Equivalent 20-year change	Change	Equivalent 20-year change	Yield
1820-50	11.1	7.4	−2.4	−1.6	2.2
1850-70	19.0	19.0	−6.1	−6.1	3.2
1870-90	22.4	22.4	−3.6	−3.6	1.6
1890-1910	27.1	27.1	−6.1	−6.1	2.3
1910-29	21.9	23.0	−9.3	−9.8	4.3
1929-50	16.6	15.8	17.3	16.5	−10.4
1950-70	51.3	51.3	−12.4	−12.4	2.4
1960-80	42.9	42.9	−4.6	−4.6	1.1
1970-90	28.2	28.2	−14.6	−14.6	5.2
1980-90	11.2	22.4	−13.6	−27.2	12.2
1990-2000	12.6	25.2	−9.7	−19.4	7.7
1980-2000	23.8	23.8	−23.3	−23.3	9.8
Mean		**25.7**		**−9.4**	**3.5**
Standard deviation		**11.6**		**11.5**	**5.6**

a. When a time period is either less or more than 20 years, the 20-year "equivalent" income or head count ratio change is presented, i.e., the actual change is multiplied by a fraction equal to (20 divided by the number of years); e.g., figures for 1910-29 will be multiplied by (20 divided by 19).

Note: The yield of growth is defined as the decline in poverty (head count ratio) brought about by each 10 percent growth in per capita incomes (data up through 1950) or per capita consumption (data for 1950 to 2000). Both income and consumption figures are national-accounts based. The poverty line used is $1.50 a day, national accounts means, 1993 prices, for data for 1950-2000.

Sources: Deininger and Squire (1996); World Income Inequality Database, available at http://www.wider.unu.edu/wiid; Asian Development Bank (2002); World Bank, World Development Indicators, CD-ROM; for years prior to 1950, data taken from Bourguignon and Morrisson (2001).

In 1820, global poverty was close to 84 percent of the world's population, and more than a century later, it had declined to 56 percent (in 1929). Twenty years later, it was approximately at this same level. There has been a constant drift downward in the poverty ratio since 1950, and by 1992, only a fifth of the world's population was poor. The number of poor people in the world shows a different trajectory; not until the start of globalization (and consistently high growth rates in China and India) in the 1980s does it begin to decline. From a peak of 1.589 billion people in 1982, the number has declined by almost a billion.

Table 9.3 attempts to answer a simple question: In the past almost 200 years, when was there the maximum bang for the buck in poverty reduction? The table's first two columns give estimates of consumption growth (income growth for the period 1820-1950) for each (approximate) 20-year period. The second two columns give the estimated change in the head count ratio. The final column gives the poverty reduction yield of growth (i.e., the amount of poverty reduction brought about by each 10 percent growth in incomes). For example, during the 1820-50 period, income grew by 11.1 percent and the head count ratio declined by 2.4 percent; the yield, therefore, is 2.4 divided by 11.1, or 0.216 for each 1 percent of growth; for 10 percent, it is 2.16 or 2.2.

The highest yield in 190 years is observed for the 20-year globalization period, 1980-2000. In this golden age, world poverty declined by 23.3 percent, a (log) consumption growth of only 23.8 percent. In other words, each 10 percent in growth brought about a 9.8-percentage-point reduction in poverty. The next-best period (not overlapping with the globalization years 1980-2000) was 1910-29; it had a yield less than half; at that time, each 10 percent in growth brought about a reduction of "only" 4.3 percentage points in the head count ratio.

Not only were the years 1980-2000 the best for development, but they were the best by far. A slightly lengthy, and perhaps somewhat distracting, heuristic explanation of the phenomenon that we have all been privileged to witness is as follows. The only reason for this involved digression is that, ironically, though great strides were being made in the reduction of poverty, the world and its leaders—especially aid-giving and development research organizations—seem to have completely missed noticing this progress.

A Digression: How Do You Assess the Best?

Throughout the text, we have emphasized the importance of cleaning the data, of consistency checks, of checking for "smell" tests, and so on. So how can one assess if a particular period was remarkable, a genuine outlier? Let us look at an equivalent question from the world of sports: How can one determine whether a particular player was the best in his or her field? But you might justifiably object and say—that cannot be done; apples and oranges, or Tigers and Jordans. Worse, you cannot even compare a Wilt Chamberlain with Michael Jordan or Sachin Tendulkar with Don Bradman. And why not?

Let us make the problem very simple—let us compare players at a point in time. Clearly, Tiger Woods dominates the game of golf today, just as Muhammad Ali dominated boxing in the 1960s, or Jesse Owens dominated athletics in the 1930s. But who dominated *more*, that is the question.

The answer is only slightly complicated. If an index of performance can be constructed for each sport,[1] then how good a player is will be indicated by the distance between him and the number two player, in

---

1. For a first attempt for the sport of cricket, see Bhalla (1987).

standard deviation terms. The larger the distance, the better the player. Now apples and oranges can be compared, or Bradman and Jordan.[2]

Now back to globalization. Table 9.3 also reports the standard deviation for the poverty yield of growth—it is large and equal to 5.6. Given the second-best yield of 4.3 observed in 1910-29 (the overlapping period of 1970-90 does not count), it appears that the best period was ahead of second best by almost 1 standard deviation! That is like the second-best player after Tiger Woods having a handicap of 2. That is how good globalization was for the poor. It is difficult to find any other statistic that shows that the globalizing 1980s and 1990s were indeed the golden age of development.

Regional Poverty Trends

Table 9.4 documents the poverty levels in different regions of the world, according to the $1.50 poverty line and using national accounts data. This line is approximately the same as that used in 1979 by Ahluwalia, Carter, and Chenery (with a $1.25 consumption line, 1985 PPP, and also national accounts).

All areas of the world show significant declines in poverty, except sub-Saharan Africa. The two largest, and formerly poorest, regions of the world—East and South Asia—show parallel declines, and both regions had a poverty ratio in 2000 of less than 10 percent. In Latin America, the head count ratio was down from 16 percent in the 1960s to only 5 percent in the 1990s. In the Middle East and North Africa, the decline was more rapid—from 24 percent in the 1960s to 8 percent in 2000.

One major region of the world, sub-Saharan Africa, has been most unfortunate. Poverty rates there are at the same level as in the 1960s—about half the population then, and about 55 percent in 2000. The reality is even worse. The population has more than doubled during the past four decades, which means that the absolute number of poor people has also more than doubled, to reach about 362 million—more than half of the world's poor people.

Time to Raise the Poverty Line

The first important implication of the finding that poverty today is less than 15 percent is that the poverty line is too low. What should the new poverty line be? A common, and correct, presumption is that poverty lines tend to rise with economic development.

---

2. Work on this project is under way; preliminary results indicate that the Australian cricketer Donald Bradman might just have been the best athlete ever.

Table 9.4 Poverty in the world, 1950-2000

Region[a] and measure	Poverty line (PPP, $1.50 a day)						Poverty line (PPP, $2.00 a day)					
	1950	1960	1970	1980	1990	2000	1950	1960	1970	1980	1990	2000
Head count ratio (percent)												
East Asia	86.6	77.5	71.1	67.2	31.3	6.0	91.1	86.0	82.0	78.3	49.2	16.1
South Asia	44.3	37.2	32.1	34.4	18.5	7.8	64.3	58.1	55.2	56.3	39.3	21.1
Sub-Saharan Africa	59.3	53.2	52.2	49.9	55.3	54.8	70.2	65.4	63.4	62.3	67.1	66.8
Middle East and North Africa	26.3	24.3	13.4	4.3	5.2	7.8	40.3	37.2	23.3	10.4	10.2	14.0
Latin America	22.0	16.0	9.4	3.6	5.3	5.2	31.3	24.5	15.4	8.2	10.8	10.4
Eastern Europe	17.8	9.2	3.3	1.7	0	0	28.4	16.4	6.7	2.8	3.2	3.1
Developing world	**63.2**	**52.5**	**46.4**	**43.5**	**25.4**	**13.1**	**73.8**	**65.2**	**59.9**	**56.3**	**40.4**	**23.3**
Number of poor people (millions)												
East Asia	830	729	833	955	521	114	873	809	959	1114	820	306
South Asia	208	209	229	310	207	105	303	326	392	508	441	286
Sub-Saharan Africa	104	118	150	188	279	362	123	145	181	235	339	441
Middle East and North Africa	27	32	23	10	16	29	41	49	40	24	31	53
Latin America	36	35	27	13	23	27	51	53	44	30	48	54
Eastern Europe	49	29	12	7	0	0	78	52	24	11	13	13
Developing world	**1,223**	**1,131**	**1,262**	**1,479**	**1,056**	**647**	**1,429**	**1,406**	**1,631**	**1,917**	**1,680**	**1,147**

PPP = purchasing power parity

a. For the classification of regions, see appendix C.

Note: Calculations are based on national accounts means. In many cases, income distribution data may not be available for decade-end years. In such cases, the table presents either the closest earlier year for which data are available, or, where earlier data are not available, data for the earliest later year. For example, if the latest survey took place in 1995, the 2000 figures reflect these values; if the first survey took place in 1975, the 1960 figures reflect those values.

Sources: Deininger and Squire (1996); World Income Inequality Database, available at http://www.wider.unu.edu/wiid; Asian Development Bank (2002).

The first estimates of world poverty were reported for 1975 by Ahluwalia, Carter, and Chenery (1979). Since then, per capita consumption in the developing world has increased by 50 (log) percent—from $3.38 per day to $5.57 (in 2000). The elasticity of the poverty line with respect to average consumption is 0.54, as revealed by the following regression for 51 countries in 1993 (above, an analogous regression for 1964 was given):

Log (poverty line) = 0.043 + 0.54*(log per capita consumption)

51 countries; R^2 = 0.46; standard error of log consumption = 0.083

Thus, the poverty line needs to be raised by 0.27 (log) percent. Given an original poverty line of $1.50 (and this poverty line incorporates adjustments for undercoverage, etc.), this yields $1.96 as the new poverty line. Rounding off, one obtains $2 as the new poverty line to use for developing countries.

Additional support for the $2-a-day poverty line is obtained by noting that for the 50 developing countries for which we have data, the mean national poverty line (population-weighted) was equal to $1.96 per day. Finally, this poverty line ($2) has been in use in Latin America for some time; the average country-specific poverty line there is a high PPP $6.11 a day; in sub-Saharan Africa, the average country-specific line is about $1.50.

The alternative, not raising the poverty line, does not make much sense. As is shown throughout the book, poverty has declined significantly, and the concept of absolute poverty is from a bygone era. Absolute poverty is relative, hence the new poverty line.

Poverty in the world at $2 a day translates into 23.3 percent of the world's population, or 1.147 billion people. Coincidentally, this level is identical to the "official" World Bank poverty numbers for a considerably lower (by log 62 percent) poverty line of $1.08 a day.

Forecasts for 2000 and 2015

Using various assumptions, Ahluwalia, Carter, and Chenery (1979) forecast poverty levels for 2000 for the developing world excluding China: "Although in relative terms these projections represent impressive progress in reducing poverty—from about 50 percent of the population of developing countries in 1960 to 16 percent in 2000—they fall considerably short of the results that might be expected with more effective policies" (p. 320).

By estimating global poverty for the above country classification, and with an equivalent poverty line at 1993 prices ($1.50 a day), one obtains almost exactly the result forecast: 13.1 percent of the developing world's population. The individual region forecasts of Ahluwalia and his colleagues were not all correct—a greater decline in poverty was assumed for sub-Saharan Africa, a smaller decline for South Asia. Fortunately for the forecast, the errors canceled out. But it is still very surprising that Ahluwalia and his colleagues got it right more than 20 years ago.

Recent documents of international financial institutions suggest a halving of the world's head count ratio to 15 percent by 2015. But as is shown above, this target has already been achieved—using a poverty line that is considerably higher ($1.08 vs. $1.50). With poverty at only 13.1 percent of the developing world's population in 2000, what should realistic targets be for the international community and organizations for 2015?

This important question is taken up in the next chapter. It involves various methodological assumptions, as well as interpretations of the correct relationship between economic growth and poverty reduction.

10

Reinventing the Kuznets Curve:
Propoor Growth

Dissatisfaction with the fruits of economic growth—most likely based on a misinterpretation of data on growth and poverty reduction and on the use of problematic consumption purchasing power parity 1993 exchange rates—led the international research community to look for alternatives to "traditional" growth-based models of development. The study of growth was not junked, however; it became a search for models of development in which growth was propoor.

But what is "propoor growth"? How does one measure it? How is it different from stating that propoor growth is that which results in an increase in equality and that antipoor growth is that which results in an increase in inequality?

In a fundamental sense, the result that all the growth reflected in GDP had not been reflected in an adequate decline in absolute poverty ratios brought back fears of the debate that had raged in the 1970s. At that time, Fishlow (1972) had suggested that the growth in Brazil had really not trickled down to the poor, that the growth had been of the inequality-enhancing type, and that the gains of growth had been frittered away in increases in inequality. In short, the growth had not been propoor. It was an example of growth without poverty reduction, not unlike similar claims today. The reality was confirmed to be otherwise (see Pfeffermann and Webb 1983).

But the concern with growth being irrelevant for poverty reduction is (thankfully) not the concern today. Precious few economists, and even fewer politicians, are arguing that countries should not pursue growth. But all are arguing for a growth process that enhances poverty reduction.

Mathematically, the only manner in which, ceteris paribus, a given amount of growth will lead to a larger than expected reduction in poverty is if inequality declines. This is no different from stating that "growth with equity" or the Kuznets curve is invalid. It very well might be, but it should be recognized that today's "propoor" growth is identical to both yesterday's "growth with equity" and the day before yesterday's debate on whether the Kuznets curve exists.

It cannot be argued that the Kuznets curve prediction will be true, and that there can be "propoor" growth. Nor can it be simultaneously argued that country inequality has not changed or that "growth is good for the poor" (Deininger and Squire 1996; Roemer and Gugerty 1997; Timmer 1997; Gallup, Radelet, and Warner 1998; Dollar and Kraay 2000) or that there is need for propoor growth or a better "quality" of growth. Propoor growth is growth that lowers inequality. So why the change to a new nomenclature?

There is a further important problem with the concept of propoor growth. What if it is the case that higher growth for poor people can only be obtained if inequality increases? This is not just a theoretical possibility, and the growth consequences of inequality have been explored by many, with inconclusive results. There is the further correct and somewhat intractable problem of simultaneity—does high growth lead to worsening inequality, or does low inequality lead to high growth? Or is it the other way around? Ultimately, concern is (or should be) with poor people's incomes, and whether such an increase comes about through increasing inequality should not be a concern of those who are concerned about improving the lives of poor people.

Ignoring the general equilibrium considerations, the isolated question can still be asked: Given a certain average level of growth, did poor people share equally in the fruits of growth? But if this is the goal, then it is much more involved to answer the question "How much poverty reduction is consistent with a given amount of growth?" than to answer the question "Did inequality change?" As it turns out, the answer to the first question involves the correct interpretation of several statistical questions (the shape of the distribution, and particularly its shape around the point where the poverty line is positioned), whereas the answer to the second question is a straightforward documentation of what happened to different quintile shares.

The problems with employing the involved "propoor" growth calculations can be illustrated as follows. Assume that one had perfect data on growth and poverty reduction for all the countries in the world. For country A, it is observed that there is a 10 percent growth in income, and a 10 percent reduction in the head count ratio (HCR). For another country, B, identical in all respects (except inequality), it is observed that a 10 percent income growth leads to only an 8 percent reduction in poverty.

Is growth in country B not propoor? No. It is likely that if the poverty lines were the same, then the difference arose because of initial conditions; that is, country B was more unequal *around the poverty line*. In which case, the growth process is not flawed, nor antipoor; rather, the initial conditions were disadvantageous.

Now assume a different, let us say higher, poverty line, and exactly the same "reality." In this instance, it might well be that country B shows a poverty reduction of 10 percent and country A one of 8 percent. Now what should one conclude about the growth process? Again, nothing, except to note that the extent of poverty reduction expected with a given amount of growth is a function of the distribution of income *around the poverty line*. In other words, inequality per se may not have much to do with the relationship between growth and poverty reduction.

Apart from correctly identifying and estimating propoor growth, this chapter also suggests using a straightforward procedure (and one not used to date) for estimating whether growth during any time period was propoor or not.[1] This procedure identifies a fixed *proportion* of poor people at a point in time within each country for any given poverty line.

This proportion obviously varies for different countries; for example, according to the $1.50 poverty line, the poverty rate was 45 percent in Indonesia in 1980, 36 percent in India, and 82 percent in China. If growth was neutral, then the bottom 36 percent of Indians should show approximately the same growth as the top 64 percent of Indians. Analogously, the top 55 percent of Indonesians should experience the same growth as the bottom 45 percent for growth in Indonesia to be neutral. Propoor growth is identified as such when the growth in incomes of poor people exceeds the growth in incomes of nonpoor people.

It was not possible to conduct this simple test by earlier researchers because intertemporal data for consumption percentiles were not available. The simple accounting procedure method makes available such data, and allows for this simple test to be conducted.

The Search for Propoor Growth

By definition, there are only two sources of change in the HCR of poor people—either through growth or through a change in the distribution of consumption. It is realized that positive propoor income distribution changes are difficult to bring about, politically and/or through economic processes. So economic growth is the only method, and to increase the

---

1. Again, this simple calculation does not, and cannot, answer the mutatis mutandis question of what would have happened to aggregate (and poor) growth due to the simultaneous relationship between inequality change and growth.

"bang for the buck" of growth, it is important for it to be of the propoor variety.

The identification, and advocacy, of propoor growth has itself become a growth industry, and several articles oriented toward the notion of propoor growth have been published.[2] It would not be an exaggeration to state that much like the expansion of research into the area of poverty in the 1970s, this is a parallel movement—a second coming of sorts. The first coming—in the mid-1970s—involved a research and policy enterprise aimed at determining who poor people were, how many of them there were, and what policy initiatives were needed to reduce poverty.

The second enterprise,[3] since the mid-1990s, states five premises. First, though growth is necessary for poverty reduction, it is nowhere close to sufficient. Second, the reason poverty has been stagnant is not that there has not been any growth, but that the growth has been distinctly of the prorich variety. Third, this prorich growth pattern has exacerbated inequalities, and this pattern needs to be corrected through income distribution policies. Fourth, it is realized that bringing about income redistribution may be politically difficult. Fifth, hence, there is an intensified search (and research) for policies that will provide "better quality" growth[4] that is manifestly propoor.[5]

Moreover, most of this research homes in on the tautology that countries with more equal distribution of income allow poor people to obtain a larger share of any given amount of growth. Hence, propoor growth means growth that is accompanied by a redistribution of income. "Faced with this picture of global poverty and inequality, . . . attaining the international development goals will require actions to spur economic growth and reduce income inequality" (World Bank, *World Development Report 2000/2001: Attacking Poverty*, 6).

The Growth-Poverty Connection

The key to understanding whether the growth process is operating in a neutral manner is whether poor people participate evenly in the growth

---

2. See World Bank, *World Development Report 1990: Poverty and Development* and *World Development Report 2000/2001: Attacking Poverty*; Ravallion and Datt (1991); Ravallion and Lipton (1993); Kakwani (1997); Warr (2000); and the scores of references in these documents.

3. Most of these articles are motivated by the (erroneous) finding of "growth, growth everywhere, and not a drop in poverty."

4. An excellent exposition of this view is contained in Thomas (2000).

5. One indication of this trend is provided by the proliferation of articles that contain "propoor growth" in the title. The pattern of research in this area is almost identical to the previous pattern of research on the caloric determinants of poverty in the early 1980s. It is similarly, conceptually and empirically, flawed.

process; and "evenly" is defined as the elasticity of the incomes of poor people with respect to average growth. If poverty is now defined not by the level of poor people's incomes but rather by the *proportion* of population with incomes below a specific level P (the poverty line), the answer becomes more complex, not least because there is now a nonlinear cumulative distribution function relating the proportion of population that is poor, HCR, to the income (Y) involved. HCR now is censored above at 100 and below at 0; that is, it ranges between no poor people (HCR = 0 percent) to the entire population being poor (HCR = 100 percent).

With HCR as the variable in question, how can one determine if the growth process has been even or neutral ("equivalent" to an elasticity equal to 1 in the incomes-of-poor-people model), propoor (equivalent to an elasticity greater than 1), or prorich (equivalent to an elasticity of less than 1)? Because we are talking about income poverty, the relationship should be "exhaustive"; that is, the entire growth in income should be accounted for. By definition, changes in HCR are equal to the sum of changes caused by rising incomes—holding the distribution of income, $I = F(Y)$, constant—and the changes caused by the changing distribution of income, holding the level of income constant. In terms of first differences in logs, one obtains

$$d \log HCR = a^* d \log y + b^* d \log I \qquad (10.1)$$

where, by definition, $(a + b) = 1$.[6]

This equation has been estimated by several researchers, and though intuitive, it yields the wrong answers. It is argued, incorrectly, that the ratio of a to $(a + b)$ is indicative of whether the nature of growth is propoor. This is elaborated on below.

Propoor Elasticity

The problem is caused by the fact that both coefficients a and b in the above equation are a *function* of poverty line P. The problems this can cause for estimation are explained in heuristic terms as follows. Assume the maximum income of poor people in a society is $0.50 per capita per day, and P is double this amount, $1. Now if all incomes go up by 10 percent, there will obviously be no decline in HCR from 100 percent; the maximum income goes up to $0.55, still far below P. So the elasticity of HCR with respect to income growth (a in equation 10.1) is zero.

---

6. Ravallion and Datt introduce an error here; they suggest that there is a third "residual" term in equation 10.1, when conceptually there is not one. Kakwani (1997) correctly argues that there is no residual. The problem with both interpretations is that they are defining the left-hand side in log first-difference terms, rather than arithmetic first-difference terms; see below.

Figure 10.1 World cumulative distribution of per capita consumption, 1987 (1993 PPP dollars)

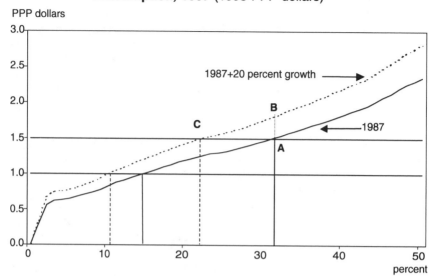

PPP = purchasing power parity

Note: The solid line indicates the actual cumulative distribution for world consumption in 1987; the dotted line indicates what the distribution would have been with an additional 20 percent of consumption growth at each percentile level.

Using a $1.50-a-day poverty line, we find that this additional consumption growth would have caused a decline in poverty from point A to point C, or about 10 percent. A $1-a-day line suggests a smaller decline.

Sources: Deininger and Squire (1996); World Income Inequality Database, available at http:// www.wider.unu.edu/wiid; Asian Development Bank (2002).

Now assume that the mean (not maximum) income of poor people is $0.50, and that the standard deviation of their incomes is 0.1. Again, a 10 percent increase in income will not make any dent in HCR (i.e., the elasticity is zero). Now assume that *all* poor people have an income equal to $0.99. A 1.1 percent increase in income will now mean that HCR will move from 100 percent to 0 percent in one fell swoop—close to an infinite elasticity, or a equal to infinity.

These are unrealistic, but informative, examples. What they all point to is the importance of incorporating into the calculations the knowledge of where the mean income of poor people, and the nature of its distribution, is with respect to the poverty line, P. This is a nonlinear affair, which perhaps is one reason analysts have not attempted to compute it.

Figure 10.1 shows the cumulative distribution for the developing world for 1987, as well as the same distribution "shocked" with a 20 percent across-the-board increase. An increase in income of 20 percent will involve a movement from point A to point B; the difference in the head count ratios is given by the movement from A to C. *The calculation of how much poverty reduction is expected is dependent on the amount of growth, the poverty line, and where the poverty line is at the point of impact or the point of departure.* These are not simple calculations, and they definitely do not yield anything even approximating the model that has traditionally been estimated. The propoor mathematics below illustrate this.

Propoor Mathematics

Mathematically, the above relationship between growth and poverty reduction can be shown as follows. HCR (or H) can be expressed as

$$H = F(P) \tag{10.2}$$

where $F(P)$ is the distribution function evaluated at the poverty line P. Differentiating with respect to P, one obtains

$$dH = f(P)\, dP \tag{10.3}$$

where $f(P)$ is the first derivative of $F(P)$ or the density at point P. Multiplying the numerator and denominator by P, one obtains

$$dH = P^*f(P)^*(dP/P) \tag{10.4}$$

where dH is the change in HCR in percentage points, not percent, when *incomes at the poverty line* change by (dP/P).

Equation 10.4 relates the arithmetic change in HCR and suggests that it is a nonlinear function of the log change in the poverty line, P, or equivalently, in the log (change) in the incomes of the poor at the poverty line. These changes are computed at the poverty line, and because incomes change, the magnitude of $P^*f(P)$ will change with growth and/or the poverty line.

Equation 10.4 is *not* the equation estimated by the authors of the propoor literature (e.g., Kakwani, Ravallion, and Datt). These authors estimate equation 10.1. That equation has log change of HCR on the left-hand side. Converting equation 10.4 to the same dependent variable as equation 10.1, one obtains

$$(dH/H) = (P/H)^*f(P)^*(dP/P) \tag{10.5}$$

Now the dependent variable in equation 10.4 matches with that in the "original" propoor model, but the rest of the equation does not. Note that there is no separate inequality term on the right-hand side in equation 10.5, which is theoretically derived. Equation 10.1 is an artificial, reduced-form equation, one that must hold in an identity sense, but one that does not follow from any theoretical model. The separate effects of income change and inequality change *cannot* be isolated by equation 10.5.

What equation 10.5 (and equation 10.4) yields is the expected change in poverty given a certain amount of growth *around the poverty line*. Whether growth is propoor or not is yielded in an ex-post fashion; that is, if the actual reduction in poverty was greater than the expected reduction, growth was propoor; if less, it was antipoor.

Rewriting equation 10.4,

$$dH = \gamma^* dY/Y \qquad (10.6)$$

where γ is a function of the income distribution and the poverty line P in the *previous* (lagged) time period, $(t - 1)$, and dY/Y is the mean growth in incomes from $(t - 1)$ to time period t, around P. If income distribution does not change, then a given change in income—"adjusted" or "filtered" by γ, also called the "shape of the distribution elasticity" (SDE)—will lead to an identical change in HCR. If this elasticity is low (e.g., 0.3), then a 10 percent growth in incomes will only lead to a 3 percent reduction in HCR, provided that the distribution stays constant.

It does not matter how equal the distribution is at an initial point for the predicted decline in poverty to be larger, or smaller. Sometimes, the interaction between a highly unequal distribution and a given poverty line can yield a high γ; sometimes, the interaction between a highly equal distribution and the poverty line can yield a low γ. It is the level of γ that translates a given amount of growth into an "expected" poverty reduction.

If interest is in whether growth was propoor or not, it can either be observed by noting the change in inequality (e.g., quintile shares), or by noting whether the actual decline in poverty was greater than the expected decline. Terming the propoor elasticity as the trickle-down elasticity (TDE), it is derived as the ratio between the actual and the "predicted" reduction in poverty, where the predicted reduction is based on no change in inequality; that is,

$$TDE = dH/dH^* = dH/[P^*f(P)^*dP/P] \qquad (10.7)$$

If the absolute value of TDE is greater than 1, this indicates that the decline in poverty was greater than expected; that is, growth was propoor. If the absolute value of the ratio is less than 1, growth was antipoor.

Empirical Estimates of Propoor Growth

The wrong model (equation 10.1) has been estimated by several researchers to derive the propoor elasticity. The most prevalent result is that this elasticity varies from 1.5 to 3, with the mode around 2.[7]

---

7. See Collier and Dollar (2000), Kakwani (1997), Kakwani and Pernia (2000), Ravallion and Datt (1999), and Martin Ravallion, "What Is Needed for a More Pro-Poor Growth Process," *Economic and Political Weekly*, March 25, 2000, 1089-93.

What meaning one should attach to this estimated elasticity is not clear, however. The model states that for each 10 percent increase in incomes, HCR is expected to decline by 20 percent (an elasticity of 2). This may seem large, and indicative of the growth process being massively propoor. But, of course, the elasticity, whatever its magnitude, is silent on the important question of whether the growth process is propoor. Left unanswered is the question of by how much *should* HCR have declined if the growth was neutral (i.e., unaccompanied by any change in inequality).

The dependent variable is a percentage change in a ratio. If the initial value of HCR was 30, then a decline of 20 percent is equivalent to a decrease of only 6 *percentage points*. Thus, a 10 percent increase in incomes in this example will lead to a 6-percentage-point reduction in poverty. But what should have happened? A reduction of 8 percent, or 10 percent, or perhaps 4 percent? We do not know, unless we know the value of γ. If γ equals 0.5, a 10 percent increase in incomes is expected to (consistent with neutral growth) lead to a 5-percentage-point reduction; if γ equals 1, the expected reduction (consistent with neutral growth) will be 10 percentage points.

In the above correct formulation (equation 10.6), the expected reduction in poverty is equal to the change in *adjusted income* (γ multiplied by income change). The value of γ varies with where the poverty line is with respect to the distribution. If income distribution stays the same, and incomes increase (e.g., in India, during the past 20 years) γ can decline, increase, or stay the same, even with the same poverty line! On average (and this is a more circumspect average than most), a given amount of neutral growth is consistent with half that amount in reduced poverty; for example, 10 percent neutral growth is typically associated with a decline in HCR of only 5 percentage points.

Because the discussion is exclusively about income (consumption) poverty, then, ceteris paribus, every adjusted income change *has* to translate into an equivalent amount of poverty change. If the coefficient deviates from unity, then this deviation represents the effect of changes in income distribution. This model, therefore, is the appropriate vehicle for examining not only whether income distributional changes are important, but also their magnitude (deviation from unity). Again, we are back at the Kuznets question, but with quite a few pyrotechnics.

Estimating Propoor Elasticity

Although it is conceptually simple, estimating equation 10.6 is not an easy task. It involves estimating the density function around the poverty line, and that for each survey year and each poverty line. What can be done, and the approach used here, is that the coefficient γ is estimated for *each* distribution for each year and for each of the different poverty

Table 10.1 Shape of the distribution elasticity (SDE), 1960-2000

Measure	Poverty line		
	$1.08	$1.50	$2.00
Mean	**0.46**	**0.50**	**0.50**
Standard deviation	0.20	0.21	0.20
10th percentile	0.21	0.22	0.24
90th percentile	0.74	0.79	0.76

Note: The expected change in poverty, for small changes in mean incomes at the poverty line, is equal to the product of income change and the SDE, keeping the income distribution fixed. For example, using a $1.50-a-day poverty line, a 10 percent increase in income will, on average, be associated with a 5 percent decline in poverty, given an SDE of 0.50. Figures are derived from consumption and income distributions, 1960-2000.

Sources: Deininger and Squire (1996); World Income Inequality Database, available at http://www.wider.unu.edu/wiid; Asian Development Bank (2002).

lines used. The estimation is done by "shocking" the distribution by plus and minus 2.5 percent (for a total of 5 percent) for the distribution *at the particular poverty line* and by calculating the resulting change in HCR. This change, divided by 5, is an estimate of the arc elasticity, γ.[8]

The correct model of estimation, therefore, has change in HCR on the left-hand side, and the product of the *lagged* shape of the distribution effect (γ or SDE) and income growth on the right-hand side. The latter (product of lagged SDE and growth) is the "correct measure" of income growth in equations involving the change in HCR and income growth. In the traditional model, the difference in HCR is regressed only on growth.[9]

Table 10.1 reports on the estimated SDE coefficients for three different poverty lines—$1.08, $1.50, and $2, all in purchasing power parity 1993 prices. They all show a consistent pattern—the means are clustered around 0.5, and the 10th and 90th percentiles are about 0.25 and 0.75, respectively.

This robustness leads to the following two conclusions. First, a given amount of consumption growth, ceteris paribus, and no distribution change, will lead to a change of only about half that amount in HCR. Thus, the statement should not be that a 20 percent growth in consumption led to a decline of "only" 10 percentage points in HCR. If this happens, growth has certainly been neutral if not propoor. Second, this result holds at an average level, and is highly nonlinear, and judgments about whether

---

8. Deaton and Tarozzi (1999) present estimates of "gamma", γ, for state-level consumption distributions in India for the period 1993-94. In the literature, they are the only ones to present this elasticity. They do not translate this computation into a relationship between growth and poverty decline, and/or say whether the growth was neutral, propoor, etc.

9. This is the important difference, and nonequivalence, between the income coefficient of the traditionally estimated model and the new formulation. To reiterate, the model estimated by Kakwani, Ravallion, et al. simply has the growth term on the right-hand side; the correctly specified model has the growth term multiplied by the highly nonlinear coefficient gamma.

particular growth episodes have been propoor or antipoor must be filtered by knowledge of what the shape of the distribution function was for that time period.

Has Global Growth Been Propoor?

The correct propoor or not-propoor growth model (equation 10.6) can now be estimated for the developing world, and different countries, for any time period after 1950. Table 10.2 reports both the traditional model and the new model where consumption growth is filtered by the lagged shape of the distribution elasticity. The model is estimated for three sets of data: the developing world for 1950-2000, states of India for 1983-99, and all of India for 1950-2000. The rural and urban areas of each state in India are considered as separate economies. The reason results for the Indian data are reported is because a considerable amount of the propoor "theory development" has been caused by the (mis)interpretation of the Indian experience; that is, India's economy showed considerable economic growth and no change in poverty rates between 1987 and 1998.[10]

The dependent variable in the estimated models can either be the first difference in HCR (the preferred model) or the log percentage change in HCR (the coefficients in this model are not easy to interpret). The correct independent variable is "predicted poverty reduction" or "'effective growth," which is the observed growth in consumption multiplied by the *lagged* value of γ, the shape of distribution elasticity. The "traditional" method of estimating such a regression is to regress the percentage change in poverty (HCR) on the percentage change in consumption growth— that is, the specification of both the dependent and independent variables is different!

There are thus four possible regressions, and results for all four are presented. During the past 16 years, consumption growth has been neutral in India; the trickle-down elasticity is equal to -0.97, with a standard error of .07. Note that this elasticity, according to the incorrect model, is only -0.57, with a standard error of .13—that is, it incorrectly appears that income distribution changes became more unequal in India and indeed thus negated more than a quarter of the growth effect! The data for the states of India reveal a similar story, though the average trickle-down elasticity is now -0.85, not significantly different from unity.

Data for the developing world suggest an elasticity whose magnitude is considerably greater, -1.2 to -1.3, for the four poverty lines considered. In no instance, however, is the elasticity significantly different from

---

10. The vagaries of survey data are best illustrated by the Government of India's estimate of poverty in India at 42 percent in 1998 and 26 percent 12 months later in 1999! No one in the government is arguing that all that poverty reduction took place in 1 year.

Table 10.2 Estimates of the growth model, India and the developing world, 1950-2000

Poverty line (1993 purchasing power parity dollars per day)	Dependent variable: Arithmetic difference in head count ratio[b]		Dependent variable: Log change in head count ratio[b]	
	Correct model	Incorrect model	Correct model	Incorrect model
Developing world[a] (survey data, 1950-2000)				
1.08				
Coefficient	-1.28	-0.76	-5.01	-3.16
Standard error	0.22	0.06	0.96	0.50
Number of countries	40.00	41.00	39.00	39.00
1.30				
Coefficient	-1.21	-0.81	-3.38	-2.38
Standard error	0.20	0.06	0.79	0.41
Number of countries	46.00	48.00	46.00	46.00
1.50				
Coefficient	-1.27	-0.50	-3.30	-2.42
Standard error	0.23	0.24	1.13	0.56
Number of countries	49.00	51.00	49.00	49.00
2.00				
Coefficient	-1.28	-0.50	-3.56	-2.30
Standard error	0.20	0.16	1.22	0.75
Number of countries	55.00	55.00	54.00	54.00
States of India (survey data, 1983-99)				
Coefficient	-0.85	-0.57	-3.39	-2.53
Standard error	0.22	0.13	0.81	0.51
Number of states	51.00	51.00	51.00	51.00
All of India (survey data, 1950-2000)				
Coefficient	-0.97	-0.75	-2.53	-1.96
Standard error	0.07	0.05	0.23	0.17

a. The developing world is defined to exclude the industrialized world and Eastern Europe.

b. The specification of the correct model involves the product of lagged gamma (the shape of the distribution elasticity) and consumption growth; the traditional, and incorrect, model simply has consumption growth, unfiltered by gamma, on the right-hand scale.

Note: See the text and Bhalla (2000a) for further details.

Sources: Indian National Sample Survey Consumption Expenditure Surveys for 1983-84, 1987-88, 1993-94, and 1999-2000.

unity. For all the four poverty lines, the incorrect specification (relating reduction in poverty to just the consumption growth—(i.e., growth not filtered by γ) is estimated at less than half that obtained by the correct model, and always significantly less than unity. It is this misspecification result that has possibly led to the popular conclusion that growth during the golden age of development (1980-2000) was not propoor.

The results for the incorrect and correct specification of the log-log model (log poverty change versus log change in income change or income change adjusted) also underline the importance of γ. As modeled by others, the incorrect elasticity is observed to be near 2—actually about 2.3, with the lowest poverty line yielding this elasticity to be 3.2. In each instance, however, the correct specification yields an elasticity that is significantly higher, and higher by about 50 percent—centered on 3.4, and equal to 5 for the $1.08 poverty line.

Figure 10.2 models actual and predicted poverty reduction for the developing world according to the $1.50 poverty line (national accounts) and the $1.30 poverty line (survey data). The fit in both cases is very good. All the results point to the crucial importance of incorporating the shape of the distribution elasticity into the estimation; all models suggest that the entire amount of poverty reduction that has been observed can be accounted for by growth. Indeed, for developing countries as a class, the estimated reduction in poverty has always been observed to be propoor, and by a 25 percent plus margin, though the excess margin is not significantly different from zero.

Using Consistent Data

The disillusionment with the processes of growth was in large part an unintended outcome of a revolution, a changed paradigm, in the measurement of poverty, a paradigm that carried no less a signature than that of the World Bank. A large part of this disillusionment is an illusion. The consistent use of national accounts data, with a 39 percent "higher" poverty line ($1.50 vs. $1.08), was shown to still result in considerably lower poverty than that indicated by World Bank estimates based on the consistent use of survey data. This removes the first source of illusion. The second source is the tendency to mix survey data on poverty with national accounts data on income.

This unwarranted mix is *the* source of popular disillusionment. The mixed-up observation (a large increase in consumption and little reduction, perhaps even an increase, in poverty) was shown above to be due to the mix-up of using Peter's poverty (from survey data) and Paul's income (from national accounts data). What is the relationship between growth and poverty reduction if a correct pairwise analysis is done with

Figure 10.2 Growth is sufficient: Actual and predicted poverty reduction in the developing world, 1950-2000

national accounts; poverty line = $1.50 a day (PPP)

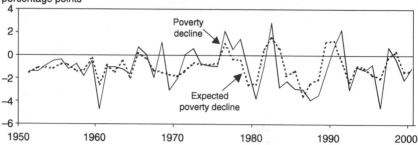

household surveys; poverty line = $1.30 a day (PPP)

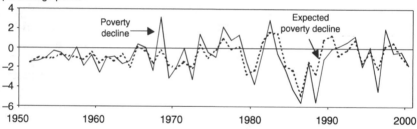

PPP = purchasing power parity

Note: The figures for expected poverty decline reflect both income growth and the shape of distribution elasticity; see table 10.1. The developing world is defined as the world, excluding the industrialized world and Eastern Europe.

Sources: Deininger and Squire (1996); World Income Inequality Database, available at www.wider.unu.edu/wiid; Asian Development Bank (2002); World Bank, *World Development Indicators*, CD-ROM.

survey data (i.e., both consumption and growth in consumption from surveys)?

Table 10.3 conducts this exercise for two large sets of data. The first is based on data for the 15 major states in India (the same data as were used for table 10.2). These data yield several spell pairs (i.e., the change in expenditure and the change in HCR). Similar kinds of spells are constructed using country data for the years after 1960, but most of the data are for the past two decades.

**Table 10.3 Relationship between growth and poverty reduction:
Evidence from India and international sources** (percent)

Source	Neutral growth[a]	Propoor growth[b]	Prorich growth[c]	Total number of spells[d]
Developing countries (survey data, poverty line = $1.30)				
1960-80	27.4	64.4	1.4	6.9	73
1980-2000	36.0	50.0	5.0	8.0	222
Indian states (survey data)				
1983-99	30.9	49.7	10.7	8.7	383

a. Neutral growth is defined as an event where positive growth is accompanied with poverty reduction, or negative growth with an increase in poverty.

b. The clearest evidence of propoor growth is a spell when poverty declines in spite of negative growth.

c. Prorich growth is when growth is accompanied by an increase in poverty.

d. A "spell" is defined as any pair of survey observations in different years. For example, two surveys, in 1983 and 1987, would constitute one spell; three surveys—in 1983, 1987, and 1993—would be defined as two spells. A single observation, e.g., a one-off survey in 2000 with no preceding surveys, would not constitute a spell. The total number of spells, in India's case 383, is the sum of all state-level spells.

Sources: Deininger and Squire (1996); World Income Inequality Database, available at http://www.wider.unu.edu/wiid; Asian Development Bank (2002); World Bank, *World Development Indicators*, CD-ROM; Indian National Sample Survey Consumer Expenditure Surveys: 1983-84, 1987-88, 1993-94, 1999-2000.

Four sets of results are possible. The first two relate to neutral growth—growth and poverty reduction are negatively related (e.g., poverty goes up with decline in average consumption levels, and goes down with increase in per capita consumption). The third is propoor growth—poverty goes down with a decline in average consumption levels. The fourth is prorich growth—poverty goes up even though average consumption levels have gone up. Note that if growth and poverty were loosely related, one would expect almost 25 percent in each cell.

The reality is that growth and poverty are strongly related. In the case of the Indian state data, for close to 80 percent of the cases, the "traditional" result occurs—that is, when growth occurred, HCR went down; when consumption declined (negative growth), HCR went up. The bad result—prorich growth—is observed for only 9 percent of the cases for the past 20-plus years, and these bad cases are more than evenly matched by the super-good result of propoor growth (negative growth and poverty reduction).

For the developing-world data, there is an even stronger indication of propoor growth. Close to 90 percent of the cases have been neutral—that is, there is a one-to-one relationship between growth and the incomes of poor people. Again, the cases of propoor growth are balanced by cases of prorich growth, and both have a very small magnitude.

Is the Initial Income Distribution Important?

It turns out that the case for a more equal distribution of income as a poverty reduction device is vastly overstated. As was observed above, intracountry distributions do not change that much, with Eastern Europe having been a significant exception. But it also went through a larger structural change. So for a country to move from an unequal to a substantially more equal distribution is close to an impossibility, especially given all the confirmation that was observed on the Kuznets curve.

Flaws in model specification have prevented the conclusion from emerging that growth has been sufficient to reduce poverty, and that, on balance, it has been neither prorich or propoor.

But does not inequality affect the value of SDE, and therefore affect the impact of growth on poverty reduction? It does, but the impact effect is very small. A separate regression of SDE on the (log) consumption share of the bottom 20 percent, using survey data, with a poverty line equal to $1.30 and observed poverty of at least 5 percent (to get a relationship not at the extremes), yields:

$$SDE = -.07 + 0.31*\log(\text{consumption share of first quintile})$$
$$(.09) \quad (.061)$$

Number of observations = 184; R^2 = .41; robust standard errors

Inequality does have a significant effect; the higher the share of the bottom 20 percent, the higher the impact on the poor. The estimated coefficient suggests that each 10 percent increase in the share of the bottom 20 percent leads to an approximately 3.1 percent increase in SDE. This magnitude is small, as is illustrated by the following example. Assume that there is a 10 percent increase in consumption and no change in distribution. If SDE is assumed to be 0.5 (see table 10.1), the expected decline in poverty is 5 percentage points.

Now assume that the distribution of income improves by 10 percent, a large change (e.g., the share of the bottom 20 percent goes up from 7 to 7.7 percent). In this scenario, SDE will not be 0.5 but 3 percent higher, or 0.515. The resulting change in poverty would be a reduction of 5.15 rather than the 5 percent observed with a flat distribution. If income distribution worsens by 20 percent (a very large change), this will reduce SDE by 6 percent, from 0.5 to 0.47. Thus, a 10 percent income change will now result in a decline of HCR of 4.7 percent instead of the 5 percent expected in the no-income-distribution change.

These results put a big question mark on the conclusion that a redistribution of income is necessary to help poor people. If the correct growth elasticity is twice as large as is commonly estimated, and if it has helped to reduce poverty as much as could be "expected," then clearly the need for explicit redistribution policies is not there. Further, income distribution has not been an inhibiting factor, contrary to this assertion by the World Bank: "The sensitivity of poverty to growth depends a great deal on initial inequality in poor people's access to opportunities to share in this growth" (*World Development Report 2000/2001*, 55)—and its echo from Stewart: "The sensitivity of poverty to growth depends on a country's income distribution" (2000, 3).

What remains is the tautological conclusion that a more even distribution of income is better for poor people. This is true, of course—but the magnitude "depends." It is correct to assert this conclusion with the ceteris paribus condition. If all other things are not equal (as is invariably the case), it can very well be observed that an economy that is more equal observes a lower SDE with respect to a particular poverty line. And even if a higher SDE is present, the difference between this higher SDE and, for the same mean level of income, a distribution with a lower SDE— well, the differences are just not large.

A corollary of these results is that all the hyperbole about the importance of income inequality in affecting the change in poverty is just that— hype. In a section titled "Why are similar rates of growth associated with different rates of poverty reduction?" *World Development Report 2000/2001* argues that

> the general relationship between economic growth and poverty reduction is clear. But there are also significant differences across countries and over time in how much poverty reduction occurs at a given rate of economic growth . . . there can be large variation in poverty reduction for the same growth rate in per capita consumption. . . . What explains these large differences? For a given rate of growth, the extent of poverty reduction depends on how the distribution of income changes with growth and on initial inequalities in income, assets, and access to opportunities that allow poor people to share in growth. (p. 52)

This argument is also echoed by the International Monetary Fund:

> Some analysts have raised concerns that the positive link between growth and poverty reduction, evidenced in the past, may have weakened in the 1990s. Critics contend that, although the reforms in the early 1990s raised economic growth markedly, benefits in terms of poverty reduction were relatively muted. (*World Economic Outlook*, November 2001, 35)

A Simple Method for Estimating Propoor Growth

The availability of simple accounting procedure data for mean expenditures for different percentiles over various years allows a simple test of the hypothesis of propoor growth. This method does not involve any pyrotechnics about the availability of SDE or the position of the poverty line, or about changes in inequality. The method follows definitions; each country is divided into two groups, poor and nonpoor people. By keeping the proportion poor, and proportion nonpoor, fixed to a level at a particular time (e.g., 1980) the growth of the mean expenditures of the poor group are compared with the mean expenditures of the nonpoor group. If the ratio is greater than 1, then the process can be deemed propoor; if it is less than 1, the process can be deemed antipoor.

Table 10.4 computes this elasticity for different regions of the world.[11] Taking the developing world as one group, it is observed that the growth process during the past 20 years of globalization has been highly propoor; the elasticity is considerably greater than 1 and equal to 1.8; that is, poor people increased their consumption at almost twice the rate experienced by nonpoor people. For the world, the elasticity is a very high level of 2.3—i.e., for every 10 percent rise in consumption by the nonpoor, the consumption by the poor increased by 23 percent. This is the "purest" test of whether growth was propoor or not—observe how the incomes of poor people have fared with respect to nonpoor people. The results unambiguously suggest that the globalization period favored the world's poor.

Forecast of Poverty in 2015

Collier and Dollar (2000) undertook an exercise to measure the efficacy of foreign aid and forecast poverty in 2015. They reached the following, possibly wrong conclusion: "Poverty in the developing world will decline by about one-half by 2015 if current growth trends and policies persist" (p. 1). Apart from the fact that different answers are obtained for a point in time depending on whether surveys or national accounts data are used, the "true elasticity" of poverty reduction with respect to economic growth is also more than twice as high as the one they assume (table 10.2). Thus, given their assumptions of growth and so on, their target for poverty reduction will be reached twice as soon!

Table 10.5 contains forecasts for population and per capita consumption growth (these forecasts match and are somewhat lower than those contained in the latest IMF *World Economic Outlook*). The distribution of consumption is assumed to be constant, under the assumption that some worsening has already taken place in the past 20 years (it is likely that now the right

---

11. Two different elasticities are reported. The first is a simple ratio of the growth of consumption by the poor relative to the growth of consumption by the nonpoor, and the second is obtained via a log-log regression of the poor and nonpoor consumption. Unless otherwise specified, the latter elasticity is discussed in the text.

Table 10.4 Changes in income and consumption, 1980–2000

	Percent change in per capita levels					Propoor elasticity 1	Propoor elasticity 2
	Income (NA)	Consumption (NA)	Consumption (survey)	Consumption (poor)	Consumption (nonpoor)		
East Asia	204.5	182.6	180.8	238.4	160.1	1.49	1.17
South Asia	81.9	68.0	34.7	60.7	69.0	0.88	0.89
China and India	218.2	179.1	157.6	188.9	173.4	1.09	0.98
Sub-Saharan Africa	−17.6	−10.5	−17.8	−10.7	−10.5	1.02	0.77
MENA	−1.1	11.1	1.8	−23.0	11.2	−2.05	−2.70
Latin America	0	−1.5	−22.4	−13.6	−1.5	9.07	0.54
Developing world	51.4	45.4	25.2	103.3	38.8	2.66	1.82
Developing world excl. China and India	8.4	10.8	−6.3	10.8	10.8	1.00	0.64
Eastern Europe	−26.0	−14.0	−29.5				
Nonindustrialized world	31.9	33.1	18.8	101.1	27.0	3.74	2.37
World	23.5	26.8	17.5	97.8	24.1	4.06	2.29

NA = national accounts
MENA = Middle East and North Africa

Notes:

1. Columns 2 and 3 report the simple growth rate computed between the level of per capita income and consumption, PPP 1993 prices, for the two years 1980 and 2000. Column 4 reports an analogous computation for survey measured consumption between the two years.

2. Columns 5 and 6 report the consumption growth (NA data) of the fraction of poor and nonpoor observed in 1980. No such computation is reported for Eastern Europe since in this region, there were less than 2 percent poor in 1980.

3. Two elasticities of propoor growth are reported; the first is a simple ratio of columns 4 and 5; the second is obtained from a simple log-log regression between the consumption of the fraction of 1980 poor and nonpoor for the period 1980–2000.

Sources: World Bank, *World Development Indicators*, CD-ROMs, 1998, 2001; Maddison (2001); Penn World Tables, various years; Deininger and Squire (1996); World Income Inequality Database, available at http://www.wider.unu.edu/wiid; Asian Development Bank (2002); Milanovic and Yitzhaki (2001).

Table 10.5 Forecast of poverty ($2 poverty line), 2015

Region	Population (millions)	Per capita consumption (1993 PPP dollars)	Head count ratio, 2000 (percent)	Annualized projected growth rate, 2000-15[a] (percent)	Average SDE, 2000-15	Implied poverty decline, 2000-15[b] (percentage points)	Head count ratio, 2015 (forecast) (percent)
East Asia	1,894	5.68	16.1	3.5	0.34	17.9	0.0
South Asia	1,355	3.78	21.1	2.5	0.47	17.6	3.5
Sub-Saharan Africa	661	2.89	66.8	1.5	0.50	11.3	55.6
Middle East and North Africa	374	7.84	14.0	1.5	0.25	5.6	8.4
Latin America	518	11.47	10.4	1.0	0.20	3.0	7.4
Eastern Europe	408	9.58	3.1	2.0	0.35	10.5	0.0
Developing world	**4,928**	**5.54**	**23.3**	**2.5**	**0.38**	**14.2**	**10.1**

PPP = purchasing power parity
SDE = shape of the distribution elasticity

a. Annualized projected growth rates closely match IMF forecasts that were published in IMF, *World Economic Outlook*, November 2001.

b. The implied poverty decline for 2000-15 is obtained from the product of annual growth and the average projected SDE for this period. For instance, a 2.5 percent annual income growth in South Asia translates, given an SDE of 0.47, to a 17.6-percentage-point reduction in poverty over 15 years.

Sources: Deininger and Squire (1996); World Income Inequality Database, available at www.wider.unu.edu/wiid; Asian Development Bank (2002); World Bank, *World Development Indicators*, CD-ROM.

leg of the Kuznets curve should come into operation—i.e., intracountry income distribution should improve between now and 2015—but this is not assumed for purposes of the forecast).

SDE is assumed to be that pertaining to the 10th percentile level in 2000. The poverty line chosen is $2 a day. The results: the HCR of world poverty in 2015 is likely to be only 10 percent—that is, substantially below the target set by the World Bank and other financial institutions, *and lower according to a poverty line that is almost twice (85 percent) as high as the poverty line in use today, $1.08 per capita per day.*

How accurate is the above forecast likely to be? In terms of the growth assumptions, our average of 2.5 percent a year is in line with experience during the past two decades and is substantially lower than the 3.6 percent average contained in the IMF forecast. Nor does it seem that the regional composition of the growth is "out of line"; East Asia is assumed to grow at 3.5 percent a year, and South Asia at 2.5 percent; if anything, these forecasts are likely to be at the lower end of the eventual reality. By the laws of compounding, average consumption in East Asia is expected to be higher by 73 percent, and that in South Asia by 47 percent. As is well documented in the next chapter, a very reasonable assumption is that each 1 percent of growth translates into a *half-percentage-point* decline in HCR. So given initial levels of poverty in Asia around 20 percent, an increase in per capita consumption upwards of 30-40 percent should virtually eliminate $2 poverty in these regions by 2015.

One calculation that is consistent with the above result (the simple accounting procedure may not always be right but it is to be hoped is always consistent) is the following: Average consumption of the less than $2 Asian[12] poor in 2000 was $1.52. The consumption level of each of the first six percentiles was as follows: $0.72, $0.91, $1.02, $1.12, $1.21, and $1.27. The average growth rate assumed in the forecast for Asia is 3.1 percent a year, or a 58 percent increase during 15 years. This means that the 6th percentile would be consuming 1.27 multiplied by 1.58, equal to approximately $2 in 2015—and therefore become nonpoor. Thus this method predicts 5 percent poor in 2015—a level close to the 3 to 4 percent poverty forecast yielded by a different method described above.

But this calculation assumes that income distribution stays the same. There is room in the forecast for some deterioration to take place, and still have Asian poverty in the low to mid single digits. The only basis for rejecting the forecast of less than 5 percent poor people in Asia in 2015 is to reject the growth assumptions—and not too many economists, policymakers, or even left-wing intellectuals are prepared to do so at present.

---

12. Asia here includes the countries of South Asia, East Asia, and Central Asia.

Zero $2 poverty is likely in all parts of the world in 2015, except in sub-Saharan Africa. This region's share of the world's poor people is expected to rise from 36 percent today to almost 90 percent in 2015. This phenomenon, if it occurs, is likely to have deep social and political significance, and on that ground alone, it is to be hoped that it can be ruled out.

Policy is endogenous, and policymakers are likely to act to prevent this catastrophe from happening. Educational advances and a greater opening up are likely to ensure that the sub-Saharan African growth rate during the next 15 years is likely to be higher than the assumed 1.5 percent a year. If this growth is closer to a more realistic 2 percent, absolute poverty in sub-Saharan Africa, in 2015, is likely to be less than 40 percent. Not zero, but beginning to be more manageable.

11

Inequality as It Is

There are at least four "legitimate" estimates of world individual inequality. Official and consumption purchasing power parity (PPP) exchange rates, and survey and national accounts estimates of mean income are the four components that can yield these estimates. As debate rages on as to whether inequality has improved or not, it is important to identify precisely what definition, and what measures of inequality, are being used.

The simple accounting procedure (SAP) system allows one to test the behavior of inequality according to virtually any method. It is this attribute that has allowed us to reproduce the received results, and therefore also to identify the problems with earlier methods. It was observed that the published PPP 1993 exchange rates, along with published national accounts figures, provided the best basis for estimating world inequality. There are at least three advantages to such a combination: It is transparent (everybody can reproduce the results), it provides a consistent series (the survey-national accounts ratio does not meander), and the estimates of growth and so on derived from such a series are estimates that everyone is familiar with (e.g., GDP growth in local currency).

The story told by such a consistent estimation of world and regional inequality is radically different from received wisdom. Far from world inequality worsening, it actually improved with globalization. The peak of world inequality occurred in 1973; today, it is at its lowest in the past 50 years. This is likely the result of catch-up and convergence; there are no signs of this inequality trend slowing, either. Though undoubtedly there will be fights for shares of the pie, the convergence trend should

Figure 11.1 World individual income and consumption inequality (Ginis), 1950-2000

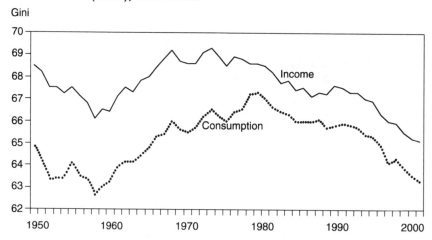

Note: The simple accounting procedure method is used to derive world income distribution from individual country distributions.

Sources: Deininger and Squire (1996); World Income Inequality Database, available at www.wider.unu.edu/wiid; Asian Development Bank (2002); World Bank, *World Development Indicators*, CD-ROM.

ensure that in 10 years, inequality will be where it started off a hundred years ago in 1910. A similar trend is observed for consumption inequality.

On a regional basis, both the developing and the industrialized worlds show a strong trend toward equality—this despite several large economies (e.g., China, the United States) showing an increase in inequality in the past 20 years.

SAP Results for World Inequality, 1950-2000

Figure 11.1 plots the movement of both the income and consumption Gini for the past 50 years. Both patterns are roughly the same. The time pattern is a normal U-shaped curve from 1950 to 1980, and since then there is a trend decline (i.e., the globalization period is the one where there is a decline, and a sharp one at that, and for both income and consumption). In 2000, global income distribution was at its lowest level in the postwar period, lower than the previous trough in 1958. These pictures illustrate the move toward equality much better than even a thousand words.

SAP estimates for world inequality indicate a Gini of 66.4 in 1960, a level that became more unequal until a peak of 69.3 was reached in 1973.

**Figure 11.2   An inexorable trend toward less inequality?
World income distribution, 1973 and 2000**

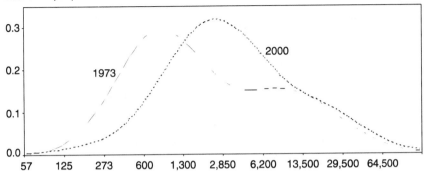

fraction of people

annual per capita income
in nominal PPP 2000 dollars (1993 base)

Note: Per capita income is calculated at 2000 prices. An 18 percent increase in prices between 1993 and 2000 (equal to US inflation for the period) is used to convert 1993 prices to 2000 prices. The simple accounting procedure method is used to derive world income distribution from individual country distributions.

Sources: Deininger and Squire (1996); World Income Inequality Database, available at http://www.wider.unu.edu/wiid; Asian Development Bank (2002); World Bank, *World Development Indicators*, CD-ROM.

It stayed at these highly unequal levels for more than a decade, and then inequality started to improve. World individual income inequality has been trending lower since then, and is estimated to have reached its lowest level of 65.1 in 2000.

How unequal is a Gini of 65.1? It is slightly more unequal than the Gini of Brazil in 1990 (Gini of 63.7) and slightly less unequal than a Gini of 69.0 observed for the Central African Republic in 1993. Ginis are hard to relate to; in terms of quintile shares, Brazil in 1993 showed the following: income shares of 2.2, 4.8, and 67.1 percent for the first, second, and fifth quintiles. The world shares in 2000 were as follows: 1.8, 4.3, and 70.3 percent.

Figures 11.2 and 11.3 show the world individual income inequality (W3i) density distribution for selected years. Figure 11.2, comparing 1973 and 2000, compares the most unequal with the most equal year. The trend toward lesser equality is apparent from the sharp movement toward a more log normal distribution. Figure 11.3 documents how the distribution has shifted during the past 40 years, and how it has become more equal.

Regions and Indices

Income inequality Ginis are reported for various regions of the world for three years, 1960, 1980, and 2000, in figures 11.4 and 11.5. Three results

Figure 11.3 World income distribution, 1960, 1980, and 2000

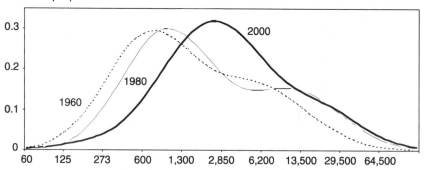

fraction of people

Note: Per capita income is calculated at 2000 prices. An 18 percent increase in prices between 1993 and 2000 (equal to US inflation for the period) is used to convert 1993 prices to 2000 prices. The simple accounting procedure method is used to derive world income distribution from individual country distributions.

Sources: Deininger and Squire (1996); World Income Inequality Database, available at www.wider.unu.edu/wiid; Asian Development Bank (2002); World Bank, *World Development Indicators*, CD-ROM.

emerge. First, the most equal part of the world in 1960 was Eastern Europe, and relatively more equal by a wide margin (a Gini of 29.9 versus a Gini of 40 for South Asia). In 2000, the two regions have the same inequality index—thus, Eastern Europe was witness to the largest increase in inequality recorded for any region, or any time, globalization or not. This increase, of 37 percent in the slow-moving Gini, is a huge, huge increase. The one area with the sharpest decrease in inequality is the developing world, a region making up about four-fifths of the world's population. And the decrease is large—almost 7 percentage points.

Second, the most equal part of the world today consists of the industrial countries, which, despite major inequality increases *within*, show only a small increase since 1980 (from 36.4 to 38) but a 4-Gini-point decline since 1960. Third, inequality in most subregions of the world is as it was in 1960, or somewhat worse; but between 1980 and 2000, there is improvement. So when generalizations are tricky, one can say that broadly, both legs of the inverted Kuznets U-curve were witnessed—the left leg 1960 to 1980, the right leg 1980 to 2000. This is mirrored in both the developing-world inequality and the world inequality—these two "regions" display the Kuznets curve in its most classic form.

The construction of percentile-level data allows one to be more sophisticated, and more accurate, in the analysis of "convergence." Recall that the popular (but wrong) method of determining convergence was by

Figure 11.4 Simple accounting procedure (SAP) regional measures of income inequality (Ginis), 1960-2000

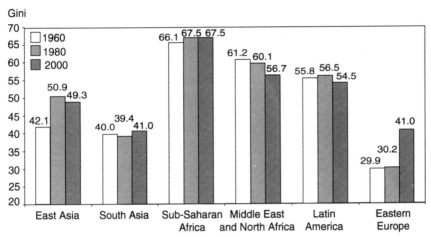

Note: To obtain regional distributions of income, country data are pooled using the SAP method.

Sources: Deininger and Squire (1996); World Income Inequality Database, available at http://www.wider.unu.edu/wiid; Asian Development Bank (2002); World Bank, *World Development Indicators*, CD-ROM.

looking at the ratio of incomes of the richest country in comparison with those of the poorest country. What is more appropriate is to compare the incomes of the rich (e.g., the 20th percentile in the United States) with the poor (the 20th percentile in the developing world)—or to compare the median income in the two sets of countries. According to both indices, figure 11.6 documents that there has been a huge increase in equality, a definite trend toward convergence. In 1960, the US 20th-percentile person was about 18 times richer than the 20th-percentile person in the developing world; in 2000, this ratio had almost been halved to 11. The 50th percentile shows a greater decline—from a relative level of 19.1 in 1960 to a relative level of only 11.7 in 2000.

Individual Inequality Studies Compared

The results for W3i, however, are at sharp variance with received wisdom. On inequality, a strong negative trend is observed, it has been downhill since the peak reached in 1973; the 2000 estimate is an improvement of about 6 percent since then. Thus, for more than 20 years, and coincident with the globalization period, world individual inequality has been declining—a result different from what one has been led to believe.

Figure 11.5   Simple accounting procedure (SAP) regional measures of income inequality (Ginis), 1960–2000

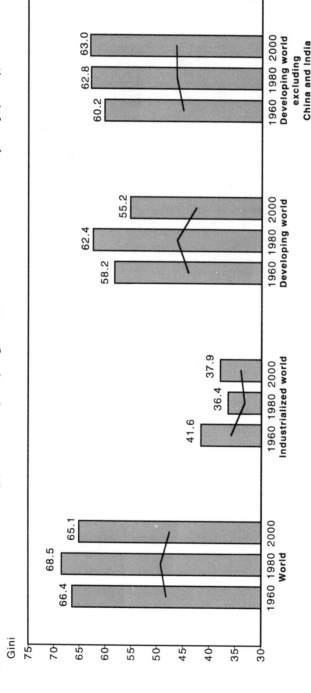

Note: To obtain regional distributions of income, country data are pooled using the SAP method.

Sources: Deininger and Squire (1996); World Income Inequality Database, available at www.wider.unu.edu/wiid; Asian Development Bank (2002); World Bank, World Development Indicators, CD-ROM.

Figure 11.6 Proper tests of intercountry convergence, 1950-2000

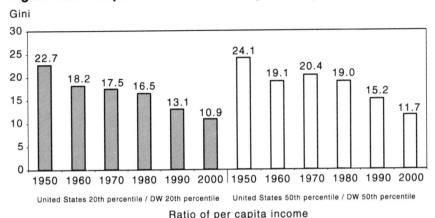

Gini

United States 20th percentile / DW 20th percentile   United States 50th percentile / DW 50th percentile

Ratio of per capita income

DW = developing world

Note: The figures above the bars represent the ratio of incomes at the 20th (shaded bars) and 50th (unshaded bars) percentiles, respectively, comparing US incomes with incomes in the developing world. To obtain the distributions of income across the developing world, country data were pooled using the simple accounting procedure method.

Sources: Deininger and Squire (1996); World Income Inequality Database, available at www.wider.unu.edu/wiid; Asian Development Bank (2002); World Bank, *World Development Indicators*, CD-ROM.

The set of estimates discussed here is the third set of estimates on world inequality (besides Bourguignon and Morrisson 2001 and Milanovic 1999), and it updates those reported in June 2000 (see Bhalla 2000d). What does a joint reading of the three results tell us? First, the time periods considered are vastly different: The Bourguignon and Morrisson study's (an extension of the Berry et al. 1983 study done for a single year) scope is exhaustive, from 1820 to 1992, and results for about 10 selected years are reported; SAP constructs inequality indices for all the 50 years from 1950 to 2000, and for both consumption and income; and Milanovic constructs income inequality estimates for only 2 years, 1988 and 1993. The welfare indicator used by the three studies is the same (PPP incomes). All three studies use essentially the same income distribution data.[1]

Are the results of the studies the same, at least for the overlapping periods? No, and not necessarily so. For three reasons: the level of aggrega-

---

1. As discussed in appendix B, for some countries more than one estimate of income distribution is available; this is truer for earlier years than the post-1970s period. I have selected a procedure to "filter" out the "bad" estimates of income distribution, and it is not clear what methods of filtering the other authors undertake. Nevertheless, it is highly unlikely that the selection of data would make much difference to the results, or trends, in world income inequality.

tion, the cleaning of the raw data, and the use of national accounts means versus survey means. SAP is the most disaggregated, and likely to be the cleanest; SAP and Bourguignon and Morrisson use national accounts means; and Milanovic alone uses survey means as the estimate of mean income.

The SAP estimates overlap with Bourguignon and Morrisson's estimates for the period 1950-92, and though there are differences (they observe a marginal increase in inequality, 1970-92, while I observe a decline), the common element is very large—both in the method and in the results.

The level of inequality estimated by Berry and his colleagues and SAP are similar for 1970 (the base year for Berry et al.), yet quite different. Berry and his colleagues estimate the Gini to be 64.9, while the SAP estimate is almost 6 percent higher at 68.6. While a 6 percent difference may appear small, it is actually quite large. Several reasons point to its largeness; first, as Bourguignon and Morrisson's analysis shows for a period of 170 years, the Gini moves like an elephant—slow to change, and slow to accelerate, but once it gains momentum, the speed (change) can be large as we saw above for Eastern Europe for 1980-2000.

The three studies reach very different conclusions on the *trend* in inequality. The Bourguignon and Morrisson study suggests that inequality worsened till 1980 and since then has remained relatively flat at 65.7. Milanovic shows a huge increase in inequality in the space of just 5 years, 1988 to 1993—an increase from 62.5 to 65.9 and to a level almost identical to that of Bourguignon and Morrisson in 1992. The SAP method results in the highest level of inequality for any year common to the three studies; in 1950, SAP reports a Gini level of 68.5, considerably higher than the 64.0 level reported by Bourguignon and Morrisson; in 1980, the levels are 65.7 and 68.5, respectively.

The differences in estimates between SAP and Bourguignon and Morrisson are most likely due to the disaggregated nature of this study, disaggregated to the percentile level in *each* country. The SAP method is also the only study to suggest that globalization has led to a sharp decline in inequality, a decline that leads to the result that inequality in 2000 was the lowest in the past 50 years (but still higher than the levels reached by either Bourguignon and Morrisson or Milanovic for 1992 or 1993).

Let us look at pictorial differences among different methods and estimates of W3i. Figure 11.7 shows the time pattern of inequality according to the two different methods of obtaining estimates of mean income— national accounts (Berry et al.; Bourguignon and Morrisson; and SAP) or surveys. The two methods reveal a similar pattern for most of the past 50 years, with the survey estimates being higher (until recently) and more exaggerated. The exaggeration is to be expected because changes in the survey capture *create* inequality changes even when none exist. Note the

Figure 11.7   World individual income inequality estimates, according to surveys and national accounts, 1950-2000

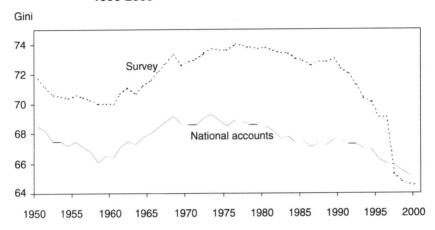

Sources: Deininger and Squire (1996); World Income Inequality Database, available at www.wider.unu.edu/wiid; Asian Development Bank (2002); World Bank, *World Development Indicators*, CD-ROM.

sharp decline in the survey-based estimate of the world Gini from a level of 72.6 in 1988 to less than the national-accounts-based estimate of 65.1 in 2000! Besides the survey capture ratio, differences can also arise with use of internal or "consumption" PPP exchange rates and thus cause havoc with the estimates of inequality (and poverty). But figure 11.7 uses only the published PPP exchange rates; hence, the entire effect documented in the figure is due to the use of survey means rather than national accounts means.

How Accurate Are the SAP Estimates?

Different regional distributions have been computed to partly identify why SAP indicates that inequality has improved when most are saying the opposite.[2] Is there a particular bias in the SAP method? There cannot

2. Two recent international conferences—sponsored by the World Institute for Development Economics Research and the Organization for Economic Cooperation and Development— have been held on the determinants and consequences of worsening world inequality. Not one of these studies (at least to my knowledge) questions the conclusion that world inequality has worsened. Note that *it is quite possible for a large number of countries to show worsening inequality and yet for the world itself to show improving equality.* Indeed, it is theoretically possible for all countries to show worsening inequality and yet the world to show improvement.

be, because, as the name suggests, the procedure is one of simple counting, and simple accounting. SAP is far from rocket science, though there is some methodological improvement[3] in constructing percentile distributions from exclusive use of just quintile data (appendix B). So why are SAP results different from others? One possibility is that the conclusion of the *other* studies that income inequality has worsened since the 1980s is incorrect.

Poor People Have a High Elasticity of Connection

Some support for the proposition that world inequality has improved in the globalization period is provided by the results on the "elasticities of connection" for the first and fifth quintiles for different regions of the world. These elasticities have been computed on the basis of aggregations of the data for the individual countries (unlike the computations undertaken by Roemer and Gugerty (1997), Timmer (1997), Gallup, Radelet, and Warner (1998), and Dollar and Kraay (2000), the results portrayed in figure 11.8 do not need any assumptions or inference); the reported figures are the elasticities of the bottom 20 percent (and top 20 percent) of individuals in each region.

Let us consider some results for the bottom 20 percent: The world as a whole shows an elasticity of 1.58 in the globalization period, more than *twice* as high as that observed for the period 1961-80. The elasticity for the preglobalization period was 0.74, signifying that this period was associated with worsening world inequality, whereas the next 20-year period was associated with a significant increase in equality, at least as measured by the share in incomes of the first quintile.

This elasticity for the globalization period is higher than that observed by any of the studies attempting to estimate the impact of growth on the poor. Unlike studies that use country data, in our formulation, the bottom 20 percent *are* the poor of the world. This striking result can only be revealed by a Lorenz curve that aggregates individual percentile incomes, and not by country quintile averages.

And consider some results for the top 20 percent: The results tell a similar story; the 1961-80 elasticity is 1.12; absence of globalization was good for the rich. The 1981-2000 elasticity was 0.85; the presence of globalization was bad for the rich.

In a most striking way, this result indicates the improved inequality effects of globalization, and the importance of China and India to the calculations. For the classification of the developing world excluding

---

3. The basic method is outlined in the pioneering study of Kakwani (1980); the SAP improvement is simply to impose consistency checks on the Kakwani Lorenz distributions.

Figure 11.8 Elasticities of connection: Quintile 1 (Q1) and quintile 5 (Q5) to mean income, 1960-2000

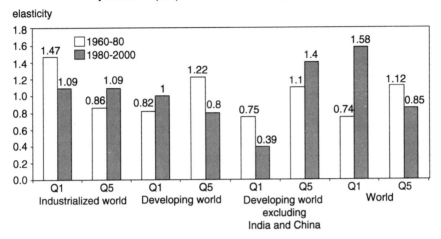

Note: The elasticities above are derived by regressing the mean income of the first and fifth quintiles as a function of the mean income in each region. To obtain regional distributions of income, country data are pooled using the simple accounting procedure method.

Sources: Deininger and Squire (1996); World Income Inequality Database, available at www.wider.unu.edu/wiid; Asian Development Bank (2002); World Bank, *World Development Indicators*, CD-ROM.

China and India, the elasticity of quintile 1 is significantly below unity for both periods, and *declines* during the period 1980-2000. For the rich, there is a continuous improvement, from an elasticity of 1.1 in the 1960-80 period to about 1.4 in the globalization period.

What are the major results emerging from the connection elasticities? It is not the case that globalization has been bad for poor people—just the opposite. It is not the case that the quality of growth has been not good, or that the growth has been antipoor—just the opposite. It is not the case that relatively poor people (defined as the bottom 20 percent) share equally in the downturns as in the upturns. It is the opposite, at least for the unit of analysis called the world, or the developing world.

What Happened with Global Inequality?

The beginning point of globalization is dated by most observers to be in the 1980s. But no matter what year is chosen, there is a definite positive association between globalization and improving global income distribution. In this regard, the critics of world inequality today have to be careful as to what they find wrong—high inequality per se (in which case, just look at the 1970s for considerably worse inequality) or trends in inequality (in which case, the only legitimate complaint can be that inequality is not declining as fast as one would like).

Why should we have expected things to get worse? Along with the United States, China is the other major economy whose own income distribution has significantly worsened in the past two decades. It is very possible that this worsening is associated with an improvement in world distribution; however, a worsening US distribution is unambiguously associated with worsening inequality. Again, one needs to be careful about the inequality measure one is concerned with. Most Americans (upward of 60 percent) are in the top decile of world population; a worsening US distribution only makes a difference if one is concerned about the top 10 versus the top 12 percent. It is true that one percentile's ceiling is another percentile's floor.

The result that world individual inequality has improved significantly since the 1960s is a major conclusion of this book. It is different from all other studies, and naturally subject to scrutiny. However, let me offer some reasons why the result of greater world equality *has* to be accepted. This conclusion requires three very minor assumptions: first, that China has a large population, approximately 1.3 billion people; second, that China was a poor country in 1980 with more than half its population classified as absolutely poor; and third, that this large poor country has experienced economic growth rates in significant excess of the growth rates experienced by most countries that were richer than China in 1980. Though there are quibbles about whether China's average per capita growth rate since 1980 has been as high as 7.5 percent,[4] all analysts agree that the figure is at least upward of 6 percent, or some 4.5 percent a year higher than the world non-China average; and higher per year for 20 years!

There is one additional troublesome aspect for those arguing that world income distribution has deteriorated during the so-called globalization period of the 1980s and 1990s. It is the acceleration in India's annual per capita income growth rate to 3.8 for 1980-2000, from less than half that pace in the previous two decades (1960-80).[5] If this information is added to the China pot, then one has more than conclusive proof—one has incontrovertible proof—that W3i *has* to have improved since 1980.

---

4. In a footnote contained in Bhalla (1997a), and *not* considered "politically correct" (at that time), I observed that existing estimates for China's growth implied that "China had a per capita income of approximately \$92 in 1960, 1987 prices. This figure is put in perspective by noting that with this income, China ranks as the *poorest* developing country in 1960 followed by Lesotho (\$93), Burundi (\$99) and Ethiopia (\$103). The Summers-Heston data are not so ridiculous—out of 118 countries China ranks 66 from the bottom."

5. See Virmani (2000) for an excellent discussion of the growth story about the Indian elephant during the past 20 years.

The China-India logic has an important bearing on calculations of global inequality. If large numbers of those in the first five deciles (China and India) are growing at a faster pace than the rest of the world, then even if presence in deciles does not change (e.g., 20 percent of China's population remains in the second and third deciles), then the share of income accruing to these deciles will, or rather must, *increase*; that is, global inequality must decline.

But what about all the megarich people of the world; what about all the genuine stories of the rich getting richer? All of them are true, but perceptions sometimes are based on absolute increases, whereas the reality being discussed here (inequality) is about relative performance. A heuristic explanation for what has happened is as follows. Growth has brought about income increases. The average poor person in the world enjoyed a higher rate of income growth than the average rich person. The poor person is still miles away from the entry gates; but she is getting closer.

If world inequality must have improved, and has indeed improved, and if conventional and journalistic wisdom say the opposite, then what should one believe? And from where comes the conclusion that globalization has induced large inequality changes in the past 20 years? How is it that researchers have missed this simple point? The constancy of paradigms in economics is a subject explored in some detail in Bhalla (2002c).

The Relationship between Growth and Inequality

Is there any relationship between high growth and changes in inequality? East Asian experience suggests yes, but South Asian experience suggests no; all of Asia reveals that inequality increased sharply in the slow-growth period, 1960-80, but then increased only marginally during the period 1980-2000. Latin America had high growth in the 1960-80 period, and stagnant income levels thereafter, yet showed a constant Gini level throughout. Sub-Saharan Africa also showed an unmoved Gini, regardless of growth or declining per capita incomes for the period 1980-2000.

Is there any relationship between initial inequality levels and income growth? There has been a considerable literature on this issue; a fair summary is that the research has been inconclusive. Nevertheless, cursory evidence suggests that there is a strong negative relationship. Look at sub-Saharan Africa—high inequality and no growth. Look at Latin America—equally high inequality and (almost) equally low growth. Look at Asia—low inequality and high growth.

There is a perfect fit—too perfect. Almost as perfect as the fit observed by some about the association between dictatorship, or Confucianism, or both, and high growth. The reason India did not grow well is because of the conflicts in decision making that arise due to democratic politics; the reason China grows is because it does not have those constraints. As discussed extensively in Bhalla (1997a), and even in *World Development Report 1991: The Challenge of Development,* for every successful dictatorship there are at least 10 unsuccessful brothers. What most likely explains India's lack of progress before (along with other economically failed democracies like Costa Rica, Jamaica, and Sri Lanka) is the restraints it put on the economic freedom of its citizens; what explains its recent economic success is the beginnings of its participation in globalization.

The Middle Class

The definition of, and concern with, the middle class has been almost the same as that with the poor. Different definitions abound (see Bhalla and Kharas 1991; Birdsall, Graham, and Sabot 2000; and Milanovic and Yitzhaki 2001). Using a poverty line as the starting point, Bhalla and Kharas suggest the following simple construction of the different income classes. Let the poverty line be P, and then construct multiples of two with this poverty line as the base; for example, the first level is P, the next is $2P$, the next is $4P$, the next is $8P$, ... $16P$, ... $32P$, ... $64P$, and $128P$. These relative income levels can then be grouped to "fit" the sociological and/or economic definition of the middle class.

For poor people in the developing world, a poverty line of $2 was suggested. But this line ignores poor people in the industrialized world. In the United States, the poverty line is about $10 a day. This is a convenient "market given" point for the beginning of the middle class in the world. The end-point is provided by PPP $40 per capita per day, at 1993 prices. At current 2000 prices, and in US dollars, this is approximately $70,000 for a family of four (i.e., if you earn more than that, you are no longer middle class—you are rich).

The advantage of an absolute middle-class category (unlike the relative definition of the 25th to 75th percentiles adopted by Birdsall, Graham, and Sabot) is that one can actually note the different magnitudes of the people in this class; relative definitions will always have the same percentage of people, for all times, and all income ranges. Further, by tying the definition to an absolute poverty line, the Bhalla and Kharas formulation has the advantage of allowing the notion of middle class to also rise with development.

A definition is only as good as its "feel"; it is only good if it passes "smell" tests (not unlike obscenity tests à la a US Supreme Court judge, who opined about the definition of obscenity: "I know it when I see it"). Figure 11.9 documents the trend in the share of the middle class within

Figure 11.9   Middle-class share in own population

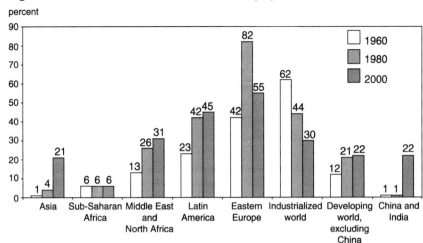

Note: "Middle class" is defined as average per capita daily incomes in the range of $10-$40 (1993 purchasing power parity dollars). To obtain regional distributions of income, country data are pooled using the simple accounting procedure method.

Sources: Deininger and Squire (1996); World Income Inequality Database, available at www.wider.unu.edu/wiid; Asian Development Bank (2002); World Bank, *World Development Indicators*, CD-ROM.

each region of the world; the sum of the shares of the three classes (poor, middle class, and rich) within each region is equal to 100.

The miracle of Asia is one of the most prominent results. This region alone contains more than half (54.4 percent) of the world's population, and more than two-thirds of the population of the developing world. During the period 1960-80, Asia had a negligible number of middle-class or rich people. But in 2000, middle-class people constituted 21 percent; and rich people, 2 percent! (Poor people are 77 percent, but this is according to a poverty line almost eight times the popular $1-a-day line).

The changing world landscape is recorded by figure 11.10, which documents the composition of the three classes in the world population for 1960, 1980, and 2000. In 1960, 6 percent of the world's middle-class population came from Asia; today, that share is 52 percent. If the world's middle class was basically white in 1960 (industrialized-world residents constituted 63 percent), today it is basically Asian.[6] This gives one explanation for the crisis of growth in Latin America (more explanations are given in the next chapter). This region had twice the market size of Asia in 1960; it had an equal market size in 1980; and today has less than one-third the market size of Asia.

---

6. See Asian Development Bank (2002) for details about the miracle that *is* Asia.

Figure 11.10 Share of each region in various income levels

Share of each region in world's lower-class population (annual income is less than or equal to $3,650, PPP at 1993 prices)[a]

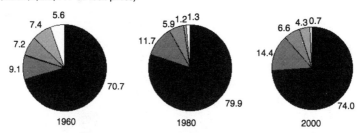

Share of each region in world's middle-class population (annual income is between $3,650 and $14,600, PPP at 1993 prices)[b]

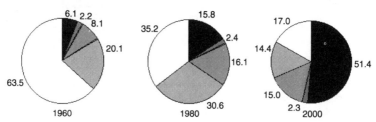

Share of each region in world's upper-class population (annual income is more than $14,600, PPP at 1993 prices)[c]

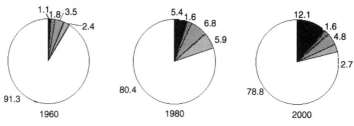

☐ Industrialized world

▨ Eastern Europe

▨ Latin America

▨ Sub-Saharan Africa

■ Asia, Middle East and North Africa

PPP = purchasing power parity

a. "Lower class" is defined as average per capita daily incomes below $10, or below $3,650 a year (all in 1993 PPP dollars).

b. "Middle class" is defined as having an income in the range of $10-$40 a day or $3,650-$14,600 per year.

c. "Upper class" is defined as having an income greater than $40 a day or $14,600 a year.

Note: To obtain regional distributions of income, country data were pooled using the simple accounting procedure method.

Sources: Deininger and Squire (1996); World Income Inequality Database, available at www.wider.unu.edu/wiid; Asian Development Bank (2002); World Bank, *World Development Indicators*, CD-ROM.

12

Globalization: A Second Look

Having considered the data, definitions, and methodology, it is now time to revisit some of the conclusions of received wisdom reported in chapters 2 through 4. Several (actually all) conclusions get overturned. There is strong evidence of convergence; there is also consistent and strong evidence that globalization is helping to equalize wages for similar productivity levels, and that the major beneficiaries are people in the developing world. There is even stronger evidence that global inequality is in a declining mode for the first time in 200 years.

There is plenty of reason to believe that all of this should have been "expected" or forecast. There is one major force: globalization. Neither national nor language boundaries matter anymore. The economics is the trend toward the law of one price and law of one wage—for goods, and all factors of production. Obviously, the world is not there yet, and the most important factor, labor, is differentiated by quality of education and differences in ability. But the trend is inexorable—and a leading indicator for this trend is the decline in worldwide inflation levels over the last decade or so—and induced primarily by productivity growth in China and India.

If movement is there toward one price, and if productivity growth in poor nations is large and in excess of growth in industrialized economies, then this is a manifestation not just of catch-up but of catch-up with a vengeance, or Convergence, Big Time. The prime beneficiaries of this convergence are poor nations, and as we saw in earlier chapters, poor people in poor nations. Several indicators of well-being (education, health, and political and civil liberties) point to the fact that the golden age of development has perhaps only just started.

It is not all a happy story, however. There has been stagnation in Latin America, at least in income growth. Partly, this is likely a result of the competitive forces of globalization. Countries that refused to let wages and incomes adjust (Argentina being the worst example) have had to allow employment and output to adjust; convergence for these countries has meant a stagnation, if not decline, in incomes. Yet those that have faced up to the challenge (Chile, and now Mexico) have benefited handsomely.

The genuine, and mostly self-inflicted, tragic story is that of sub-Saharan Africa. It is little realized, but in 1960 this region had more than double the per capita income of Asia. Today, Asia has double the income of Africa. The reasons for this stagnation are many. For the world community, this should be the major target of attention. On a positive note, there is no reason why the positive forces of globalization should not also catch up with Africa.

Income: Before and After

In chapter 2 it was noted that though the developing world lagged behind in terms of per capita income growth during the preglobalization period, it more than caught up during the globalization era. During the 50-year period 1950-2000, growth in the developing world exceeded that in industrialized countries by an aggregate of 27 percent or about 0.5 percent per year. This is a narrow margin, but it does mean that the developing world has gained both absolutely and *relatively*.

These figures help answer one noticeable anomaly in the discussion on globalization. At the risk of being politically incorrect, but with the accuracy of being factual, it is a reality that one does not witness any brown, or yellow, or black people in the vanguard of the antiglobalization debate, or in the attacks on the operations of international institutions.[1] All the leaders and operators are white, come from rich countries, and are fighting the cause "in the name of [nonwhite] poor people."

Convergence: New Results

Did worldwide individual and country inequality worsen during the period of globalization? The contention of Pritchett (1997, 2001), the United Nations (*Human Development Report 1999*), the IMF (World Economic Outlook, November 2001), the World Bank (*World Development Report 2000*), and Stewart (2000) was that there was divergence in per capita output—though the simple data on per capita output in developing and industrial-

---

1. To be sure, one does witness nonwhite intellectuals articulating antiglobalization theses; why this is so is more a question for a psychiatrist to answer, rather than an economist.

ized countries indicated just the opposite, and did so in a convincing fashion. Are the divergent results a function of the time period chosen? No. Note that if one goes sufficiently far back, especially to before the Industrial Revolution, one will tautologically define and find divergence. Today, countries are rich and poor; back then, all countries were the same.

The real source of the difference between the distinguished divergent tribe and those that argue that there has been overwhelming convergence is not in terms of the time period but in the set of statistics chosen. In particular, the divergent calculation is often done in terms of the relative incomes of those residing at the technology frontier (the richest country, typically the United States) and those residing in the poorest country (one that is changing continuously over time).

This ratio suffers from a severe self-selection bias and may be about as accurate as stating that there is convergence in looks because no one today comes even close to the beauty of Greta Garbo or Ingrid Bergman (but look at Aishwarya Rai of India, and you will get an example of convergence). Or that inequality has widened because the relative income of Bill Gates has gone up relative to you, me, or the poorest peasant in the world. The second and equally severe problem with this self-selection analysis is that its unit of analysis is the poorest country rather than the poorest *people*. And even if it were the poorest people, it should be the poorest *fraction* of people.

Figure 12.1 tries to rectify some of these deficiencies by reporting ratios for two different classifications. The nonconventional (but improved) statistics on the trend in convergence are indicated by the trends in income of the 20th and 50th percentiles in the United States, with corresponding percentiles in different regions of the world. The median American earned 26 times the level of his East Asian counterpart in 1960; today that ratio is down to only 9. For both Latin America and South Asia, the ratio has declined by about 10 percent; the picture is not as stark as in East Asia, but there is a definite trend (at least for the much more numerous millions in South Asia). Only sub-Saharan Africa has seen divergence—but one does not need complicated convergence calculations to tell us that development has *not* occurred there.

Catch-Up with Globalization

The tests reported in figure 12.1 are better than those in the literature, but only marginally. It is still not a like-with-like comparison. The *real* test of convergence, and one not published in the literature to date, requires the groups to be chosen on the basis of their skills, which should be approximately equal, and their incomes (wages), which are not. In particular, wages in catch-up countries should be substantially *below* those of residents (with similar skills) in comparator countries at an initial point

Figure 12.1 US income relative to that of developing regions, 1960–2000

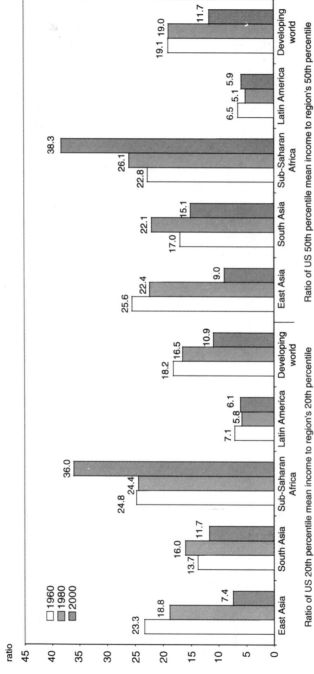

ratio

Note: The figures above represent the ratio of incomes at the 20th and 50th percentiles, respectively, comparing US income with income in regions of the developing world. Hence, a (20th percentile) ratio of 11.7 for South Asia in 2000 indicates the US income at the 20th percentile was 11.7 times the income at the 20th percentile in South Asia. To obtain the distributions of income across the developing world, country data were pooled using the simple accounting procedure method.

Sources: Deininger and Squire (1996); World Income Inequality Database, available at www.wider.unu.edu/wiid; Asian Development Bank (2002); World Bank, *World Development Indicators,* CD-ROM.

in time, say 1960 to 1980. If globalization has helped convergence, then the relative gains for the poorer group should be larger in the past 20 years than in the previous 20.

The top 10 percent of developing countries constitute approximately 500 million people. These are the elites, and it is likely that elites always had the means to acquire education and training. In a converging world, developing-world elites should witness a narrowing of the gap between their incomes and those of a comparison group. But who are their comparators in the industrialized world? The size of this parallel group is known—it should be approximately 500 million. This rules out the top 10 percent (or the richest country!) as the comparator, because the total population of industrialized countries is less than a billion. Should the top 10 percent in the industrialized world be part of the comparator group? It would be unlikely, though additional data are needed for a precise calculation.

The following procedure was used to identify the comparator group. Per capita incomes in the industrialized world were computed for 5 deciles (approximately making up the population of elites in the developing world) on a sliding basis from the top; for example, the top 5 deciles, the next five (40th to 90th percentiles), and the next five (30th to 80th). This last group was finally chosen as the comparator—there were approximately the same number of people, and they had incomes about 35 percent above the developing-world elites (the top 10 percent). This group (30th to 80th percentiles) has a ring of plausibility. It contains the industrialized-world middle class, and it likely is a group with the same skills as elites in the developing countries—at least back in the preglobalization 1960s and 1970s.

Some evidence that the skills of these two groups are comparable is yielded by Barro and Lee's (2001) data on educational attainment. In 1960, mean school attainment in the industrialized world (30th to 80th percentiles) was approximately 7 to 8 years; that for developing-world elites, 3.5 to 5 years; in 2000, the ranges were 9 to 12 years and 6 to 10.5 years, respectively. Not an exact match but not indicating incomparables, either.

Figure 12.2 provides convincing evidence about convergence and the angst of those losing out to globalization. Countries are organized according to the ratio of the incomes of elites relative to the industrialized-world middle class in 1960. A ratio of less than 1 would indicate competitive advantages, ceteris paribus. A ratio greater than 1 would indicate that there was no benefit to be derived from the competitive forces of globalization; that is, wages were too high (relative to the industrialized world) for comparable skills. Indeed, for such countries globalization should mean a *decline in the relative wage*. To an amazing degree, the forecast that globalization means convergence is accurate—for both countries with ratios less than 1 and those with initial ratios greater than 1.

From 1960 to 1980, elites in Asian countries had income (wages) relative to their comparators of approximately 41 percent; that is, the middle-class

Figure 12.2 Globalization and big-time convergence

log change in the ratio of mean income of the top 10 percent
in each country to the industrialized world's middle 50 percent

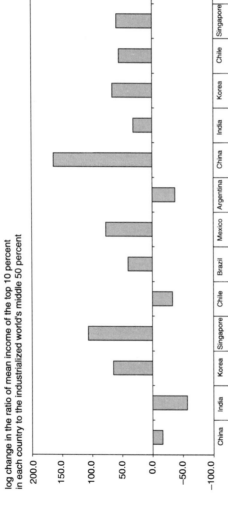

Notes: For each time period, the graph above presents data for eight developing countries. A ratio of less than 1 indicates that the top 10 percent in each country (90th–100th percentiles) was earning less, at the beginning of the period, than the middle 50 percent (30th–80th percentiles) in the industrialized world; a ratio of more than 1 indicates the opposite.

The numbers above represent the log change in this ratio for each country. Positive values indicate a convergence between that country's top income earners and the middle 50 percent in the industrialized world; negative values indicate a divergence.

The two groups (top 10 percent in the developing world, middle 50 percent in the industrialized world) are chosen for their high level of comparability for many factors, including educational opportunities. To obtain the distributions of income across the developing world, country data were pooled using the simple accounting procedure method.

Sources: Deininger and Squire (1996); World Income Inequality Database, available at www.wider.unu.edu/wiid; Asian Development Bank (2002); World Bank, World Development Indicators, CD-ROM.

people in the industrialized world had incomes approximately two and a half times those of Asian elites. During this golden age of the industrialized-world middle class, real incomes almost doubled, registering an annual growth of 3.2 percent. Aspirations are built on experience, and the experience was very good. Asian elites (constituting about three-fourths of developing-world elites per se) also matched the progress of their industrialized-world counterparts; their relative income had inched up to 43 percent from 40 percent.

The next 20 years turned out to be the golden age for Asia. While the growth in the absolute incomes of the industrialized-world middle class slowed down to a crawl—only 1.2 percent a year, a third of that experienced by their parents—that of Asian elites slowed down only marginally—to 2.9 percent relative to 3.5 percent in the 1960-80 period. However, the relative incomes of Asian elites (the one of concern for tests of convergence) *accelerated* to 60 percent of their counterpart incomes in 2000. This relative income, as mentioned above, was 43 percent in 1980.

This *is* the predicted effect of globalization. Firms cannot afford to be nationalistic or racist; if they are, they will lose out to the competition. The search for lower costs has meant looking for Indians, Chinese, Bangladeshis, and Malaysians to do the work, rather than middle-class Dutch people, Danes, Swedes, or Americans. This looking has meant a rise in the relative wage of developing-country, particularly Asian, elites. And firms have gone to wherever the wages are lowest, relative to the skills possessed. Thus, Latin Americans have not witnessed a surge in their relative wage—indeed, their relative incomes today (after globalization) are 70 percent of the preglobalization value in 1960.

One should be witnessing Latin Americans as the leaders of the antiglobalization brigade, but one does not. Perhaps they realize that in the uncompetitive world of the pre-1980s, they derived rents from their closeness to industrialized-world markets, and that with lower transaction costs (almost zero in the age of the Internet and instant communication) these rents have disappeared. One should not be seeing Asians in the antiglobalization camp, and one does not. One should be seeing middle-class people from industrialized countries disappointed with what globalization has brought them—more competition for their skills, a decrease in their rents, and a sharp fall in their expectations for future growth—and one does. These people are facing a collapse from 3.2 percent annual growth (or a doubling in real incomes in one generation) to an increase of only 1.2 percent a year (or a doubling in 58 years or three generations, and perhaps not even in one's working life).

There is an explanation for why there is a protest against globalization—only it does not have anything to do with the poor getting poorer, or the rich getting richer faster. The explanation is that because of globalization, the entire middle class in the industrialized world has had to lower its expectations of a *better* life. It is the "poor elites" in the developing world (as well as the poor) who are getting richer at a faster pace than that experienced by almost any such large group of people (500 million) in history. The middle class in the industrialized world feels that this is at their expense, and they are at least partially right. Globalization is a democratic force; it is the ultimate leveler—a force not kind to those "unnaturally" at the top of the heap.

Is There a Poverty-Terrorism Connection?

The events of 11 September 2001 have made it fashionable, in some quarters, to suggest a link between poverty and terrorism, particularly Islamic terrorism. The data on incomes and distributions can be used, along with information about the percentage of Muslims in each country, to generate distributions for residents of Muslim and non-Muslim "regions" of the world. This is obviously an approximation, and requires the assumption that both the mean and distribution of Muslims in mixed societies are approximately the same as those of non-Muslims. If this assumption is made, and particularly if the high growth in mean incomes of China and India is excluded, then one can assess both mean incomes and poverty in the two "regions" from 1950 to 2000. The poverty line of $1.30 per capita per day, at 1993 prices (equal to the popular $1-a-day line) was chosen for this analysis; the choice of a particular line does not affect the results.

The results, given in table 12.1, suggest that the pattern of growth and poverty is virtually indistinguishable in the two "regions." Indeed, predominantly Muslim nations show a slightly higher growth rate between 1980 and 2000 (2.3 percent) than predominantly non-Muslim nations (−4 percent). Muslim nations also show a decline in the head count ratio of 4 percent compared with a smaller decline of only 1.5 percent for non-Muslim nations. These data are suggestive at best—but what they do suggest is that non-Muslim Africans, Burmese, Cambodians, or North Koreans should be leading the terrorist charge if poverty were really related to terrorism.

The Evolution of Living Standards, 1960-2000

Tables 12.2 and 12.3 present summary data for various indices of living standards for the preglobalization and globalization periods, 1960-80 and 1980-2000. The data are given both for the world, in table 12.2, and for the developing world, in table 12.3. As has been mentioned throughout, the attempt here is not to identify causation; just association will suffice for the moment.

Table 12.1 Muslim and non-Muslim incomes in the developing world (DW), 1950-99

Year	Number of Muslims (millions)	PPP mean income, per capita per day, 1993 prices[a]				Head count ratio (percent) at $1.30, PPP, 1993 prices[b]			
		DW	DW, excluding China and India	Muslim DW, excluding China and India	Non-Muslim DW, excluding China and India	DW	DW, excluding China & India	Muslim DW, excluding China and India	Non-Muslim DW, excluding China and India
1950	539	2.59	4.37	2.92	5.28	62.8	35.5	45.4	33.8
1960	613	3.69	5.56	3.83	6.44	50.7	29.8	39.5	28.8
1970	815	4.82	7.52	5.29	8.54	37.1	21.3	27.4	22.5
1980	1,041	6.19	9.75	6.83	11.24	35.0	19.1	24.0	20.5
1990	1,312	7.07	9.69	6.80	10.48	18.2	16.5	19.9	19.7
1999	1,562	8.81	10.02	6.99	10.83	9.8	16.3	19.9	18.9

PPP = purchasing power parity

a. The mean incomes have been computed according to the expenditure distribution for a poverty line of $1.00 a day at 1985 prices or $1.30 a day at 1993 prices.

b. The head count ratio has been calculated on the basis of the total population of the region and not the world's population.

Note: The aggregation involves the computation of mean incomes in each country according to its Muslim and non-Muslim population. Within each country, no distinction is made between the incomes of the Muslims and non-Muslims. The proportion of Muslims today is close to 25 percent of the world's population; 32 percent of the developing world's population; and 60 percent of the developing world's population excluding China and India.

Sources: PPP and national accounts data from World Bank, World Development Indicators, CD-ROM; for the methods used and other variables, see appendix A.

Table 12.2 Indices of living standards for the world, 1960-2000

Measure[a]	Level			Change (percent)	
	1960	1980	2000	1960-80	1980-2000
Income					
Mean income	8.81	14.34	17.71	62.8	23.5
Share of 1st quintile	1.66	1.43	1.84	−13.9	28.7
Share of 5th quintile	70.57	72.83	70.33	3.2	−3.4
Consumption					
Mean consumption	5.56	8.54	10.83	53.6	26.8
Share of 1st quintile	2.11	1.61	2.50	−23.7	55.3
Share of 5th quintile	67.77	71.40	69.50	5.4	−2.7
Distribution					
Gini (income)	66.4	68.5	65.1	3.2	−5.0
Gini (consumption)	63.2	67.0	63.3	6.0	−5.5
Head count ratio, according to national accounts (percent)					
Country poverty line	64.9	58.0	39.9	−10.6	−31.2
$2.00 poverty line	48.0	43.5	19.0	−9.4	−56.3
$1.50 poverty line	38.4	33.8	10.5	−12.0	−68.9
$1.08 poverty line	31.9	27.0	6.4	−15.4	−76.3
Poverty: Nonincome indicators					
Political and Civil Liberties Index[b]	3.8	4.0	4.1	5.5	1.3
Infant mortality (deaths per 1,000 births)	107.2	63.5	43.3	−40.7	−31.9
Life expectancy at birth (years)	51.2	62.7	66.4	22.4	6.0
Illiteracy (percent)	45.8	38.5	26.0	−16.0	−32.4
Middle schooling completed (percentage of adults)	8.9	13.2	18.3	49.3	38.3
Average educational attainment (years)	3.9	4.6	6.0	18.8	29.7

a. For computations of Ginis, shares of consumption, income, and the other variables, see the text and appendices A, B, and C.

b. The Freedom House Political and Civil Liberties Index ranks countries on a number of indicators, on a scale of 1 (worst) to 7 (best).

Sources: National accounts data, purchasing power parity exchange rates, living standards data: World Bank, *World Development Indicators*, CD-ROM, 2001; for data on average educational enrollment and middle-school completion: Barro and Lee (2001); Political & Civil Liberties Index: Freedom House data.

One can begin to identify causation only after one has identified association. The data suggest a strong association. No matter what the indicator, progress during the globalization period was greater. Infant mortality in the developing world declined from 140 to 80 deaths per 1,000 births in the preglobalization period; and declined further, to 52, by the end of 2000 (table 12.3). The table also reports on the (log) percentage changes,

Table 12.3 Indices of living standards for the developing world, 1960-2000

Measure[a]	Level			Change (percent)	
	1960	1980	2000	1960-80	1980-2000
Income					
Mean income	3.63	6.09	9.22	67.8	51.4
Share of 1st quintile	3.49	3.03	3.12	−13.2	3.0
Share of 5th quintile	64.05	68.51	59.55	7.0	−13.1
Consumption					
Mean consumption	2.60	3.81	5.54	46.5	45.4
Share of 1st quintile	3.90	3.20	4.38	−17.9	36.9
Share of 5th quintile	59.93	65.70	56.29	9.6	−14.3
Distribution					
Gini (income)	58.2	62.4	55.2	7.2	−11.5
Gini (consumption)	54.5	60.1	50.5	10.3	−16.0
Head count ratio, according to national accounts (percent)					
Country poverty line	68.1	60.1	28.0	−11.7	−53.4
$2.00 poverty line	65.2	56.3	23.3	−13.7	−58.6
$1.50 poverty line	52.5	43.5	13.1	−17.1	−69.9
$1.08 poverty line	43.9	35.0	9.1	−20.3	−74.0
Poverty: Nonincome indicators					
Political and Civil Liberties Index[b]	2.9	3.4	3.6	13.9	6.3
Infant mortality (deaths per 1,000 births)	140.0	79.6	52.1	−43.1	−34.5
Life expectancy at birth (years)	43.3	59.4	64.2	37.0	8.0
Illiteracy (percentage of adults)	52.9	43.0	28.3	−18.8	−34.2
Middle schooling completed (percentage of adults)	5.1	7.1	13.8	39.6	94.4
Average educational attainment (years)	2.4	3.2	5.0	33.2	54.2

a. For computations of Ginis, shares of consumption, income, and the other variables, see the text and appendices A, B, and C.

b. The Freedom House Political and Civil Liberties Index ranks countries on a number of indicators, on a scale of 1 (worst) to 7 (best).

Sources: National accounts data, purchasing power parity exchange rates, living standards data: World Bank, *World Development Indicators*, CD-ROM, 2001; for data on average educational enrollment and middle-school completion: Barro and Lee (2001); Political & Civil Liberties Index: Freedom House data.

and it is observed that such changes were larger in the preglobalization period (i.e., 43 percent). As discussed in Bhalla (1988) and Bhalla and Glewwe (1985) and Asian Development Bank (2002), there is a problem with using log changes for variables with a ceiling (or floor). The move from, let us say, 100 to 50 is a lot easier than bringing about a decline in infant mortality from 50 to 0.

Independent of ceiling or floor considerations, there has been a larger decline in illiteracy in the past 20 years than possibly ever before. Compared with the period 1960-80, the decline has been at double the rate. Today, illiteracy in the developing world is down to 28 percent of adults, down from 43 percent in 1980 and 53 percent in 1960 (table 12.3).

All the countries of the world show a large improvement in political and civil liberties. These data are from Freedom House, and are available for most countries for every year since 1973. Part of the impact of globalization has meant increasing democratization in developing countries. This is revealed by an increase in Freedom House's Political and Civil Liberties Index (which is population weighted) from 2.9 in 1973 to 3.4 in 1980 and 3.6 in 2000. An index of 7 represents political and civil liberties as enjoyed in the industrialized world (e.g., the United States).

What these figures indicate, at a minimum, is that freedom has not brought about a decline in the rate of growth of living standards in developing countries. This reality is the opposite of those who argue (e.g., Quibria 2002) that the miracle of growth is associated with authoritarianism. This thesis was explicitly examined in Bhalla (1997a); there it was shown that there was a confusing Confucian hypothesis at play. East Asian economies had Confucianism, authoritarianism, and higher growth; democratic countries like India had plenty of liberties and democracy, but no growth. The convenient conclusion was reached by many. However, if freedom is decomposed into its separate political and economic components, then the mystery of both the slow growth in India and fast growth in authoritarian regimes is explained. The contribution of economic freedom was low in, for example, India and high in, for example, China; this large effect swamped the positive effect of political and civil liberties.[2]

It does not matter what index is chosen for poor countries: income growth, consumption growth, inequality change, health standards, educational attainment, or poverty decline. The past 20 years were a golden period for poor people. It was shown above that statistically speaking, the past 20 years were a clear outlier in terms of poverty decline. It is unlikely that the world's poor people will ever again witness such a large transformation in such a short space of time. It is, in fact, not only unlikely—it is almost impossible. What the world has witnessed is a miracle for poor people. The irony is that their champions—elites in the industrialized world—not only do not realize this simple fact, they believe the opposite has happened. If this book has helped to clarify this simple point—how poor people have fared in an era of globalization—it will have achieved its major objective.

---

2. See World Bank, *World Development Report 1991: The Challenge of Development*, for an early exposition of this thesis; Bhalla (1997a) for a detailed investigation; and Bhalla (1999) for a follow-up analysis.

13

Conclusion: Roads Not Taken

This book has attempted to evaluate the data and to draw conclusions on four important and related subjects: the nature and level of economic growth; the level and change in world income distribution; the level and change in absolute poverty; and the effect of globalization on all of the above. Globalization was identified as a time period, the period of the past 20 years. What are the major conclusions, the megatrends?

There is no welfare indicator for which the world economy has not done better in the past 20 years. And poor people do better, much better than the average with globalization. They began the process of catch-up, and in 2000 mean incomes in the developing world were 14 percent of mean incomes in the industrialized world—up from a ratio of 12.6 percent two decades earlier.

Today, these poor nations account for almost 50 percent of world output, their education levels are reasonably high, and their wages relative to their productivity are relatively low. Globalization has meant that Stolper-Samuelson (or the law of one price and one wage) is in easy play—the drive toward greater competition, and greater convergence, is inexorable. This same force has led to a reversal of a centuries-old global trend of greater inequality; since 1973, the trend is down, and by the end of this decade, world inequality is likely to be lower than what it was in 1910—with a Gini of about 61. Today, the world inequality level has a Gini of 65.1—almost the lowest in 100 years.

It is a firm and happy ending to the twentieth century. On virtually every measure, the past 20 years have witnessed tremendous progress, to great improvement for all, and especially for the world's poor people.

Using the old $1-a-day poverty line ($1.50 at 1993 prices), there are "only" 650 million poor people in the world today, and they constitute 13 percent of the developing world's population. On the basis of the lower "official" World Bank poverty line of $1.08 a day, at 1993 prices, there are 450 million poor people, and they constitute only 9.1 percent of the developing world's population, or 6.4 percent of the world's population. On the basis of the higher and recommended $2 a day poverty line, the developing world has a poverty rate of 23.3 percent, or 1.15 billion poor people.

This result on poverty—both on the level today, and its trend—is at odds with the "official" World Bank results on world poverty for the $1.08 poverty line. The official results are 23 percent, or 1.15 billion, poor people in 1999; this book finds the same level of poverty, but for a poverty line that is 85 percent higher! Only one of the two conclusions can be right.

This exploration of world poverty and inequality started off with some puzzling conventional wisdom on globalization and its not-so-good side effects. Was their divergence as revealed by the divergent growth rates in poor and rich countries? No, because the developing world exceeded the growth of the industrialized world for 50 years, from 1950 to 2000. And for the globalization subperiod, the average developing country grew at almost twice the rate of the average (all population weighted) industrialized country—3.1 versus 1.6 percent.

The puzzle of only a slow, painful reduction in world poverty during the period from 1987 to 1999, in the face of this high per capita growth, was the result of puzzling methods and puzzling data. A conventional, and straightforward, use of widely available data shows poverty to have declined by at least triple the rate indicated by the official statistics—by about 16 percentage points, to a level of about 13 percent, rather than by 5 percentage points to a level of 23 percent.

No matter what statistic is used, the revealed truth is that we have just witnessed the 20 best years in world history—and doubly certainly the 20 best years in the history of poor people. Yet this is not the perception of many, if not most, of the participants in the global debate on globalization. It certainly is not the perception of most nongovernmental organizations to the left of the Cato Institute—which means more than 99 percent of the world's nongovernmental organizations. It certainly is not the perception of the media, the liberal press. It is not the perception of international institutions dedicated to bringing about the miracle we have all witnessed. Most interesting, and perhaps most important, it is not the perception of most academics, the intellectual elite, the women and men who are supposed to know better.

Different Forks for Different Folks

Why do so many have this distorted perception of reality? One explanation, if not *the* explanation, is that at every moment of methodological choice, the wrong one was made. The wrong fork in the road was taken by the guardians of conventional wisdom. In no particular order, the following points stand out. First, we were mesmerized into believing that instead of convergence, there had been divergence; and instead of a measure of divergence, there had been "big-time" divergence. This clarion call echoed throughout the institutions inside the Washington Beltway and, if I may be excused for saying so, at apparently all the left-of-center policy outposts of the world.

The intellectual basis for this conclusion: that the relative income of the United States had widened with respect to that of the poorest country, Tanzania in 1950 and Sierra Leone in 2000. A better alternative would have been to compare the trend in relative incomes of the richest and poorest countries, benchmarked to a particular date, say 1960. This would still not have been correct, but it would have been a better method—and it would have shown a trend toward convergence. This choice was not made. Instead, we were told about the relative incomes of the always changing top and bottom 20 countries, with China conveniently, and perhaps deliberately, excluded from the calculation.

When a defendable method, however, was used—comparing relative incomes of the 20th percentile in the United States with the 20th percentile in the developing world (the people might change, but not the percentiles) or relative incomes of the medians in the two sets of countries—the result was quite different. Rather than divergence, one obtained an even bigger-time convergence.

The next fork in the road involved the measurement of absolute poverty. After being employed for the first two decades in the new field of "poverty economics," the method of measuring a country's mean incomes got changed. Instead of continuing to rely on national accounts data—the bread and butter of most (good and bad) economists—the institution in charge of measuring poverty, the World Bank, decided that henceforth only survey data would be used.

But a funny thing happened after this edict was handed down in the late 1980s. Survey data started capturing fewer and fewer of the changes revealed by national accounts. In one of the largest countries of the world, with the largest concentration of poor people, India, the survey method showed that between 1987 and 1998, mean per capita consumption had *declined* by about 10 percent, in real terms. The national accounts data, in contrast, suggested that there had been an *increase* in consumption of more than 40 percent. Even in Indonesia, a country affected the most by the financial crisis, per capita income in 1998 was 21 percent higher than in 1987. (Indonesian survey data also show a similar increase, because the survey capture ratio has stayed relatively constant at a low 50 percent.)

This methodological mistake also led researchers to take another wrong fork and miss another forest. Exclusive reliance on survey data meant that South Korea was deemed richer than the United Kingdom in 1993; and the Central African Republic was richer than India. These same assumptions yielded the result that not only had inequality worsened, but worsened at an unprecedented pace—more than 1 percent a year for 5 continuous years, from 1988 to 1993.

In the initial eureka moment of discovering this "forbidden inequality truth," analysts did not stop to note that such a fast change for the world's 5.5 billion people was not only unlikely but impossible. The last such documented change took place between 1910 and 1950 and encompassed the Great Depression and two world wars. An analogous change between 1988 and 1993 was just not possible—even as an academic, one must state this. Yet we all lapped up this "revealed" truth and started looking for explanations as to how it might have happened.

Yet another wrong fork on the methodological road was taken in 1999. The revised 1993-base purchasing power parity (PPP) exchange rates had just been released, and the World Bank distributed these data to all the researchers and policymakers in the world. Its own staff, however, used the then-unpublished PPP "consumption" exchange rates for calculations of global poverty.

There was no backing for this choice, and its results were peculiar; it inexplicably showed South Asia to have 18 percent lower consumption than that revealed by the existing, and official, PPP data. Thus it was no surprise that, according to the World Bank, South Asian poverty was much higher than believed by anyone (e.g., for a higher national poverty line, equal to PPP $1.25 a day, official statistics showed a 26 percent poverty rate in India for 1999, rather than the 36 to 39 percent suggested by the World Bank).

Then came the time to interpret what had happened to growth and poverty. Here again, note was not taken of the warning signals—warnings about possibly a wrong method. Suddenly, it was observed that growth was not delivering. But no one paused to ask why. Instead, new models of development were offered, the quality of growth was emphasized, and policymakers and development specialists were asked to look for policies pertaining to the redistribution of income. Left unattended was the reality that if a proper method had been used, it would have been observed that growth had been propoor, and especially so during the globalization period 1980-2000; that these years were the best in the past 200 years in terms of poverty reduction; that poverty reduction in other periods had been less than half as much for every given unit of growth; and that the Millennium Development Goal of 15 percent poverty by 2015 had already been reached in 2000.

Answers to Often-Asked Questions

In closing, let us consider answers to four often-asked questions. *First, what is happening to global individual inequality?* Global individual (as opposed to country) inequality has shown a gradual, but significant, decline since 1973. The Gini coefficient of individual income inequality has declined from an average level of about 68 before the 1980s to close to 65 today. This surprising *reduction* in inequality during the globalization period (mid-1980s to now) has not been uniform. Industrialized countries have witnessed no change, Asia has recorded more than a 10 percent increase, and the postcommunist structural change in Eastern Europe has not been good for growth or for inequality. Per capita incomes are lower, and inequality has increased by an unprecedented amount—from an average Gini level of 32 before the 1990s to an average of almost 50 today.[1]

Several heuristic arguments have been made above to emphasize that the conclusion that *the world is becoming more equal* must be accepted if one believes that there are more than 1 billion people in China and that their incomes are rising at a faster rate than the average. And if one adds the fact that Indian incomes are also rising faster than the average, then the conclusion of increasing world equality is even more inescapable.

Another way to look at the reality is as follows. What the data suggest is that while the average poor country may be losing ground (the divergence literature), the average *person* in a poor country is gaining ground because her income is increasing at a faster rate than the income of the average rich person in a rich country. This is a result of several big, poor countries doing very well—the giants, China and India, and also Indonesia and Vietnam. There is no room for the fiction that the world is becoming more unequal if the revealed facts of growing big, poor countries are incorporated into the analysis.

Second, is there divergence or convergence? Divergence is a myth. If data on income distribution are available, then calculations of divergence based on differences in average country income growth are not that significant. Yet differences in individual income growth are very significant. For the globalization period, 1980 to 2000, the relative incomes of poor people soared: The elasticity of the bottom 20 percent is estimated to be 1.58 (i.e., for a 10 percent increase in average global income, the incomes of poor people increased by 15.8 percent). This is in large part due to the high growth experienced by the many poor people in China and India.

Third, has growth been propoor? A proper response to this question is twofold—theoretical and empirical. Theoretically, how much poverty reduction *should* a given amount of growth be associated with? What is neutral—is a 5 percent reduction in the head count ratio okay with 10 percent growth in consumption? Or is it 10 percent? It depends—on the "shape of the distribution elasticity," a concept introduced to help estimate the neutral impact of growth. This elasticity varies with the level

---

1. These inequality levels are for the distribution in Russia and Eastern and Central Europe, which is considered as one region or "country."

of the poverty line, and where in the distribution the poverty line is at any point in time. Typically, the value of this elasticity is about 0.5 (i.e., 10 percent neutral growth is associated with a 5-percentage-point reduction in poverty).

Moreover, empirically, there is no evidence to suggest that growth has been biased against the poor. In more than 80 percent of cases, gains (or losses) in consumption have resulted in declines (or increases) in the head count ratio. Further, the pattern of growth has almost invariably been at least neutral—poverty has declined by as much as it was expected to, given the poverty line and the shape of the distribution elasticity.

Further, according to a simple measure of propoor growth—comparing the consumption growth of poor people with the consumption growth of nonpoor people—poor people in the developing world (defined as the fraction of people who were poor in 1980, approximately the bottom 45 percent) have enjoyed much higher growth than nonpoor people (for every 10 percent growth in consumption of the nonpoor, the poor have increased their consumption by 18 percent). Little additional evidence is needed to suggest that globalization has been manifestly propoor. In a causal sense, globalization has made it possible for the developing world to compete with (and sometimes outcompete) the industrialized world in the global marketplace.

Fourth, can growth alone be sufficient for poverty reduction? Yes. If the discussion is about income poverty, then by definition, only two factors can affect the head count ratio: output growth and a change in income distribution. Given that within countries income distribution changes have tended toward inequality, it definitionally follows that growth has been more than sufficient to reduce poverty. In this important regard, the conclusion differs from the conventional wisdom that "attacking poverty requires actions beyond the economic domain."[2] Such actions are not needed. Growth is sufficient, period.

---

2. World Bank, *World Development Report 2000/2001: Attacking Poverty*, 33; emphasis added.

APPENDICES

Appendix A
The Simple Accounting Procedure Dataset

The research on which this book is based involved assembling data on per capita incomes and consumption for 149 countries for the 50-year time period 1950-2000. An attempt was made to get consistent data on five basic variables: population, income, consumption, the distribution of income, and distribution of consumption. Once information on these five variables is available, on a continuous basis, then questions about levels and changes in the distribution of income and economic growth can effectively be answered.

Unfortunately, there is no single source from which all of these data can be obtained. This appendix describes how the data were assembled, and the assumptions that were made.

Population: Information for this variable involved virtually no assumptions and was taken from two major sources: World Bank, *World Development Indicators* CD-ROM, referred to as *WDI*; and Maddison (2001), referred to as M2001.

Income: All country income and consumption data have been converted to purchasing power parity (PPP) data, at 1993 prices. Along with the above two sources, the following additional four references have been used to help construct a consistent series for 1950-2000: Penn World Tables, 1985-base PPP prices, referred to as PWT 5.6; *WDI* 1998, which has PPP data, 1987 base, at both constant and current prices; PPP data, 1975 base, from Summers and Heston (1988), Heston and Summers (1991), referred to as HS; and IMF, *International Financial Statistics* CD-ROM, 2002.

Two questions remain: When data are available from more than one source, which one is chosen; and how are the data linked. The hierarchy of preference for data available from more than one source is as follows: first the *WDI* CD-ROM, which contains the latest, 1993-base PPP estimates. When these are not available, the 1985-base data are used (PWT 5.6), failing which *WDI* 1987 CD-ROM, failing which HS and finally the M2001 dataset are used. Data were linked via the *rate of growth* for the lower-order series.

Consumption: National accounts data (*WDI*) were used to derive the share of consumption in income. When such data were not available, the share contained in PWT 5.6 was used. For missing observations, the most recent estimate was used. If no consumption data were available, then the regional share was imputed.

The above provides us with data on incomes and consumption and population. It remains to obtain data on the distribution of income or consumption. There are close to 50 countries for which income distribution data are available for the 1950s; the number increases to about 75 countries for the mid-1970s, and to more than 100 countries for the mid-1990s. The number of countries for which distribution data are available is steadily increasing, and for 2000 it had increased to 124 countries (i.e., at least one distribution observation was available by the end of the 1990s). Thus, a fair amount of data are available for estimating, with a reasonable degree of confidence, both the level of world income distribution and its change for the period 1950 to the present.

Since the mid-1970s, collection and documentation of income distribution data has been accorded high-priority status by development economists. The first such collection was by Paukert (1973) and the second by the World Bank (Jain 1975). Both of these datasets were "rough," in that it was felt that a compilation was more important than verification or cleaning. In the 1990s, two important distribution datasets emerged—that of Deininger and Squire (1996) and of the World Institute for Development Economics Research's World Income Inequality Database. Both these datasets have been used to generate data on distributions. These two sources of data have been supplemented by data available from the Web (World Bank poverty monitor, worldbank.org/research/povmonitor; and Milanovic's data on Eastern European countries), as well as data gathered for 18 Asian countries (Asian Development Bank 2002). Table A.1 documents the coverage of these data.

One problem remains. For some countries only an income or consumption distribution is available. Since both distributions are needed (consumption distribution for poverty calculations and income distribution for calculations of world individual income distributions), data from one distribution were transformed into the other via a simple regression between consumption and income shares for each quintile. Such regressions were estimated for 27 country-year observations when data on both consumption and income distribution were available.

Finally, for some countries (e.g., Afghanistan), no survey data are available. For these countries, the average regional quintile shares were imputed.

Table A.1 Data for the simple accounting procedure

Region	Countries[a]	Population coverage (percent)	Surveys[b]	Survey means Consumption	Survey means Income	Gini index Consumption	Gini index Income
1950-80							
Asia	15	52.4	79	3	6	47	29
East Asia	10	24.2	38	0	4	36	2
South Asia	5	98.2	41	3	2	11	27
Sub-Saharan Africa	12	29.2	16	0	0	16	0
Middle East and North Africa	5	39.5	7	0	1	6	1
Latin America	20	88.6	62	3	12	60	2
Developing world	52	53.5	164	6	19	129	32
Developing world, excluding India and China	51	68.0	140	3	18	129	9
India and China	1	40.5	24	3	1	0	23
Eastern Europe	5	20.2	26	0	0	26	0
Nonindustrialized world	57	51.2	190	6	19	155	32
Industrialized world	20	99.0	127	0	4	126	1
World	77	58.9	317	6	23	281	33
1980-2000							
Asia	18	97.0	126	48	37	62	58
East Asia	13	96.3	85	23	28	47	28
South Asia	5	98.2	41	25	9	15	30
Sub-Saharan Africa	31	77.6	72	30	3	3	61
Middle East and North Africa	9	66.9	22	9	2	1	18
Latin America	25	85.6	104	28	29	81	19
Developing world	93	96.7	357	134	78	169	168
Developing world, excluding India and China	91	93.0	323	114	63	147	153
India and China	2	100.0	34	20	15	22	15
Eastern Europe	25	97.8	131	39	39	105	32
Nonindustrialized world	108	97.0	455	154	110	252	188
Industrialized world	22	100.0	149	0	42	138	9
World	130	94.0	604	154	152	390	197

a. The countries column designates the number of countries in the region with either expenditure or income data. Population covered signifies the coverage of the surveys; if all countries have at least one survey during the designated period, the coverage is 100 percent.

b. The survey means column reports the number of countries for which data on survey means are available for either consumption or income; and analogously for Gini coefficients.

Appendix B
Estimation of the Lorenz Curve, and Its Accuracy

The data on distribution are available at mostly the quintile level (i.e., with only five observations per distribution). If a Lorenz curve (relationship between shares of population and shares of income) can be estimated, then this five-observation distribution can be converted into a 100-observation distribution. This appendix explains how.

Briefly, the estimation of a Lorenz curve follows the following procedure: If the Lorenz curve can be parameterized (i.e., given a mathematical formulation), then the study of the determinants of inequality can "begin." Unfortunately, there are an infinity of "patterns" of distribution, so where can one start? The Lorenz curves can cross, in which case it is a priori ambiguous which distribution is more unequal. In a pioneering study, Kakwani (1980) discusses methods of approximating the Lorenz curve, and methods of estimating the same from the limited data (share in income of different income groups and/or shares of individual quintiles).

His preferred formulation, and the one used by the simple accounting procedure (SAP), is

$$p - a^* \left[p^\alpha\right] * \left[(1 - p)\right]^\beta \tag{B.1}$$

where p represents the bottom p percent of the population and $L(p)$ is the corresponding share in income. Taking logs and rearranging terms, one obtains a form fit for regression:

$$\log\left[p - L(p)\right] = \log a + \alpha\,{}^*\!\log(p) + \beta^*\!\log(1 - p) \tag{B.2}$$

The parameters obtained from the above equation can be used to generate the estimated incomes of each percentile of the population. Often, only four independent observations are available for each distribution (the quintile shares—the fifth quintile is derived from the other four and is equal to 1 minus the sum of the other four); thus three parameters (a, α, and β) are estimated from four observations, leaving only 1 degree of freedom.

The results of equation B.2 are *filtered* by the SAP procedure to satisfy the theoretical boundary constraints (i.e., the sum of the estimated shares of each quintile is actually equal to the observed shares, and the share of each percentile is equal to or larger than the share of the previous percentile). The filtering is done through an iterative procedure, in which at the end of the first round, the shares of the first percentile get estimated and fixed; then the next quintile; then the next; and so on.

Regardless of the estimation procedure, the resulting distribution exactly reflects the underlying exact quintile shares. So errors that might creep in do not affect estimates of quintiles. Thus, this procedure cannot contain *more* errors than a study that uses quintile shares (e.g., Milanovic 1999; or log-variance). The question remains: How accurate is this procedure?

If the procedure is accurate, then the resulting world income distribution would also be more accurate than hitherto available. Note what happens now when only quintile data are available. Each data point for China represents the average income of 350 million people; for India, 250 million; for the United States, 70 million. For a world distribution, it does not matter if for a small country distribution is in quintiles; but it does matter if it is one of the many countries with a population above 20 million (when each data point represents 4 million people). If a percentile distribution were available, then each data point for India would still represent 10 million people, but the error for a global distribution would be a lot smaller.

The data construction is now complete. Percentile distributions of income and consumption are available for each year after 1950. These data are the most complete and exhaustive of any income distribution dataset assembled to date. These data are used throughout this book to estimate the world income, and also consumption distribution for each year after 1950, regional distributions, distributions for each country over time (which will only change with each new survey), the composition (by country) for each percentile, the poverty ratios for each country according to an international poverty line, and so on.

How Good Is SAP?

The different sources (Deininger and Squire 1996; World Institute for Development Economics Research's World Income Inequality Database;

World Bank, *World Development Indicators* CD-ROM and Web site) yielded more than 2,500 distributions for more than 120 countries, with several countries having more than one distribution for each survey year.

This procedure still left the choice to be made among competing estimates of the distribution (quintile shares and Ginis) for the *same country* and *same year*. For these survey country years, the quintile shares corresponding to the survey with the minimum absolute error in the Gini coefficient were selected.

Errors in Survey Inequality Measures

But this begs the question: How is the error in the Gini identified? Access to most raw (unit observations) survey data is not available for most surveys conducted before the mid-1980s. Researchers have to rely on the tabulations of income (or expenditure) distributions from published sources. In some instances, the official documents contain estimates of Ginis as well.

The trail of income distribution data from source to publication is as follows. The original tabulations of income ranges and percentage households are converted by researchers into quintile distributions.[1] The error involved at this stage involves errors at the "cusp" (e.g., if the income ranges of two adjoining cells overlap, then some adjustment is needed to allocate households between the two quintiles). These adjustments introduce error, but one of low intensity. Often, researchers have transformed household distributions into per capita distributions, or income before taxes into a distribution that reflects income after taxes. The researchers have been careful to document what distribution is being reported, though it is unclear whether the reported Gini reflects the "official" Gini, or the Gini for the converted distribution. A reasonable hypothesis for the reported data is that the distribution characteristics (quintile shares) are reasonably accurate, but that there is a question mark about the Ginis.

Errors in Published Inequality Data

In their study on the Kuznets hypothesis, Anand and Kanbur (1993b) noted that simple reclassifications or "corrections" to the data resulted in the inverted U-curve relationship between income distribution and development becoming a normal U-curve! More recently, Atkinson and Brandolini (1999) have discussed the possibility of errors in the inequality

---

1. The quintile distribution is selected for expositional purposes only, though decile distributions are rare for data from before the 1980s.

data reported in Deininger and Squire (1996) and by implication in the World Institute for Development Economics Research tabulations.

It is quite possible that the SAP method of generating the Lorenz curve from reported quintile data may also contain large errors in the Ginis. Access to 8 years worth of household survey data for 15 major states in India (1983 to 1998) provides a vast laboratory to test methods of constructing Ginis. Two Ginis were calculated for each distribution—a Gini based on the original distribution, and a Gini based only on the calculated quintile shares. Analogously, there are two estimates for the mean expenditure level at each percentile—the true estimate derived from unit-level data, and the synthetic estimate derived from the quintile shares through use of the SAP method. Table B.1 reports on the errors for 21 different percentiles for 210 different distributions spanning 16 years of per capita expenditure data in India.

The SAP method is seen to be shockingly accurate. The constructed Ginis are within 1 percent of the true value in almost 90 percent of the cases. The largest error is only 3.7 percent; the standard deviation of Gini errors is about 0.4 percent.

Analogously, table B.2 reports the more extreme errors (Gini error > 5 percent) observed with reported Ginis for different regions, and the different sources of data. Note that both the Deininger-Squire and WIDER datasets have relatively large numbers of country-year errors (>100 percent of the sample) whereas "other" sources are considerably "cleaner" (<5 percent of the sample) by comparison.

Even more telling are the values at *individual* percentile levels. Accuracy at the individual percentile level is a very strict test of the method, because it does not allow for errors to "cancel" out, as might very well be the case for the Ginis.

Where accuracy is most needed for the generation of world inequality is at the percentile level. To reiterate, four observations are used for each distribution (the fifth quintile share is unity minus the sum of the shares of the first four quintiles); from just these four observations, and knowledge of the mean, levels of expenditure for 100 percentiles are derived. Table B.1 reports on the error involved for every 5th percentile; no percentile error is more than 3.5 percent, and the average error is less than half a percent. However, the errors at the extremes—the 1st and 100th percentiles—are large; the 1st percentile is overstated by almost 4 percent, whereas the richest percentile's expenditure is overestimated by a large 21 percent! This large error simply means that, on average, the last few percentiles are underestimated, and this underestimation is reflected in the share of the richest percentile. Note that this "error" does not in any way affect the share of the richest quintile.

Because all the distributions used in this study have been transformed using the SAP method, the low level of error achieved with more than 300 test distributions is very reassuring.

Table B.1 How good is the simple accounting procedure (SAP)? Testing with National Sample Survey data from India, 1983-98

Percentile	Percentile error			
	Mean	Maximum	Minimum	Standard deviation
1	3.8	274.6	−100.0	36.1
5	1.5	14.3	−7.5	3.0
10	−0.3	8.5	−12.5	2.3
15	−0.7	8.7	−9.1	2.2
20	−0.7	7.0	−9.1	2.1
25	−0.1	4.7	−3.3	1.1
30	−0.1	3.6	−3.1	0.8
35	0.2	3.2	−3.0	0.9
40	0.3	4.0	−4.4	1.0
45	−0.1	3.2	−3.2	0.9
50	0.1	3.7	−2.5	0.7
55	0.1	2.4	−2.5	0.7
60	0.0	2.5	−4.4	0.9
65	0.5	5.9	−3.3	1.2
70	0.2	3.7	−4.1	0.8
75	−0.2	3.8	−4.3	1.0
80	−0.9	4.9	−10.7	1.8
85	−2.0	6.3	−24.0	3.1
90	−3.1	15.7	−21.3	4.0
95	−3.4	24.5	−17.2	5.2
100	20.3	102.0	−30.1	20.8

Percentile distribution of errors in SAP Ginis

	Gini	Percentile
Largest error	**3.7**	**274.6**
Smallest error	**−1.3**	**−100.0**
Mean error	**0.4**	**−0.2**
5th percentile	−0.4	−5.2
25th percentile	0.2	−1.1
50th percentile	**0.4**	**−0.1**
75th percentile	0.7	0.6
95th percentile	1.3	3.2

a. For each percentile, the "true" value is known, and the error reflects the deviation of the predicted SAP value from the true value.

Note: 210 distributions are from seven National Sample Surveys frorn 1983 to 1998 and 15 states, and a total of separate urban-rural distributions were used for testing the SAP method of constructing Lorenz curves and associated statistics or inequality.

Table B.2 How error free are published Ginis?

Region	D-S[a]		WIDER		Others[c]	
	Number of surveys	Percentage with 5 percent error[b]	Number of surveys	Percentage with 5 percent error[b]	Number of surveys	Percentage with 5 percent error[b]
Industrialized countries	428	15.9	512	13.7	54	5.6
Asia	113	14.2	132	12.1	51	2.0
Eastern Europe	128	8.6	164	9.1	85	5.9
Latin America	130	17.7	166	13.9	90	1.1
Sub-Saharan Africa	13	23.1	24	12.5	16	6.3
Developing countries	71	5.6	80	5.0	50	4.0
Percent, excluding China and India	49	20.4	102	14.7	68	7.4
All observations	**932**	**14.5**	**1,180**	**12.4**	**414**	**4.3**

WIDER = World Institute for Development Economics Research

a. D-S is Deininger and Squire (1996).

b. Absolute error > 5 percent, between Ginis as officially *reported* and Ginis as *computed* by the SAP method; see the text.

c. Others—*World Development Report*, World Bank Web site and individual papers.

Appendix C
Basic Data for the Simple Accounting Procedure

The following table summarizes the dataset used to derive the results presented in the book. The regional classification is East Asia, South Asia, sub-Saharan Africa, Middle East and North Africa, Central Asia, Latin America and the Caribbean, Eastern Europe, and the industrialized world.

The definitions for most of the regions are self-explanatory. The four Central Asian economies are Kazakhstan, Kyrgyz Republic, Mongolia, and Uzbekistan. These four countries are also included in the developing-country classification (all countries excluding Eastern Europe and the industrialized world). The 21 economies making up the Middle East and North Africa are Algeria, Bahrain, Cyprus, Egypt, Iran, Iraq, Israel, Jordan, Kuwait, Lebanon, Libya, Malta, Morocco, Oman, Saudi Arabia, Syrian Arab Republic, Tunisia, Turkey, United Arab Emirates, West Bank and Gaza, and Yemen. The distribution data reflect the data of the nearest preceding year, if survey data were not available for 1960, 1980, or 2000. Table C.1 presents data for each country for 1960, 1980, and 2000. The survey type column depicts whether surveys for that country were expenditure ("exp.") or income ("inc.") surveys. The next six columns present annual per capita income and consumption in purchasing power parity dollars at 2000 prices (1993 base) for the 3 selected years. The next six columns present shares of consumption or income for the 1st and 5th quintiles. If the survey type is expenditure, the quintile shares are expenditure shares; otherwise they are income shares; the same pattern is analogously followed for the data on the Gini. The last column presents the survey/national accounts ratio (i.e., the ratio of the survey consumption mean to the national accounts data on private final consumption expenditure, or the ratio of the survey mean to the national accounts data on per capita GNP, at market prices).

Table C.1 Basic SAP data on incomes and distribution, 1960-2000

Region and economy	Survey type[a]	Per capita income			Per capita consumption			Share of 1st quintile			Share of 5th quintile			Gini			S/NA[b]		
		1960	1980	2000	1960	1980	2000	1960	1980	2000	1960	1980	2000	1960	1980	2000	1960	1980	2000
East Asia																			
Cambodia	Exp.	899	1,096	1,485	621	734	1,274	8.5	8.5	6.0	43.9	43.9	52.4	34.9	34.9	45.7	141.7	141.7	110.3
China	Inc.	563	907	4,126	387	458	1,952	7.9	7.9	5.9	36.7	36.7	46.6	29.5	29.5	40.5	56.9	56.9	38.7
Fiji	Inc.	2,900	5,001	7,431	2,025	2,859	4,934	4.0	4.0	4.0	52.3	52.3	52.3	48.1	48.1	48.1	54.4	59.3	58.8
French Polynesia	Exp.		18,749	24,257		12,564	16,062										84.4	82.1	82.0
Hong Kong	Inc.	3,589	13,449	25,828	2,512	8,030	15,006	5.7	6.2	4.4	56.2	46.5	57.3	49.5	39.8	51.9	52.7	52.7	63.5
Indonesia	Exp.	871	1,699	3,172	672	874	2,133	8.0	7.3	9.0	42.4	42.3	40.8	34.3	34.7	31.5	52.3	52.3	49.3
Korea, North	Exp.	1,464	3,763	1,762	1,082	2,521	1,154										84.4	82.1	82.0
Korea, South	Inc.	1,745	5,828	18,037	1,451	3,755	10,332	5.8	5.1	7.5	41.9	45.4	39.3	35.5	40.0	31.7	54.0	76.0	86.2
Laos	Exp.	718	927	1,674	531	621	1,364	9.6	9.6	7.6	40.2	40.2	44.9	30.3	30.3	36.8	75.1	75.1	99.3
Macao	Exp.			19,007			7,825										84.4	82.1	82.0
Malaysia	Inc.	1,894	4,704	9,396	1,175	2,413	3,992	6.5	3.7	4.4	44.0	55.8	54.3	37.4	51.3	49.3	49.7	67.0	53.0
Myanmar	Inc.	483	771	1,577	394	521	1,205	10.0	10.0	10.0	48.5	48.5	48.5	37.8	37.8	37.8	54.4	59.3	58.8
New Caledonia	Exp.		19,497	22,309		13,065	16,827										84.4	82.1	82.0
Papua New Guinea	Exp.	1,752	2,353	2,624	1,215	1,432	1,726	7.3	7.3	4.5	40.9	40.9	56.5	33.6	33.6	51.2	84.4	60.5	82.0
Philippines	Inc.	2,848	4,796	4,285	2,164	3,201	3,030	6.5	3.6	4.4	48.6	54.0	55.4	42.7	49.8	50.4	60.5	60.5	72.4
Reunion	Exp.	1,668	4,317	6,705	1,129	6,104	6,075										84.4	82.1	82.0
Seychelles	Exp.	1,921	4,438	7,111	1,686	1,961	3,659										84.4	82.1	82.0
Singapore	Inc.	2,460	11,495	24,171	2,003	5,997	9,322	7.2	6.5	5.6	42.0	46.5	48.9	35.0	39.8	42.9	35.9	35.9	35.9
Solomon Islands	Exp.		1,920	2,033		1,348	1,412										84.4	82.1	82.0
Taiwan	Inc.	1,918	6,809	21,758	1,325	3,786	12,489	7.9	8.8	7.1	41.4	37.0	38.7	33.3	28.1	31.5	69.1	69.1	64.4
Thailand	Exp.	1,260	2,891	6,777	961	1,874	3,809	6.1	6.1	5.4	50.7	50.7	50.6	44.0	44.0	44.8	72.5	72.5	82.3
Vanuatu	Exp.		4,226	3,105		2,832	1,815										84.4	82.1	82.0
Vietnam	Inc.	904	857	2,112	668	575	1,408	6.7	6.7	5.6	46.6	46.6	49.5	39.3	39.3	43.1	58.9	58.9	58.9
Western Samoa	Exp.		4,583	4,341		3,978	3,865										84.4	82.1	82.0
South Asia																			
Afghanistan	Exp.	1,322	1,193	745	1,129	952	481										87.4	87.1	72.5
Bangladesh	Inc.	1,035	1,102	1,682	1,027	991	1,305	6.9	7.4	6.2	44.5	42.9	52.1	37.4	35.3	45.1	92.9	92.9	66.9
Bhutan	Exp.		814	1,501		547	533										87.4	87.1	72.5
India	Exp.	1,213	1,310	2,512	969	951	1,708	8.4	8.5	8.7	41.4	40.9	41.8	32.7	32.2	32.7	71.1	69.4	55.7
Maldives	Exp.			5,320			2,371										87.4	87.1	72.5
Nepal	Inc.	957	990	1,429	912	814	1,107	4.6	4.6	9.1	59.2	59.2	39.5	53.5	53.5	30.2	102.6	102.6	71.3
Pakistan	Exp.	809	1,259	2,052	613	1,046	1,553	9.2	8.6	8.9	40.0	41.3	41.9	30.5	32.4	32.6	88.7	88.7	74.1
Sri Lanka	Inc.	1,750	2,071	3,680	1,343	1,662	2,656	5.2	6.6	4.1	53.8	51.1	53.0	47.7	43.4	48.2	77.1	52.8	52.8

Sub-Saharan Africa

Angola	Exp.	2,475	1,794	4,292	1,438	613	1,529	8.0	8.0	8.0	50.0	50.0	50.0	41.5	41.5	41.5	119.4	119.4	105.9
Benin	Inc.	974	975	1,015	822	952	799	3.6	3.6	3.6	58.9	58.9	58.9	54.5	54.5	54.5	76.2	77.7	57.7
Botswana	Exp.	862	3,566	7,886	743	1,639	2,448	5.6	5.6	5.5	54.7	54.7	54.7	48.3	48.3	48.8	79.1	79.1	79.1
Burkina Faso	Exp.	899	879	1,067	838	839	813	5.6	5.6	5.7	55.1	55.1	54.7	48.3	48.3	48.8	74.9	74.9	74.9
Burundi	Exp.	1,124	821	601	1,034	750	547	7.9	7.9	7.9	41.6	41.6	41.6	33.5	33.5	33.5	87.5	87.5	87.5
Cameroon	Exp.	1,403	2,334	1,700	1,137	1,600	1,208										119.4	119.4	105.9
Central African Republic	Exp.	1,782	1,607	1,263	1,283	1,506	1,026	2.0	2.0	2.0	65.0	65.0	65.0	62.0	62.0	62.0	55.0	55.0	55.0
Chad	Inc.	1,471	790	880	1,139	641	836	8.0	8.0	8.0	43.0	43.0	43.0	34.8	34.8	34.8	76.2	77.7	57.7
Comoros	Exp.	1,839	2,137	1,461	1,765	1,693	1,279										119.4	119.4	105.9
Congo	Exp.	440	771	697	426	361	155										119.4	119.4	105.9
Côte d'Ivoire	Exp.	1,543	2,512	1,765	988	1,577	1,165	5.7	5.7	7.1	47.4	47.4	44.2	41.4	41.4	36.9	97.8	97.8	77.2
Djibouti	Exp.	2,346	2,346	1,411	1,827	1,719	1,105	6.1	6.1	6.1	46.7	46.7	46.7	40.2	40.2	40.2	190.9	190.9	190.9
Equatorial Guinea	Exp.			5,779			1,777										119.4	119.4	105.9
Eritrea	Exp.			921			652												
Ethiopia	Exp.	586	734	692	523	586	560	8.6	8.6	7.2	41.2	41.2	47.7	32.2	32.2	39.9	195.3	195.3	195.3
Gabon	Inc.	3,159	8,095	5,883	1230	2,116	2,860	2.0	2.9	2.9	71.0	66.3	66.3	67.6	62.2	62.2	76.2	77.7	57.7
Gambia	Exp.	1,362	1,903	1,741	907	1,198	1,463	4.4	4.4	4.4	52.7	52.7	52.7	47.6	47.6	47.6	53.1	53.1	53.1
Ghana	Exp.	2,179	2,089	2,046	1,587	1,753	1,697	7.0	7.0	5.9	42.7	42.7	45.9	35.5	35.5	39.8	310.5	310.5	113.9
Guinea	Exp.	1,435	2,097	2,083	1,086	925	1,607	3.0	3.0	6.4	50.2	50.2	47.2	47.3	47.3	40.4	114.9	114.9	114.9
Guinea-Bissau	Exp.	595	720	760	512	528	692	2.1	2.1	2.1	58.8	58.8	58.8	56.0	56.0	56.0	138.6	138.6	138.6
Kenya	Exp.	878	1,219	1,081	632	814	818	3.4	3.4	5.0	62.2	62.2	50.2	57.7	57.7	44.6	159.8	159.8	159.8
Lesotho	Exp.	342	1,217	2,018	365	1,585	2,054	2.8	2.8	2.9	60.1	60.1	59.9	56.4	56.4	56.2	83.7	83.7	57.3
Liberia	Exp.	1,095	1,416	1,238	638	799	799										119.4	119.4	105.9
Madagascar	Exp.	1,703	1,314	913	1,454	1,174	796	5.0	5.0	5.4	52.4	52.4	52.1	46.8	46.8	46.0	51.4	51.4	51.4
Malawi	Inc.	481	750	650	427	525	535	5.8	5.8	5.8	53.2	53.2	53.2	46.5	46.5	46.5	45.3	45.3	44.2
Mali	Exp.	1,005	955	825	941	851	635	7.0	7.0	4.6	56.2	56.2	56.2	36.7	36.7	50.8	70.9	70.9	70.9
Mauritania	Exp.	1,657	1,933	1,732	519	1,126	1,345	3.5	3.5	6.4	46.3	46.3	44.0	42.4	42.4	37.4	141.4	141.4	141.4
Mauritius	Exp.	3,110	4,681	9,989	2,559	3,532	6,234	5.9	5.9	6.7	45.7	45.7	43.4	39.4	39.4	36.5	119.4	119.4	105.9
Mozambique	Exp.	985	789	986	1,192	776	811	6.5	6.5	6.5	46.5	46.5	46.5	39.5	39.5	39.5	94.5	94.5	94.5
Namibia	Exp.	5,069	8,224	6,020	2,897	3,637	3,879	1.5	1.5	1.5	78.2	78.2	78.2	75.1	75.1	75.1	101.8	101.8	101.8
Niger	Exp.	1,137	1,382	771	973	1,037	627	7.5	7.5	2.6	44.1	44.1	53.3	36.2	36.2	50.6	98.1	98.1	98.1
Nigeria	Exp.	513	1,185	964	464	669	628	6.0	6.0	4.4	45.1	45.1	55.6	39.1	39.1	50.4	95.5	95.5	107.5
Rwanda	Exp.	881	1,408	1,007	718	1,173	887	9.7	9.7	9.7	39.0	39.0	39.0	29.1	29.1	29.1	85.6	85.6	85.6
Senegal	Exp.	1,654	1,581	1,546	1,469	1,338	1,182	3.5	3.5	3.1	58.6	58.6	57.9	54.3	54.3	53.9	74.3	74.3	48.1

(table continues next page)

Table C.1 Basic SAP data on incomes and distribution, 1960-2000 (continued)

Region and economy	Survey type[a]	Per capita income			Per capita consumption			Share of 1st quintile			Share of 5th quintile			Gini			S/NA[b]		
		1960	1980	2000	1960	1980	2000	1960	1980	2000	1960	1980	2000	1960	1980	2000	1960	1980	2000
Sierra Leone	Exp.	771	1,097	497	601	982	427	1.1	1.1	1.1	63.4	63.4	63.4	62.8	62.8	62.8	126.1	126.1	126.1
Somalia	Exp.	1,684	1,136	1,174	1,455	1,105	913										119.4	119.4	105.9
South Africa	Exp.	7,838	12,627	9,977	5,401	6,857	6,243	2.9	2.9	2.9	64.7	64.7	64.7	60.7	60.7	60.7	68.2	68.2	68.2
Sudan	Inc.	1,663	1,322		1,298	1,084		5.6	5.6	5.6	48.1	48.1	48.1	42.4	42.4		76.2	77.7	57.7
Swaziland	Exp.	2,023	3,817	4,375	990	2,841	2,577	2.6	2.6	2.6	64.7	64.7	64.7	60.9	60.9	60.9	230.7	230.7	230.7
Tanzania	Exp.	356	536	563	278	393	485	2.4	2.4	6.8	62.9	62.9	45.5	59.5	59.5	38.4	197.6	197.6	197.6
Togo	Exp.	1,230	2,308	1,502	958	1,257	1,324										119.4	119.4	105.9
Tonga	Exp.			3,323			3,117										119.4	119.4	105.9
Uganda	Exp.	699	624	1,299	522	596	1,107	4.9	4.9	7.1	49.9	49.9	44.9	44.6	44.6	37.5	196.2	196.2	112.0
Zaire	Exp.	2,093	2,186	867	1,765	1,783	716										119.4	119.4	105.9
Zambia	Exp.	1,243	1,366	794	615	754	727	3.4	3.4	3.3	52.1	52.1	56.6	48.8	48.8	52.5	97.0	97.0	46.7
Zimbabwe	Exp.	2,277	2,810	3,016	1,669	1,903	2,234	4.0	4.0	4.0	62.3	62.3	62.3	57.3	57.3	57.3	92.1	92.1	92.1
Middle East and North Africa																			
Algeria	Exp.	3,992	6,280	5,505	2,475	2,709	2,824	6.5	6.5	7.0	47.2	47.2	42.6	40.2	40.2	35.5	112.0	112.0	92.3
Bahrain	Exp.	11,160	19,484	16,139	7,563	6,230	7,603										87.9	87.9	84.8
Cyprus	Inc.	3,860	10,517	21,015	2,450	6,976	13,381	8.2	8.2	8.2	38.6	38.6	38.6	30.3	30.3	30.3	69.0	69.0	59.1
Egypt	Exp.	1,144	2,656	3,876	806	1,837	2,926	8.7	8.7	6.7	41.1	41.1	46.5	32.1	32.1	39.4	92.8	92.8	75.5
Iran	Exp.	4,098	5,581	5,939	1,935	2,942	2,693										87.9	87.9	84.8
Iraq	Inc.	5,233	11,059	1,498	3,328	4,789	577	2.0	2.0	2.0	68.0	68.0	68.0	64.7	64.7	64.7	65.0	65.0	45.1
Israel	Inc.	6,812	15,444	21,471	4,638	8,202	12,141	6.9	6.9	6.9	42.5	42.5	42.5	35.6	35.6	35.6	65.8	65.8	52.9
Jordan	Exp.	1,632	5,075	4,302	1,628	4,000	3,470	5.8	5.8	7.6	51.0	51.0	44.4	44.7	44.7	36.4	84.5	84.5	84.5
Kuwait	Exp.	72,864	21,851	18,437	49,377	6,742	10,291										87.9	87.9	84.8
Lebanon	Inc.	5,357	7,920	5,060	3,630	3,807	4,973	3.0	3.0	3.0	61.0	61.0	61.0	56.3	56.3		65.0	65.0	45.1
Libya	Exp.	4,610	9,095	5,899	2,468	3,493	2,616										87.9	87.9	84.8
Malta	Exp.	2,205	7,893	17,811	1,568	5,104	11,371										87.9	87.9	84.8
Morocco	Exp.	1,478	3,261	3,688	1,138	2,216	2,443	6.6	6.6	6.5	46.1	46.1	46.8	39.0	39.0	39.9	91.5	91.5	104.6
Oman	Exp.	1,238	9,958	10,068	839	2,758	3,978										87.9	87.9	84.8
Qatar	Exp.	44,023	51,838	9,654	29,833	9,227	3,292										87.9	87.9	84.8
Saudi Arabia	Exp.	6,324	22,176	12,088	2,349	4,895	3,970										87.9	87.9	84.8
Syrian Arab Republic	Exp.	1,286	3,495	3,984	1,009	2,325	2,575										87.9	87.9	84.8
Tunisia	Exp.	2,167	4,741	6,637	1,290	2,918	4,015	5.7	5.7	5.7	49.0	49.0	47.9	42.7	42.7	41.9	74.4	74.4	92.8
Turkey	Exp.	2,744	4,913	7,205	2,278	3,786	5,031	5.9	5.9	5.8	50.0	50.0	47.6	43.5	43.5	41.4	72.0	72.0	58.8
United Arab Emirates	Exp.	47,259	50,070	19,979	32,025	8,647	11,304										87.9	87.9	84.8
West Bank and Gaza	Exp.	1,825	3,844	7,496	1,237	1,847	7,293										87.9	87.9	84.8
Yemen	Exp.	415	987	904	281	474	645	6.1	6.1	9.6	46.1	46.1	30.8	39.6	39.6	21.8	87.9	87.9	84.8

(table continues next page)

Central Asia

Country	Class																			
Central Asia																				
Kazakhstan	Inc.		5,521				3,950	9.5	9.5	6.1	35.2	35.2	43.1			36.9	31.3	31.3	31.3	31.3
Kyrgyz Republic	Exp.		2,822				2,191	4.3	4.3	10.7	48.7	48.7	34.3			23.6	66.7	66.7	66.7	97.5
Mongolia	Exp.	1,013	1,879				1,174	7.4	7.4	5.3	40.7	40.7	54.8			48.5	92.4	92.4	92.4	92.4
Uzbekistan	Inc.	1,831	2,470				1,841	10.6	10.6	7.4	35.6	35.6	40.9			33.5	74.9	74.9	74.9	52.0
Latin America																				
Antigua and Barbuda	Exp.		5,340	11,210	6,238	3,486	7,053									44.0	74.6	74.5	74.6	73.6
Argentina	Inc.	9,361	13,565	12,953	9,239	8,773	8,981	6.8	7.0	7.0	54.8	51.9	51.9	47.0	44.0	44.0	82.0	53.9	82.0	44.0
Bahamas	Inc.	12,461	18,339	16,475	5,239	11,315	10,488	2.9	4.2	3.5	50.6	46.8	46.8	47.2	42.4	43.4	73.9	71.2	73.9	70.6
Barbados	Inc.	5,784	14,308	15,612	1,739	8,939	9,832	3.6	2.3	6.3	51.6	50.9	47.5	48.6	48.6	40.6	109.8	109.8	109.8	109.8
Belize	Exp.	2,233	4,132	6,230	10,293	2,973	4,264									48.6	119.4	119.4	119.4	105.9
Bermuda	Exp.	13,884	30,841	27,470	1,378	21,789	19,301									56.1	74.6	74.5	74.6	73.6
Bolivia	Inc.	1,720	2,814	2,588	2,158	1,883	1,971	3.5	3.5	1.9	61.0	61.0	61.8	56.1	56.1	59.0	68.4	68.4	68.4	100.0
Brazil	Inc.	3,257	7,861	7,562	1,567	5,479	4,584	3.8	2.9	3.5	54.0	61.6	56.2	49.7	57.9	52.1	84.8	84.8	80.0	66.4
Cape Verde	Exp.	1,426	2,839	5,000	3,030	3,262	3,704									47.5	74.6	74.5	74.6	73.6
Chile	Inc.	3,994	5,324	9,725	2,369	3,764	6,157	4.5	4.3	3.4	51.4	52.3	61.9	46.4	47.5	57.5	70.0	70.0	70.0	53.1
Colombia	Inc.	3,275	5,434	6,281	3,272	3,817	4,245	2.2	3.1	3.0	68.0	58.8	60.9	64.5	54.8	56.9	73.0	44.7	73.0	62.1
Costa Rica	Inc.	4,255	7,399	8,878	3,062	4,850	5,635	6.2	2.8	4.5	55.0	55.0	50.9	48.7	51.6	46.0	39.1	39.1	39.1	54.8
Cuba	Exp.	4,130	3,547	2,861		2,506	2,010									46.0	74.6	74.5	74.6	73.6
Dominica	Exp.		2,949	6,554	1,570	2,725	5,079										74.6	74.5	74.6	73.6
Dominican Republic	Inc.	2,332	4,358	6,217	1,338	3,357	3,837	5.4	5.4	5.1	47.8	47.8	53.3	42.5	44.0	47.5	72.5	72.5	72.5	72.5
Ecuador	Exp.	1,728	3,781	3,222	2,906	2,254	2,000	4.4	4.4	5.4	48.9	48.9	49.7	44.0	44.0	43.9	76.6	76.6	76.6	70.3
El Salvador	Inc.	3,695	4,649	4,704		3,339	4,139	5.5	5.0	3.7	61.4	53.2	55.3	55.1	48.2	50.9	65.8	65.8	65.8	66.6
Grenada	Exp.		3,666	7,781	2,435	3,100	5,325									50.9	74.6	74.5	74.6	73.6
Guatemala	Inc.	2,901	4,422	4,117	1,913	3,490	3,455	2.8	2.8	3.8	61.9	61.9	60.6	58.1	58.1	55.8	66.5	66.5	66.5	86.5
Guyana	Inc.	2,792	4,079	3,997	2,314	2,259	2,571	4.3	4.3	4.3	46.5	46.5	56.1	42.0	42.0	50.9	106.2	106.2	106.2	106.2
Haiti	Exp.	2,615	2,843	1,603	1,549	2,327	1,497									42.0	74.6	74.5	74.6	73.6
Honduras	Inc.	2,020	2,988	2,688	1,930	2,103	1,881	1.6	1.6	1.6	65.3	65.3	61.7	62.7	62.7	59.3	85.8	85.8	85.8	75.1
Jamaica	Exp.	2,841	4,050	3,807	3,300	2,585	2,586	4.1	4.1	7.0	50.3	50.3	43.9	45.9	45.9	36.6	72.7	72.7	72.7	72.7
Mexico	Inc.	4,169	8,838	9,532	1,845	5,751	6,486	4.4	3.1	4.0	61.4	60.2	56.6	56.0	56.2	51.8	62.4	57.5	62.4	47.0
Nicaragua	Exp.	2,727	3,741	2,534	2,146	3,087	2,309	4.2	4.2	2.3	55.1	55.1	63.5	55.1	50.2	60.1	171.1	171.1	171.1	171.1
Panama	Inc.	2,841	5,986	6,367	1,944	3,106	3,846	4.9	4.2	2.3	56.7	52.4	59.8	50.4	47.9	56.7	95.1	95.1	95.1	93.1
Paraguay	Inc.	3,864	5,534	4,797	3,956	4,190	3,993	5.9	5.9	1.9	46.2	46.2	61.0	40.1	40.1	58.3	57.4	57.4	57.4	89.8
Peru	Exp.	4,737	6,025	5,079		3,463	3,587	4.9	4.9	4.9	51.4	51.4	50.4	46.0	46.0	45.1	94.1	94.1	94.1	48.7
Puerto Rico	Inc.		10,573	17,524		7,878	11,700	4.5	2.9	2.9	50.6	52.6	53.2	45.6	45.6		73.9	73.9	73.9	70.6
St. Lucia	Inc.		3,261	5,893		2,458	4,413	5.2	5.2	5.2	48.3	48.3	46.3			42.7	71.2	71.2	71.2	70.6
St. Kitts and Nevis	Exp.		4,610	12,646		3,282	9,575									42.7	74.6	74.5	74.6	73.6

Table C.1 Basic SAP data on incomes and distribution, 1960-2000 (continued)

Region and economy	Survey type[a]	Per capita income 1960	Per capita income 1980	Per capita income 2000	Per capita consumption 1960	Per capita consumption 1980	Per capita consumption 2000	Share of 1st quintile 1960	Share of 1st quintile 1980	Share of 1st quintile 2000	Share of 5th quintile 1960	Share of 5th quintile 1980	Share of 5th quintile 2000	Gini 1960	Gini 1980	Gini 2000	SNA[b] 1960	SNA[b] 1980	SNA[b] 2000
St. Vincent and the Grenadines	Exp.		2,867	5,932		2,552	3,658	10.7	10.7	10.7	42.4	42.4	42.4	31.6	31.6	31.6	74.6	74.5	73.6
Suriname	Inc.	3,283	4,081	3,526	1,811	2,354	1,309	3.4	2.7	5.5	48.6	49.4	46.0	45.3	46.4	40.4	73.9	71.2	70.6
Trinidad and Tobago	Inc.	4,473	8,854	9,255	2,704	4,061	5,749	5.4	5.4	5.4	48.3	48.3	48.3	42.5	42.5	42.5	38.6	38.6	38.6
Uruguay	Inc.	6,810	8,924	9,349	5,053	6,764	6,968	4.4	5.0	3.7	47.7	42.8	53.1	43.2	38.1	48.9	72.3	72.3	73.2
Venezuela	Inc.	7,205	7,846	6,173	3,977	4,305	3,915										64.3	64.3	51.3
Eastern Europe																			
Albania	Exp.	2,348	3,998	3,614	1,317	2,241	3,264	8.7	8.7	8.7	37.9	37.9	37.9	29.3	29.3	29.3	29.0	29.0	29.0
Armenia	Inc.	2,551	4,343	2,579	1,413	2,405	2,461	1.7	1.7	1.5	40.6	40.6	68.0	39.0	39.0	65.2	106.5	106.5	106.5
Azerbaijan	Inc.	4,777	8,132	3,491	2,585	4,400	2,287	6.9	6.9	6.9	43.2	43.2	43.2	36.1	36.1	36.1	70.2	70.2	70.2
Belarus	Inc.	4,864	8,281	7,596	2,632	4,480	4,331	10.5	10.5	8.5	33.0	33.0	37.2	22.6	22.6	28.7	52.5	52.5	37.9
Bosnia and Herzegovina	Exp.	2,853	4,858	3,779	1,609	2,739	2,644	10.8	9.9	8.5	33.6	33.0	41.7	22.6	23.5	33.0	77.3	77.3	70.3
Bulgaria	Inc.	3,331	5,670	5,567	1,575	2,681	4,018	8.7	8.7	8.7	38.1	38.1	38.1	29.3	29.3	29.3	54.4	54.4	46.4
Croatia	Exp.	5,191	8,838	9,149	2,928	4,984	5,229	8.2	11.4	10.2	35.1	32.1	36.4	27.0	20.8	26.0	127.5	127.5	127.5
Czech Republic	Inc.	5,784	13,462	13,827	3,431	6,288	7,380	10.0	10.0	7.0	32.7	32.7	45.1	23.0	23.0	37.8	43.3	43.3	41.6
Estonia	Inc.	5,728	9,751	9,332	3,172	5,401	5,496	8.2	6.4	3.7	45.7	40.8	47.2	36.5	34.7	37.3	57.9	57.9	56.9
Former Yugoslavia	Inc.	2,933	8,498	5,809	1,490	4,946	3,985	6.1	6.1	6.1	43.6	43.6	43.6	37.3	37.3		77.4	77.4	58.0
Georgia	Exp.	5,552	9,452	2,649	3,075	5,235	2,378	9.2	10.8	9.9	34.8	32.4	34.5	25.8	21.6	24.6	138.8	138.8	24.7
Hungary	Inc.	3,833	10,729	12,694	2,184	6,564	8,093	10.4	10.4	7.5	32.8	32.8	40.4	22.6	22.6	32.6	56.1	56.1	30.7
Latvia	Inc.	3,389	8,501	6,843	1,829	5,051	4,484	10.6	10.6	6.7	32.9	32.8	41.7	22.5	22.5	34.7	110.0	110.0	51.5
Lithuania	Inc.	5,184	8,826	7,295	2,805	4,776	4,694	10.0	10.0	5.6	34.1	32.9	46.8	24.2	24.2	40.9	34.1	34.1	36.8
Macedonia, FYR	Exp.	3,394	5,777	5,065	2,448	4,167	3,740	9.5	9.8	7.8	35.2	34.5	40.1	25.9	24.8	32.1	77.3	77.3	70.3
Moldova	Inc.		5,776	2,069	1,879	3,199	1,700	10.0	10.0	8.7	33.2	33.2	37.3	23.3	23.3	28.6	56.5	56.5	56.5
Poland	Inc.	4,143	8,809	9,275	2,545	5,932	6,028	9.5	9.5	6.7	34.0	34.0	42.4	24.7	24.7	35.9	43.9	43.9	50.4
Romania	Inc.	2,295	8,996	6,530	1,593	5,391	4,823	10.4	10.4	9.3	34.2	34.2	38.6	23.7	23.7	29.1	58.5	58.5	58.5
Russia	Inc.	4,605	11,721	8,422	2,230	4,962	4,428	10.1	10.1	9.1	36.1	36.1	37.7	25.9	25.9	28.5	431.1	431.1	50.1
Slovak Republic	Inc.	5,658	9,632	11,351	3,106	5,288	6,059	10.0	10.0	6.7	36.6	36.6		26.7	26.7	36.0	45.0	45.0	50.6
Slovenia	Inc.	8,864	15,090	17,614	4,999	8,510	9,673										54.5	54.5	135.9
Tajikistan	Exp.	2,052	3,493		1,119	1,904											77.3	77.3	70.3
Turkmenistan	Inc.	4,411	7,508	4,060	2,223	3,784	2,534										33.6	33.6	34.0
Ukraine	Exp.	5,191	8,838	3,730	2,809	4,782	2,140	4.6	4.6	8.8	48.9	48.9		44.0	44.0	29.0	156.2	156.2	112.3

Industrialized world

Country	Type[a]																			
Australia	Inc.	12,012	19,263	27,299	7,096	10,905	16,303	6.6	4.6	5.9	38.8	43.4	41.3	32.0	39.3	35.4	44.7	44.7	45.3
Austria	Inc.	10,385	20,902	27,309	6,180	11,825	15,402	6.8	6.6	10.4	36.6	38.3	33.4	29.7	31.5	23.1	58.2	58.2	34.3
Belgium	Inc.	11,076	22,315	28,123	6,325	11,664	15,074	7.9	7.9	9.5	36.1	36.1	34.5	28.3	28.3	25.0	42.8	42.8	42.3
Canada	Inc.	12,148	23,065	29,140	7,375	12,326	16,859	6.6	6.4	7.5	38.9	37.9	39.4	32.2	31.0	31.8	58.4	58.4	57.1
Denmark	Inc.	13,309	21,940	28,531	7,886	11,782	13,641	5.0	7.0	6.4	41.2	38.0	39.5	36.4	31.4	33.5	55.4	55.4	50.9
Finland	Inc.	8,999	18,232	25,866	5,213	9,531	13,138	2.4	6.6	10.6	49.3	40.0	33.6	46.9	32.9	23.0	51.6	51.6	58.0
France	Inc.	10,068	19,819	25,123	5,772	11,067	13,765	1.9	8.3	7.2	53.7	38.5	40.2	51.4	30.0	32.9	42.3	42.3	52.5
Germany	Inc.	10,552	19,144	25,901	5,981	11,637	14,956	10.5	6.6	8.2	37.7	39.0	38.4	27.3	32.1	30.1	52.1	52.1	52.1
Greece	Exp.	4,801	13,586	16,900	3,281	8,242	11,792	6.4	6.4	6.2	41.7	41.7	41.2	35.3	35.3	35.2	101.7	101.7	78.4
Iceland	Exp.	10,762	24,041	30,689	6,901	13,856	18,383												
Ireland	Inc.	5,465	11,418	29,623	4,034	7,791	14,509	4.8	4.9	6.7	42.2	43.6	42.9	37.6	38.9	36.0	47.2	47.2	32.6
Italy	Inc.	8,633	18,669	24,242	4,538	10,866	14,435	7.0	7.9	8.7	42.0	39.1	36.3	34.9	31.2	27.6	47.9	47.9	46.8
Japan	Inc.	5,835	19,279	25,990	3,424	11,344	15,889	5.3	6.3	10.6	45.1	39.6	35.6	39.6	33.5	24.9	53.2	53.2	54.7
Luxembourg	Inc.	14,162	19,684	48,257	7,418	12,459	21,790	10.2	10.2	9.4	34.0	34.0	36.5	23.9	23.9	27.1	43.6	43.6	44.0
Netherlands	Inc.	10,962	20,044	27,709	4,794	9,401	13,888	4.0	8.4	7.3	48.4	36.7	40.0	43.8	28.2	32.6	40.9	40.9	52.1
New Zealand	Inc.	12,949	16,753	20,601	8,336	10,543	13,389	6.8	6.0	4.6	37.0	40.6	44.7	30.3	34.8	40.1	76.8	76.8	92.3
Norway	Inc.	9,990	21,592	30,927	5,188	10,110	13,449	4.5	9.7	9.7	40.5	32.8	35.9	35.9	23.0	26.1	57.6	57.6	54.1
Portugal	Exp.	4,115	11,440	18,202	3,069	7,333	11,712	5.8	5.5	7.3	46.3	42.5	43.4	40.2	37.0	35.8	33.3	33.3	53.6
Spain	Inc.	5,652	13,532	19,921	3,321	7,732	11,844	8.2	8.2	10.2	35.1	35.1	33.1	27.0	27.0	23.1	45.9	45.9	45.9
Sweden	Inc.	12,322	20,214	24,929	6,625	9,902	12,576	4.4	7.0	9.6	44.0	39.5	34.6	34.6	32.7	25.1	45.4	45.4	54.8
Switzerland	Inc.	19,175	28,383	29,684	11,166	17,690	18,191	5.9	5.9	6.9	43.9	43.9	40.2	37.4	37.4	33.1	80.5	80.5	60.1
United Kingdom	Inc.	11,976	17,494	23,968	7,862	10,248	15,773	9.4	10.2	6.6	36.9	37.6	42.9	27.7	27.4	36.2	55.5	55.5	58.5
United States	Inc.	16,469	25,399	35,427	10,475	16,132	23,770	4.8	4.3	3.6	41.3	43.6	49.4	36.3	39.7	45.7	53.9	48.5	41.5

FYR = Former Yugoslav Republic

a. There are two types of surveys; exp = expenditure surveys, and inc = income surveys.

b. The S/NA ratio is the ratio of the mean consumption (surveys, S) to mean consumption (national accounts, NA). For countries for which no survey data are available (e.g., Afghanistan), the S/NA ratios reported are the regional means.

Note: Income and consumption are annual per capita levels in purchasing power parity dollars, 1993 prices. The survey type shows whether majority of the surveys have been income or expenditure survey and the reported quintile shares, Gini, and S/NA ratio (see note a.) are either for income or consumption, depending on the survey type.

In many cases, income distribution data are not available for 1960, 1980, or 2000. In such cases, the table presents data for either the closest earlier year for which data are available, or, where earlier data are not available, data for the earliest later year. For example, if the latest survey took place in 1995, the 2000 figures reflect these values; if the first survey took place in 1975, the 1960 figures reflect those values.

References

Adelman, Irma, and Cynthia Taft Morris, eds. 1973. *Economic Growth and Social Equity in Developing Countries.* Stanford, CA: Stanford University Press.

Ahluwalia, Montek S. 1974. Dimensions of the Problem. In *Redistribution with Growth*, ed. Hollis B. Chenery et al. New York: Oxford University Press.

Ahluwalia, Montek S. 1976. Inequality, Poverty, and Development. *Journal of Development Economics* 3 (September): 307-4.

Ahluwalia, Montek S. 1977. Rural Poverty and Agricultural Performance in India. *Journal of Development Studies* 22: 298-323.

Ahluwalia, Montek S., N. Carter, and H. Chenery. 1979. Growth and Poverty in Developing Countries. *Journal of Development Economics* 6, no. 3: 399-441.

Altimir, Oscar. 1981. Poverty in Latin America: A Review of Concepts and Data. *CEPAL Review* no. 13 (April).

Anand, Sudhir, and S.M.R. Kanbur. 1993b. The Kuznets Process and the Inequality-Development Relationship. *Journal of Development Economics* 41, no. 40: 25-52.

Andic, S., and A. Peacock. 1961. The International Distribution of Income. *Journal of the Royal Statistical Society* (series A) 124: 206-18.

Asian Development Bank. 2002. Asian Drama Re-Visited: Policy Implications for the Poor. Report prepared for research project RETA-5917 by a team led by Surjit S. Bhalla. Asian Development Bank, Manila. Photocopy (July).

Atkinson, A.B. 1970. On Measurement of Inequality. *Journal of Economic Theory* 2: 244-63.

Atkinson, A.B. 1975. *The Economics of Inequality.* Oxford: Oxford University Press.

Atkinson, A.B. 1999. Is Rising Income Inequality Inevitable? A Critique of the Transatlantic Consensus. World Institute for Development Economics Research publication. Tokyo: United Nations University.

Atkinson, A.B., and A. Brandolini. 1999. Promise and Pitfalls in the Use of Secondary Data Sets: Income Inequality in OECD Countries. Nuffield College and Banca d'Italia Research Department, Oxford and Rome. Photocopy (July).

Banerjee, Abhijit V., and Esther Duflo. 2000. Inequality and Growth: What Can the Data Say? Massachusetts Institute of Technology, Cambridge. Photocopy (June).

Bardhan, Pranab K. 1974. On the Incidence of Poverty in Rural India in the Sixties. In *Poverty and Income Distribution in India*, ed. Pranab K. Bardhan and T.N. Srinivasan. Calcutta: Statistical Publishing Society.

Bardhan, Pranab K., and T.N. Srinivasan, eds. 1974. *Poverty and Income Distribution in India.* Calcutta: Statistical Publishing Society.

Barro, Robert J. 1999. Inequality and Growth in a Panel of Countries. Harvard University, Cambridge, MA. Photocopy (June).

Barro, Robert, and Jong Wha Lee. 2001. International Data on Educational Attainment: Updates and Implications. NBER Working Paper 7911. Cambridge, MA: National Bureau of Economic Research.

Baumol, W.J., R.R. Nelson, and E.N. Wolff. 1994. The Convergence of Productivity, Its Significance, and Its Varied Connotations. In *Convergence of Productivity*, ed. W.J. Baumol, R.R. Nelson, and E.N. Wolff. Oxford: Oxford University Press.

Beck, Ulrich. 2000. *What Is Globalization?* Translated by Patrick Camiller. Bodmin, UK: MPG Books.

Benabou, Roland. 1996. Inequality and Growth. In *National Bureau of Economic Research Macroeconomics Annual*, ed. Ben Bernanke and Julio Rotemberg. Cambridge, MA: MIT Press.

Bergsman, Joel. 1980. *Income Distribution and Poverty in Mexico*. World Bank Staff Working Paper 395. Washington: World Bank.

Berry, Albert, François Bourguignon, and Christian Morrisson. 1981. Changes in the World Distribution of Income between 1950 and 1977. *Economic Journal*, series 93 (June): 331-50.

Berry, Albert, François Bourguignon, and Christian Morrisson. 1983. The Level of World Inequality: How Much Can One Say? *Review of Income & Wealth* 29, no. 3: 217-41.

Bery, Suman, and Rajesh Shukla. 2002. Updated poverty estimates from market information survey of households. Paper presented at a World Bank workshop on Poverty Monitoring and Evaluation, New Delhi, January 11.

Beteille, Andre, ed. 1969. *Social Inequality*, Penguin Modern Sociology Readings.

Bhagwati, Jagdish N. 1988. Poverty and Public Policy. *World Development* 16, no. 5: 539-55.

Bhalla, Surjit S. 1971. Theories of Distributive Justice. Princeton University, Princeton, NJ. Photocopy (November).

Bhalla, Surjit S. 1980. Measurement of Poverty—Issues and Methods. Background paper for World Development Report 1980. World Bank, Washington. Photocopy (March).

Bhalla, Surjit S. 1987. *Between the Wickets: The Who and Why of the Best in Cricket*. New Delhi: Living Media.

Bhalla, Surjit S. 1988. Is Sri Lanka an Exception? A Comparative Study of Living Standards, August 1984. In *Rural Poverty in South Asia*, ed. T.N. Srinivasan and P. Bardhan. New York: Columbia University Press.

Bhalla, Surjit S. 1997a. Freedom and Economic Growth: A Virtuous Cycle? In *Democracy's Victory and Crisis*, ed. Axel Hadenius. Cambridge, UK: Cambridge University Press.

Bhalla, Surjit S. 1997b. Re-interpretation of the Evidence on Poverty in India & Impact of Economic Reforms. Research proposal submitted to the National Council of Applied Economic Research, New Delhi. Photocopy (May 30).

Bhalla, Surjit S. 1999. Hayek Rediscovered the Road to Economic Freedom. Paper presented at University of Michigan Conference on Economic Freedom, Tokyo (June 17).

Bhalla, Surjit S. 2000a. FAQs on Poverty in India. Paper presented at the Delhi School of Economics (July 20).

Bhalla, Surjit S. 2000b. Growth and Poverty in India—Myth and Reality. In *Poverty and Public Policy: Essays in Honour of Raja Chelliah*, ed. Govinda Rao. Oxford: Oxford University Press.

Bhalla, Surjit S., ed. 2000c. *New Economic Policies for a New India*. Indian Council of Social Science Research. New Delhi: Har-Anand Publications.

Bhalla, Surjit S. 2000d. Trends in World Poverty: Research and Ideology. Paper presented at the International Monetary Fund, Washington (June 28).

Bhalla, Surjit S. 2001a. How to Over-Estimate Poverty: Detailed Examination of the NSS 1993 Data. Paper presented for the 50th Anniversary of the National Sample Survey (May 8).

Bhalla, Surjit S. 2001b. Imagine There's No Country: Globalisation and its Consequences for Poverty, Inequality and Growth. Draft presented at the Rajiv Gandhi Foundation, New Delhi, January.

Bhalla, Surjit S. 2001c. Indian Poverty—Ideology and Evidence. *India 2000—A Symposium on the Year That Was*, no. 497 (January).

Bhalla, Surjit S. 2001d. Poverty and Inequality in a Globalizing World: Case Study for India. Paper prepared for the Indian Council for Research on International Economic Relations, New Delhi (December 24).

Bhalla, Surjit S. 2001e. World Poverty at 13 Percent: Time to Raise the Poverty Line. Presentation for Asian Development Bank, Manila (August 1).

Bhalla, Surjit S. 2002a. Recounting the Poor. Paper presented at a World Bank workshop on Poverty Monitoring and Evaluation, New Delhi, January 11.

Bhalla, Surjit S. 2002b. Unintended Consequences of Monopoly Funding of Research. Photocopy (May).

Bhalla, Surjit S. 2002c. Report on research project entitled "The Myth and Reality of Poverty in India." Planning Commission, Government of India. Forthcoming.

Bhalla, Surjit S., and Paul Glewwe. 1985. Living Standards in Sri Lanka in the Seventies: Mirage and Reality. Paper prepared for Central Bank, Sri Lanka Project on the Evolution of Living Standards in Sri Lanka, Colombo (May).

Bhalla, Surjit S., and Paul Glewwe. 1986. Growth and Equity in Developing Countries: A Reinterpretation of the Sri Lankan Experience. *World Bank Economic Review* 1, no. 1 (September) 35-65.

Bhalla, Surjit S., and Ravinder Kaur. 1999. Poverty in India: Towards New Policies. In *Poverty in India*, ed. S. Gangopadhyay. New Delhi: Rajiv Gandhi Foundation.

Bhalla, Surjit S., and Homi Kharas. 1991. Growth and Equity in Malaysia: Policies and Consequences. In *Malaysia's Economic Vision*. Kuala Lumpur.

Bhalla, Surjit S., and Mark Leiserson. 1982. Issues in the Measurement and Analysis of Income Distribution in Developing Countries: Some Comparative Perspectives. World Bank, Washington. Photocopy (July).

Bhalla, Surjit S., and P. Vashishtha. 1988. Income Redistribution in India: A Re-Examination. In *Rural Poverty in South Asia*, ed. T.N. Srinivasan and P. Bardhan. New York: Columbia University Press, 1988.

Bigsten, Arne, and Jorgen Levin. 2001. Growth, Income Distribution, and Poverty: A Review. Paper presented at a conference on growth and poverty sponsored by the United Nations University and the World Institute for Development Economics Research, Helsinki (May 25-26).

Birdsall, Nancy. 1998. Life Is Unfair: Inequality in the World. *Foreign Policy* 95 (summer): 76-93.

Birdsall, Nancy. 2001. Asymmetric Globalization: Outcomes versus Opportunities. Carnegie Endowment for International Peace, Washington. Photocopy (September).

Birdsall, Nancy, Carol Graham, and Richard H. Sabot. 2000. Stuck in the Tunnel: Is Globalization Muddling the Middle Class? Working Paper 14. Washington: Center on Social and Economic Dynamics.

Birdsall, Nancy, David Ross, and Richard H. Sabot. 1995. Inequality and Growth Reconsidered: Lessons from East Asia. *World Bank Economic Review* 9, no. 3: 477-508.

Bourguignon, François, and Christian Morrisson. 2001. Inequality among World Citizens: 1820-1992. World Bank, Washington. Photocopy (February).

Burtless, Gary, and Timothy Smeeding. 2000. The Level, Trend, and Composition of American Poverty: National and International Perspective. Paper presented at a seminar, Understanding Poverty in America: Progress and Problems, Madison, WI (May 22-23).

Castles, Ian. 2000. Mr. Castles Room Document. In *Report of the Friends of the Chair of the Statistical Commission,* United Nations, December.

Chen, Shaohua, Gaurav Datt, and Martin Ravallion. 1994. Is Poverty Increasing in the Developing World? *Review of Income and Wealth* 40, no. 4 (December): 359-76.

Chen, Shaohua, and Martin Ravallion. 2000. How Did the World's Poorest Fare in the 1990s? Development Research Group, World Bank, Washington. Photocopy.

Chenery, Hollis, et al., eds. 1974. *Redistribution with Growth.* New York: Oxford University Press.

Chenery, Hollis, and Moises Syrquin. 1975. *Patterns of Development, 1950-1970.* New York: Oxford University Press.

Chenery, Hollis. 1979. *Structural Change and Development Policy.* World Bank: Oxford University Press.

Cline, William R. 1975. Distribution and Development: A Survey of the Literature. *Journal of Development Economics* 1, no. 4: 359-400.

Collier, Paul, and David Dollar. 2000. Can the World Cut Poverty in Half? How Policy Reform and Effective Aid Can Meet International Development Goals. Development Research Group, World Bank, Washington. Photocopy (July).

Cornia, Giovanni Andrea, and Sampsa Kiiski. 2001. Trends in Income Distribution in the Post-WWII Period: Evidence and Interpretation. Paper presented at a conference on growth and poverty sponsored by the United Nations University and World Institute for Development Economics Research, Helsinki (May 25-26).

Dahrendorf, R. 1968. On the Origin of Inequality among Men. In *Essays on the Theory of Society,* ed. R. Dahrendorf. Stanford, CA: Stanford University Press.

Dasgupta, Partho. 1993. *An Inquiry into Well-being and Distribution.* New York: Oxford University Press.

Deaton, Angus. 1998. *The Analysis of Household Surveys: A Microeconometric Approach to Development Policy.* Baltimore: Johns Hopkins University Press.

Deaton, Angus. 2001a. Counting the World's Poor: Problems and Possible Solutions. Princeton University, Princeton, NJ. Photocopy (August).

Deaton, Angus. 2001b. Adjusted Indian Poverty Estimates for 1999-2000. Research Program in Development Studies, Princeton University, Princeton, NJ. Photocopy (November).

Deaton, Angus. 2001c. Computing Prices and Poverty Rates in India, 1999-2000. Research Program in Development Studies, Princeton University, Princeton, NJ. Photocopy (December).

Deaton, Angus, and A. Tarozzi. 1999. Prices and Poverty in India. Princeton University, Princeton, NJ. Photocopy (December 13).

Deininger, Klaus, and Lyn Squire. 1996. A New Data Set Measuring Income Inequality. *World Bank Economic Review* 10, no. 3 (September): 565-92.

Deininger, Klaus, and Lyn Squire. 1998. New Ways of Looking at Old Issues: Inequality and Growth. *Journal of Development Economics* 57, no. 2: 259-87.

DeLong, Bradford. 2001. The World's Income Distribution: Turning the Corner? http://www.J-bradford-delong.ne/.

Dikhanov, Yuri, and Michael Ward. 2000. Measuring the Distribution of Global Income. World Bank, Washington. Photocopy.

Dollar, David, and Aart Kraay. 2000. Growth Is Good for the Poor. World Bank, Washington. Photocopy (March).

Dollar, David, and Aart Kraay. 2001, Trade, Growth, and Poverty. World Bank, Washington. Photocopy (March).

Douglas, Roger. 1990. The Politics of Successful Structural Reforms. *Policy* 6, no. 1 (autumn): 235-51.

Dowrick, Steve, and Akmal Muhammad. 2001. Contradictory Trends in Global Income Inequality: A Tale of Two Biases. Australian National University, Canberra. Photocopy (March).

Dubey, A., and S. Gangopadhyay. 1998. *Counting the Poor: Where Are the Poor in India?* Sarvekshana Analytical Report 1. New Delhi: Department of Statistics, Government of India.

Eastwood, Robert, and Michael Lipton. 2001. Pro-Poor Growth and Pro-Growth Poverty Reduction. Paper presented at an Asia and Pacific forum on poverty: Reforming policies and institutions for poverty reduction, sponsored by the Asian Development Bank, Manila (February 5-9).

FAO (Food and Agriculture Organization). 1973. Energy and Protein Requirements. Report of a Joint FAO/WHO/Ad Hoc Expert Committee. Rome: FAO.

Fields, Gary S. 1980. *Poverty, Inequality, and Development.* Cambridge, UK: Cambridge University Press.

Fields, Gary S. 1989. Changes in Poverty and Inequality in Developing Countries. *World Bank Research Observer* 4, no. 2 (July) 167-86.

Fields, Gary S. 1993. Poverty and Income Distribution Data for Measuring Poverty and Inequality Changes in the Developing Countries. *Journal of Development Economics* 44: 87-102.

Firebaugh, Glenn. 1999. Empirics of World Income Inequality. *American Journal of Sociology* 104, no. 6 (May): 1597-1630.

Fisher, Gordon M. 1992. The Development and History of the Poverty Thresholds. *Social Security Bulletin* 55, no. 4: 3-14.

Fisher, Gordon M. 1996a. Is There Such a Thing as an Absolute Poverty Line over Time? Evidence from the United States, Britain, Canada, and Australia on the Income Elasticity of the Poverty Line. US Department of Health and Human Services, Washington. Photocopy (August).

Fisher, Gordon M. 1996b. Relative or Absolute: New Light on the Behavior of Poverty Lines over Time. *American Statistical Association* (summer): 10-12.

Fisher, Gordon M. 1997. From Hunter to Orshansky: An Overview of (Unofficial) Poverty Lines in the United States from 1904 to 1965. US Department of Health and Human Services, Washington. Photocopy (August).

Fishlow, A. 1972. Brazilian Size Distribution of Income. *Papers and Proceedings of the American Economics Association* 62 (May): 391-402.

Forster, Michael, and Mark Pearson. 2000. Income Distribution in OECD Countries. Paper presented at an OECD conference on poverty and inequality in developing countries: a policy discussion on the effects of globalisation, Paris (November 30-December 1).

Foster, James E. 1998. What Is Poverty and Who Are the Poor? Redefinition for the United States in the 1990s. *American Review* 88, no. 2 (May): 335-41.

Fox, Louis M. 1983. Income Distribution in Post-1964 Brazil. *Journal of Economic History* 43, no. 1 (March): 261-71.

Friedman, Thomas L. 1999. *The Lexus and the Olive Tree.* New York: Farrar, Straus and Giroux.

Gallup, John L., Steven Radelet, and Andrew Warner. 1998. Economic Growth and the Income of the Poor. Harvard Institute for International Development, Cambridge, MA. Photocopy (November).

Gangopadhyay, S., and W. Wadhwa. 2000. Poverty Policy: Old Wine in an Old Bottle. In *New Economic Policies for a New India,* ed. S.S. Bhalla. New Delhi: Hari Haran Press.

Gastwirth, Joseph L. 1971. A General Definition of the Lorenz Curve. *Econometrica* 39, no. 6 (November): 1037-39.

Ginneken, Wouter Van. 1980. Generating Internationally Comparable Income Distribution Data: Evidence from the Federal Republic of Germany (1974), Mexico (1968), and the United Kingdom (1979). *Review of Income and Wealth* 26, no. 4: 365-77.

Goodman, Alissa, and Steven Webb. 1994. For Richer, for Poorer: The Changing Distribution of Income in the UK, 1961-91. Institute for Fiscal Studies, London. Photocopy.

Goodman, Alissa, and Steven Webb. 1996. For Richer, for Poorer: The Changing Distribution of Income in the UK, 1979-92. Institute for Fiscal Studies, London. Photocopy.

Government of India. 1993. *Report of the Expert Group on Estimation of Proportion and Number of Poor.* New Delhi: Planning Division, Planning Commission, Government of India.

Grosh, Margaret, and E. Nafziger. 1986. The Computation of World Income Distribution. *Economic Development and Cultural Change* 34 (January): 347-59.

Harding, Ann. 2001. Trends in Income Inequality in the 1990s. Paper presented at a Business Council of Australia seminar on future directions, Canberra, August 13.

Hayek, F.A. von. 1976. *The Road to Serfdom.* Chicago: University of Chicago Press.

Heston, Alan, and Robert Summers. 1991. The Penn World Table (Mark 5): An Expanded Set of International Comparisons, 1950-1988. *Quarterly Journal of Economics* (May): 327-68.

Himmelfarb, Gertrude. 1984. *The Idea of Poverty: England in the Early Industrial Age.* London: Faber & Faber.

IMF (International Monetary Fund). 2000. Globalization: Threat or Opportunity. http://www.imf.org/external/np/exr/ib/2000/041200.htm, April 12.

Jain, S. 1975. *Size Distribution of Income: A Compilation of Data.* Washington: World Bank.

Kakwani, Nanak. 1980. *Income Inequality and Poverty: Methods of Estimation and Policy Applications.* Oxford: Oxford University Press.

Kakwani, Nanak. 1997. On Measuring Growth and Inequality Components of Changes in Poverty with Application to Thailand. University of New South Wales Working Paper no. 9 716.

Kakwani, Nanak, and Ernesto M. Pernia 2000. What Is Pro-poor Growth? *Asian Development Review* 18, no. 1: 1-16.

Kanbur, Ravi. 1996. Income Distribution and Development. Cornell University, Ithaca, NY. Photocopy.

Kanbur, Ravi, and Lyn Squire. 1999. The Evolution of Thinking about Poverty: Exploring the Interactions. Cornell University, Ithaca, NY. Photocopy (September).

Katz, B. Michael. 1989. *The Undeserving Poor.* New York: Pantheon Books.

Knowles, Stephen. 2001. Inequality and Economic Growth: The Empirical Relationship Reconsidered in the Light of Comparable Data. Paper presented at a conference sponsored by the United Nations University and World Institute for Development Economics Research on growth and poverty, Helsinki (May 25-26).

Kohl, Richard, and Kevin O'Rourke. 2000. What's New About Globalisation: Implications for Income Inequality in Developing Countries. Paper presented at an OECD conference on poverty and inequality in developing countries: A policy discussion on the effects of globalisation, Paris (November 30-December 1).

Korzeniewicz, Roberto P., and Timothy Patrick Moran. 1997. World-Economic Trends in the Distribution of Income, 1965-1992. *American Journal of Sociology* 102, no. 4 (January): 1000-39.

Kravis, Irving B. 1960. International Differences in the Distribution of Income. *Review of Economics and Statistics* (November): 408-16.

Kravis, Irving B., et al. 1975. A *System of International Comparison of Gross Product and Purchasing Power.* Baltimore: Johns Hopkins University Press.

Kravis, Irving B., Alan Heston, and Robert Summers. 1978. Real GDP per Capita for More than One Hundred Countries. *Economic Journal* 88 (June): 215-42.

Kravis, Irving B., Alan Heston, and Robert Summers. 1982. *World Product and Income.* United Nations International Comparison Project: Phase Three. New York: United Nations.

Kravis, Irving B., Zoltan Kenessey, Alan Heston, and Robert Summers. 1975. A *System of International Comparisons of Gross Product and Purchasing Power.* United Nations International Comparison Project: Phase One. New York: United Nations.

Kuhn, Thomas S. 1962. *The Structure of Scientific Revolutions*. Chicago: University of Chicago Press.

Kuznets, Simon. 1955. Economic Growth and Income Inequality. *American Economic Review* 45, no. 1 (March): 1-28.

Kuznets, Simon. 1963. Quantitative Aspects of the Economic Growth of Nations: VIII, Distribution of Income by Size. *Economic Development and Cultural Change*, part 2, 11, no. 2 (January): 1-80.

Lakdawala, D.T. 1977. Growth, Unemployment, and Poverty. Paper presented at an all-India labor economics conference, Tirupati (December 31).

Lal, Deepak. 1983. *The Poverty of Development Economics*. London: IEA.

Lal, Deepak, and H. Myint. 1996. *The Political Economy of Poverty, Equity and Growth*. Oxford: Oxford University Press.

Lewis, W. Arthur. 1954. Economic Development with Unlimited Supplies of Labour. *The Manchester School* 22: 3-42.

Li, Hongyi, Lyn Squire, and Heng-fu Zou. 1998. Explaining International and Intertemporal Variations in Income Inequality. *Economic Journal* 108 (January): 26-43.

Londono, Juan Luis, and Miguel Szekely. 2000. Persistent Poverty and Excess Inequality: Latin America, 1970-1995. *Journal of Applied Economics* 3, no. 1 (May): 93-134.

Lundberg, Mattias, and Lyn Squire. 1999. *The Simultaneous Evolution of Growth and Inequality*. World Bank Working Paper. Washington: World Bank.

Lustig, Nora. 1990. Poverty and Income Distribution in Latin America in the 1980s: Selected Evidence and Policy Alternatives. Brookings Institution, Washington. Photocopy (June).

Maddison, Angus. 2001. *The World Economy: A Millennial Perspective*. Paris: Development Center of the Organization for Economic Cooperation and Development.

Melchior, Arne, Kjetil Telle, and Henrik Wiig. 2000. Globalisation and Inequality: World Income Distribution and Living Standards, 1960-1998. Norwegian Institute of International Affairs, Oslo. Photocopy (October).

Milanovic, Branko. 1999. True World Income Distribution, 1988 and 1993: First calculations Based on Household Survey Alone. Development Research Group, World Bank, Washington. Photocopy (October).

Milanovic, Branko, and Shlomo Yitzhaki. 2001. Does the World Have a Middle Class? Decomposing World Income Distribution. Development Research Group, World Bank, Washington. Photocopy (February).

Minhas, B.S. 1974. Rural Poverty, Land Redistribution and Development Strategy: Facts. In *Poverty and Income Distribution in India*, ed. Pranab K. Bardhan and T.N. Srinivasan. Calcutta: Statistical Publishing Society.

Minhas, B.S. 1988. Validation of Large-Scale Sample Survey Data: Case of NSS Estimates of Household Consumption Expenditure. *Sankhya: The Indian Journal of Statistics* 50, series B, part 3: 279-326.

Minhas, B.S., S.M. Kansal, Jagdish Kumar, and P.D. Joshi. 1986. On the Reliability of the Available Estimates of Private Consumption Expenditure in India. *Journal of Income and Wealth* 9, no. 2 (July).

Orshansky, Mollie. 1965. Counting the Poor. *Social Security Bulletin* 28, no. 1 (January): 3-29.

Paukert, F. 1973. Income Distribution at Different Levels of Development: A Survey of Evidence. *International Labour Review* 108 (August-September): 97-125.

Persson, Torsten, and Guido Tabellini. 1994. Is Inequality Harmful for Growth? *American Economic Review* 84, no. 3 (June): 600-20.

Pfeffermann, Guy, and Richard Webb. 1983. Poverty and Income Distribution in Brazil. *Review of Income and Wealth* 29, no. 2: 101-24.

Plotnick, R.D., E. Smolensky, E. Evenhouse, and S. Reilly. 1998. The Twentieth-Century Record of Inequality and Poverty in the United States. Institute for Business and Economic Research & Public Policy, Berkeley, CA. Photocopy (July).

Pritchett, Lant. 1997. Divergence, Big Time. *Journal of Economic Perspectives* 11 (3): 3-17.

Pritchett, Lant. 2001. Divergence, Big Time. World Bank, Washington. Photocopy (July 7).

Quibria M.G. 2002. *Growth and Poverty: Lessons from the East Asian Miracle Revisited*. ADB Institute Research Paper 33. Manila: Asian Development Bank.

Ram, Rati. 1989. Level of Development and Income Inequality: An Extension of Kuznets' Hypothesis to the World Economy. *Kyklos* 42, no. 1: 73-88.

Rao, D.C. 1978. Economic Growth and Equity in the Republic of Korea. *World Development* 6, no. 3: 383-96.

Rath, Nilakantha. 1996. Poverty in India Revisited. *Indian Journal of Agricultural Economics* 51, nos. 1 & 2 (January-June): 74-108.

Ravallion, Martin. 2001a. Growth, Inequality and Poverty: Looking beyond Averages. Development Research Group, World Bank, Washington. Photocopy (June 3).

Ravallion, Martin. 2001b. Inequality Convergence. World Bank, Washington. Photocopy (July 17).

Ravallion, Martin, and Shaohua Chen. 1996. What Can New Survey Data Tell Us about Recent Changes in Distribution and Poverty? World Bank, Policy research working paper 1694, December.

Ravallion, Martin, and Gaurav Datt. 1991. *Growth and Redistribution Components of Changes in Poverty Measures: A Decomposition with Applications to Brazil and India in the 1980s*. LSMS Working Paper 83. Washington: World Bank.

Ravallion, Martin, and Gaurav Datt. 1996. How Important to India's Poor Is the Sectoral Composition of Economic Growth? *World Bank Economic Review* 10, no. 1 (January): 1-25.

Ravallion, Martin, and Gaurav Datt. 1999. When Is Growth Pro-Poor? Evidence from the Diverse Experiences of India's States. Paper presented at the World Bank's poverty reduction and economic management week, Washington (July).

Ravallion, Martin, Gaurav Datt, and Dominique van de Walle. 1991. Quantifying Absolute Poverty in the Developing World. *Review of Income and Wealth* 37, no. 4 (December): 345-61.

Ravallion, Martin, and Michael Lipton. 1993. *Poverty and Policy*. World Bank Policy Research Working Paper 1130. Washington: World Bank.

Rawls, John. 1958. Justice as Fairness. *Philosophical Review* 67.

Rawls, John. 1971. *A Theory of Justice*. Cambridge, MA: Harvard University Press.

Reddy, G. Sanjay, and Thomas W. Pogge. 2002. How Not to Count the Poor. http://www.socialanalysis.org.

Renaud, Bertrand. 1976. *Economic Growth and Income Inequality in Korea*. World Bank Staff Working Paper 240. Washington: World Bank.

Report of the Friends of the Chair of the Statistical Commission. 2000. An Assessment of the Statistical Criticism Made of *Human Development Report 1999*. New York, United Nations. Photocopy (December 1).

Reutlinger, S., and M. Selowsky. 1976. *Malnutrition and Poverty*. Baltimore: Johns Hopkins University Press.

Riskin, Carl, ed. 1999. *Income Distribution in China*. Draft Technical Assistance Report for the Asian Development Bank. Manila: Asian Development Bank.

Robinson, Sherman. 1976. A Note on the U Hypothesis Relating Income Inequality and Economic Development. *American Economic Review* 66, no. 3 (June): 437-40.

Rock, Michael T. 1993. Twenty-five Years of Economic Development Revisited. *World Development* 21, no. 11: 1787-1801.

Rodrik, Dani. 1997. *Has Globalization Gone Too Far?* Washington: Institute for International Economics.

Rodrik, Dani. 1998. Where Did All the Growth Go? External Shocks, Social Conflict, and Growth Collapses. Harvard University, Cambridge, MA. Photocopy (August).

Roemer, Michael, and Mary K. Gugerty. 1997. Does Economic Growth Reduce Poverty? Harvard Institute for International Development, Cambridge, MA. Photocopy (March).

Rowntree, B.S. 1901. *Poverty: A Study of Town Life*. London: Macmillan.

Sachs, Jeffrey, and Andrew M. Warner. 1995. Economic Convergence and Economic Policies. Harvard Institute for International Development, Cambridge, MA. Photocopy (February).

Sala-i-Martin, Xavier. 2002a. *The Disturbing Rise of Global Income Inequality*. NBER Working Paper 8904. Cambridge, MA: National Bureau of Economic Research.

Sala-i-Martin, Xavier. 2002b. *The World Distribution of Income*. NBER Working Paper 8933. Cambridge, MA: National Bureau of Economic Research.

Schultz, Paul T. 1998. Inequality in the Distribution of Personal Income in the World: How It Is Changing and Why. *Journal of Population Economics* 11 (3): 307-44

Sen, Amartya. 1976. Poverty: An Ordinal Approach to Measurement. *Econometrica* 44 (March): 219-31.

Sen, Amartya. 1992. *Inequality Re-examined*. Cambridge, MA: Harvard University Press.

Sen, Amartya. 1999. *Development as Freedom*. New York: Random House.

Skidelsky, Robert. 1995. *The Road from Serfdom* London: Penguin Books.

Slesnick, Daniel K. 1998. Are Our Data Relevant to the Theory: The Case of Aggregate Consumption. *Journal of Business and Economic Statistics* (January).

Srinivasan, T.N. 2001. *Growth and Poverty Alleviation: Lessons from Development Experience*. Working Paper 17. Manila: Asian Development Bank Institute.

Srinivasan, T.N., and Pranab K. Bardhan, eds. 1988. *Rural Poverty in South Asia*. Oxford: Oxford University Press.

Stewart, Frances. 2000. Income Distribution and Development, QEH Working Paper. Oxford: Oxford University Press.

Stiglitz, Joseph E. 2002. *Globalization and Its Discontents*. New York: W.W. Norton.

Sukhatme, P.V. 1977. Malnutrition and Poverty. Ninth Lal Bahadur Shastri Lecture. Indian Agricultural Research Institute, New Delhi.

Summers, Robert, and Alan Heston. 1988. A New Set of International Comparisons of Real Product and Price Levels for 130 countries, 1950-85. *Review of Income and Wealth* 30: 1-25.

Sundaram, K. 2001. Employment and Poverty in India in the Nineteen Nineties: Further Results from NSS 55th Round Employment-Unemployment Survey, 1999-2000. Delhi School of Economics, University of Delhi, Delhi. Photocopy (May).

Szekely, M., N. Lustig, M. Cumpa, and J.A. Mejia. 2000. Do We Know How Much Poverty There Is? Inter-American Development Bank, Washington. Photocopy (December).

Theil, H. 1953. Enige Kwantitative aspecten van het probleem der hulpverlening aan onderontikkeide landen. *De Economist* 11: 721-749.

Thomas, Vinod. 2000. *The Quality of Growth*. New York: Oxford University Press.

Timmer, Peter. 1997. *How Well Do the Poor Connect to the Growth Process?* CAER II Discussion Paper 17. Cambridge, MA: Harvard Institute for International Development.

Townsend, Peter. 1954. The Meaning of Poverty. *British Journal of Sociology* 13, no. 3 (September).

Townsend, Peter. 1979. *Poverty in the United Kingdom: A Survey of Household Resources and Standards of Living*. London: Allen Lane.

Triplett, Jack E. 1997. Measuring Consumption: The Post-1973 Slowdown and the Research Issues. *Federal Bank Review* (Federal Reserve Bank of Saint Louis), May/June: 9-42.

UN Economic and Social Council. 2000. An Assessment of the Statistical Criticism Made of *Human Development Report 1999*. UN Economic and Social Council, New York. Photocopy (December 1).

United Nations. 2002. *Human Development Report, 2002: Deepening Democracy in an Integrated World*. New York.

US Department of Health, Education and Welfare. 1979. Dietary Intake Source Data, 1971-1974. National Center for Health Statistics, US Department of Health, Education and Welfare, Washington. Photocopy (September).

Virmani, Arvind. 2000. *Potential Growth Stars of the 21st Century: India, China, and the Asian Century*. Chintan Occasional Paper, New Delhi.

Visaria, Pravin. 2000. Poverty in India During 1994-98: A Review of Alternative Estimates and the Database. Institute of Economic Growth, Delhi University, Delhi. Photocopy (June 9).

Warr, Peter. 2000. Poverty Reduction and Sectoral Growth: Evidence from Southeast Asia. Australian National University, Canberra. Photocopy.

Whalley, John. 1979. The Worldwide Income Distribution: Some Speculative Calculations. *Review of Income and Wealth* 25, no. 25: 261-76.

Williamson, John. 1990. *Latin American Adjustment: How Much Has Happened?* Washington: Institute for International Economics.

Williamson, John. 2001. Financing for Development: The Implications of the Zedillo Report for South Asia. South Asia Network of Economic Research Institutes, New Delhi. Photocopy (August).

World Bank. 1989. Indian Poverty, Employment and Social Services. World Bank, Washington. Photocopy (May 10).

World Bank. 1991. *Growth, Poverty Alleviation and Improved Income Distribution in Malaysia: Changing Focus of Government Policy Intervention,* Report 8667-MA. Washington: World Bank.

World Bank. 1997a. *India: Achievements and Challenges in Reducing Poverty.* World Bank Country Study. Washington: World Bank.

World Bank. 1997b. *Sharing Rising Incomes: Disparities in China.* 2020 Series. Washington: World Bank.

World Bank. 1999. *Global Economic Prospects and the Developing Countries 2000.* Washington: World Bank.

World Bank. 2002a. *Globalization, Growth, and Poverty.* New York: Oxford University Press.

World Bank. 2002b. *Global Economic Prospects and the Developing Countries 2002: Making Trade Work for the World's Poor.* Washington: World Bank.

Yotopoulos, Pan. 1989. Distribution of Real Income: Within Countries and by the World Income Classes. *Review of Income and Wealth* 35, no. 4: 357-76.

Index

absolute poverty
  calculating, correcting errors, 120-21
  changing concept, 149
  data, 6
  defining and measuring, 53
    India, 53
  in early 1960s, 55
  measuring, 44
  per capita income rise related, 23
  regression of bottom 20 percent, 43-44
  relative concept, 140
  trends, 74
absolute poverty line
  first US, 55
  first World Bank, 59, 67
  income measures related, 62
  methodology, compared, 63
  search for
    first, 57-59
    methodology, four step, 58-59
  second World Bank, 62, 67
  third World Bank, 64
Africa, globalization decline, 21
aid policies
  computing poverty line, 67
  counting poor people, 92
  flow levels, 92
Algeria, consumption per capita
  estimates, 112t, 113
alternative development patterns, 74, 151

alternative studies, need for, 87-89
antiglobalization view, 2n
Asia
  conditional convergence hypothesis, 20
  consumption distribution, 39
  daily per capita income, 1950-2000, 18t,
    19f
  elite income, 193, 195
  forecast of poverty, 2015, 171
  GDP by region, 1950-2000, 17t
  globalization effects, income, 20-21
  golden age, 195
  inequality and growth, 185
  middle class share, 187f
  per capita growth, compared, 16t
  per capita income growth,
    globalization, 20-21, 20f
  population, 1950-2000, 18t
  regional share of income and
    population, 71t
  social class, 187, 188f
Asian Drama, miracle transformation,
  142
Asian financial crisis (1997), levels of
  living before, 14
Australia
  country and regional inequality, 39t
  income per capita estimates, 112t
authoritarianism, high growth rates, 200

Bangladesh
  consumption per capita estimates, 112*t*
  country and regional inequality, 39*t*
  poverty decline, 143*t*
Bayesian process, 77
book, organization of, 6-7
  statistical base, 76
Brazil
  country and regional inequality, 39*t*
  income per capita estimates, 112*t*
  poverty decline, 143*t*
  trickle-down growth, 151

caloric consumption
  cheap vs. rich sources, 60
  critiques of approach, 61
  intra-individual variation, 61
  poverty levels, determining, 59-61
  United States, 1971-74, 59-60, 60*t*
calorie trap, 59
catch-up, 22
Central African Republic, consumption
    per capita estimates, 112*t*
Central Asia
  dataset summarized, by country, 221*t*
  differences in income and
      consumption PPP exchange rates,
      95*t*
China
  consumption PPP exchange rate, 98
  country and regional inequality, 39*t*
  equality argument related, 184-85
  growth rate, 82
  growth rates and poverty, 75
  income per capita estimates, 112*t*, 113
  inequality rising, 38, 46, 174, 184
  per capita income rise, 27
  population share, 15
  poverty decline, 143*t*
  poverty estimates, 121
  poverty line, 98
  rural and urban disaggregation, 49
  separate poverty estimates, 98
  simple inequality mathematics, 33-34
China and India
  changes in income and consumption,
      169*t*
  daily per capita income, 1950-2000, 18*t*,
      19*t*
  GDP by region, 1950-2000, 17*t*
  growth, 17, 20
  income growth and poverty change,
      85*t*
  methodological problems, 24*n*

middle class share, 187*f*
per capita growth, compared, 16*t*
per capita income growth,
    globalization, 20*f*
population, 1950-2000, 18*t*
poverty lines, 98
regional share of income and
    population, 71*t*
clothing, poverty removal, 59
common currency, stating incomes, 47,
    47*n*
conditional convergence hypothesis, 20
consistency transformation, 58
consumption
  changes in, 107
  developing countries
    HCR related, 82
    median share, 120
    recent increase, 83
    top percentile, 120
  distribution, 36
    increasing, 87
    world, 48
  distribution related to poverty line, 86
  Gini coefficient, 36
  growth
    for 1987-98, 83*n*
    for 1998-99, 83*n*
  increase 1960-1975, 68
  institutional, 108
  use of term, 9*n*
  US per capita compared to India, 55
  world cumulative distribution, per
      capita, 156-57, 156*f*
consumption distribution
  consumption PPP exchange rate,
      China, 98
  inequality trends, 39
consumption exchange rate, 8
  consumption PPP exchange rate
    basis for, 94
    estimates of poverty, 95-99
    gap undocumented, 127
    local inflation, 127*n*
  differences in income and, 95*t*
  evaluation and use, 96
  "gaps" in calculating mean
      consumption, 97-98, 97*n*
consumption surveys, updating with NA
    data, 93
convergence
  concept of, 22
  conclusions, 205

household surveys
  adjusting to national accounts, 103
  advantages, 103
  data availability, 77n
  data issues, 81
  defense of, 107-09
  exclusive reliance, 203-04
  inequality changes, 73
  as mean for national accounts, 104n
  NA data compared
    deviation errors, 104-05
    NA mean uncaptured, 105
    opportunity cost of interview, 105
  national accounts data, to adjust, 83
  new and emerging products, 105
  related to poverty line, 96
  to update NA estimates, 104
Hungary, Ginis compared: original
    source and SAP, 136f

ICP prices. See PPP prices
illiteracy, 198t, 199t, 200
IMF. See International Monetary Fund
import substitution industrialization, 57
income
  average daily, compared, 67
  by deciles, average, 49
  global, developing world share, 70
  as measure of poverty, 52
  measuring, 44
  United States, undercapture ratio, 107
  use of term, 9n
income distribution
  after-tax vs. before-tax, 36
  consumption distributions vs., 36
  data, 6
  data issues, 77
    data used for this study, 37n
    errors in published inequality data,
      213, 215
    errors in survey inequality
      measures, 213-14
  global, 70, 73
  global individual, 186-88
  India, 58
  is the initial income distribution
    important?, 166-67
  Lorenz curve, 31, 32f
  as poverty reduction device, 166-67
  quintile data, 213
  region-specific, 36
  study of 90 countries, 78
  studying, 31
  three other stylized facts, 36

world
  1960, 1980, and 2000, 176f
  1970, methodology, 48
  1973 and 2000, 175f
  methodological issues, 203
income growth, preglobalization vs.
    globalization, 190
income inequality, 22
  GDP gap, 26
  globalization, 21-22
  historical trends, UN, 26
  methodological issues, 130
  worsening, 130
    country level, 130-31
income redistribution, propoor growth
    with, 154
index of inequality, 37
index of poverty, 52
India
  absolute poverty studied, 53
  consumption
    national accounts adjustment
      multipliers for different deciles,
      117, 119f
    per capita daily, US compared, 55
    per capita estimates, 112t
    PPP data, 96, 97
  defining poor-country poverty line, 57
  15 states, pairwise analysis, 164-66
  growth
    period 1983-1999, 115
    poverty and, 75
    since 1980, 82
  head count ratio (HCR), 125
  income distribution, 58
  inequality, maintained, 46
  inflation, 115
  mismatch, survey and national
    accounts, 117, 118f
  Planning Commission of, 54, 105-06n
  poor people, alternative estimates, 123f
  population share, 15
  poverty
    alternative estimates, 88n
    measuring, 106
  poverty decline, 6n, 143t
  poverty definition, 53, 53n
  poverty estimates challenged, 121-22
    estimates for 1999, 122, 123f
    household employment and
      expenditure surveys, 122, 124-25
    other estimates (1999), 125
  poverty line, 62-63

Other Publications from the Institute for International Economics

*= out of print

POLICY ANALYSES IN
INTERNATIONAL ECONOMICS Series

65 The Benefits of Price Convergence:
Speculative Calculations
Gary Clyde Hufbauer, Erika Wada,
and Tony Warren
December 2001   ISBN 0-88132-333-0
66 Managed Floating Plus
Morris Goldstein
March 2002   ISBN 0-88132-336-5
67 Argentina and the Fund: From Triumph
to Tragedy
Michael Mussa
July 2002   ISBN 0-88132-339-X
68 East Asian Financial Cooperation
C. Randall Henning
September 2002   ISBN 0-88132-338-1

BOOKS

IMF Conditionality*   John Williamson, editor
1983   ISBN 0-88132-006-4
Trade Policy in the 1980s* William R. Cline, editor
1983   ISBN 0-88132-031-5
Subsidies in International Trade*
Gary Clyde Hufbauer and Joanna Shelton Erb
1984   ISBN 0-88132-004-8
International Debt: Systemic Risk and Policy
Response*   William R. Cline
1984   ISBN 0-88132-015-3
Trade Protection in the United States: 31 Case
Studies*   Gary Clyde Hufbauer, Diane E. Berliner,
and Kimberly Ann Elliott
1986   ISBN 0-88132-040-4
Toward Renewed Economic Growth in Latin
America*   Bela Balassa, Gerardo M. Bueno, Pedro-
Pablo Kuczynski, and Mario Henrique Simonsen
1986   ISBN 0-88132-045-5
Capital Flight and Third World Debt*
Donald R. Lessard and John Williamson, editors
1987   ISBN 0-88132-053-6
The Canada-United States Free Trade Agreement:
The Global Impact*
Jeffrey J. Schott and Murray G. Smith, editors
1988   ISBN 0-88132-073-0
World Agricultural Trade: Building a Consensus*
William M. Miner and Dale E. Hathaway, editors
1988   ISBN 0-88132-071-3
Japan in the World Economy*
Bela Balassa and Marcus Noland
1988   ISBN 0-88132-041-2
America in the World Economy: A Strategy for
the 1990s*   C. Fred Bergsten
1988   ISBN 0-88132-089-7
Managing the Dollar: From the Plaza to the
Louvre*   Yoichi Funabashi
1988, 2d ed. 1989   ISBN 0-88132-097-8

United States External Adjustment and the World
Economy*   William R. Cline
May 1989   ISBN 0-88132-048-X
Free Trade Areas and U.S. Trade Policy*
Jeffrey J. Schott, editor
May 1989   ISBN 0-88132-094-3
Dollar Politics: Exchange Rate Policymaking in
the United States*
I.M. Destler and C. Randall Henning
September 1989   ISBN 0-88132-079-X
Latin American Adjustment: How Much Has
Happened?*   John Williamson, editor
April 1990   ISBN 0-88132-125-7
The Future of World Trade in Textiles and
Apparel*   William R. Cline
1987, 2d ed. June 1990   ISBN 0-88132-110-9
Completing the Uruguay Round: A Results-
Oriented Approach to the GATT Trade
Negotiations*   Jeffrey J. Schott, editor
September 1990   ISBN 0-88132-130-3
Economic Sanctions Reconsidered (2 volumes)
Economic Sanctions Reconsidered: Supplemental
Case Histories
Gary Clyde Hufbauer, Jeffrey J. Schott, and
Kimberly Ann Elliott
1985, 2d ed. Dec. 1990   ISBN cloth 0-88132-115-X
                            ISBN paper 0-88132-105-2
Economic Sanctions Reconsidered: History and
Current Policy
Gary Clyde Hufbauer, Jeffrey J. Schott, and
Kimberly Ann Elliott
December 1990   ISBN cloth 0-88132-140-0
                            ISBN paper 0-88132-136-2
Pacific Basin Developing Countries: Prospects for
the Future*   Marcus Noland
January 1991   ISBN cloth 0-88132-141-9
                            ISBN 0-88132-081-1
Currency Convertibility in Eastern Europe*
John Williamson, editor
October 1991   ISBN 0-88132-128-1
International Adjustment and Financing: The
Lessons of 1985-1991*   C. Fred Bergsten, editor
January 1992   ISBN 0-88132-112-5
North American Free Trade: Issues and
Recommendations*
Gary Clyde Hufbauer and Jeffrey J. Schott
April 1992   ISBN 0-88132-120-6
Narrowing the U.S. Current Account Deficit*
Allen J. Lenz
June 1992   ISBN 0-88132-103-6
The Economics of Global Warming
William R. Cline/*June 1992*   ISBN 0-88132-132-X
U.S. Taxation of International Income: Blueprint
for Reform*   Gary Clyde Hufbauer, assisted by
Joanna M. van Rooij
October 1992   ISBN 0-88132-134-6

Who's Bashing Whom? Trade Conflict in High-Technology Industries   Laura D'Andrea Tyson
November 1992   ISBN 0-88132-106-0
Korea in the World Economy*   Il SaKong
January 1993   ISBN 0-88132-183-4
Pacific Dynamism and the International Economic System*
C. Fred Bergsten and Marcus Noland, editors
May 1993   ISBN 0-88132-196-6
Economic Consequences of Soviet Disintegration*
John Williamson, editor
May 1993   ISBN 0-88132-190-7
Reconcilable Differences? United States-Japan Economic Conflict*
C. Fred Bergsten and Marcus Noland
June 1993   ISBN 0-88132-129-X
Does Foreign Exchange Intervention Work?
Kathryn M. Dominguez and Jeffrey A. Frankel
September 1993   ISBN 0-88132-104-4
Sizing Up U.S. Export Disincentives*
J. David Richardson
September 1993   ISBN 0-88132-107-9
NAFTA: An Assessment
Gary Clyde Hufbauer and Jeffrey J. Schott/*rev. ed.*
October 1993   ISBN 0-88132-199-0
Adjusting to Volatile Energy Prices
Philip K. Verleger, Jr.
November 1993   ISBN 0-88132-069-2
The Political Economy of Policy Reform
John Williamson, editor
January 1994   ISBN 0-88132-195-8
Measuring the Costs of Protection in the United States
Gary Clyde Hufbauer and Kimberly Ann Elliott
January 1994   ISBN 0-88132-108-7
The Dynamics of Korean Economic Development*
Cho Soon
March 1994   ISBN 0-88132-162-1
Reviving the European Union*
C. Randall Henning, Eduard Hochreiter, and Gary Clyde Hufbauer, editors
April 1994   ISBN 0-88132-208-3
China in the World Economy   Nicholas R. Lardy
April 1994   ISBN 0-88132-200-8
Greening the GATT: Trade, Environment, and the Future   Daniel C. Esty
July 1994   ISBN 0-88132-205-9
Western Hemisphere Economic Integration*
Gary Clyde Hufbauer and Jeffrey J. Schott
July 1994   ISBN 0-88132-159-1
Currencies and Politics in the United States, Germany, and Japan
C. Randall Henning
September 1994   ISBN 0-88132-127-3
Estimating Equilibrium Exchange Rates
John Williamson, editor
September 1994   ISBN 0-88132-076-5

Managing the World Economy: Fifty Years After Bretton Woods   Peter B. Kenen, editor
September 1994   ISBN 0-88132-212-1
Reciprocity and Retaliation in U.S. Trade Policy
Thomas O. Bayard and Kimberly Ann Elliott
September 1994   ISBN 0-88132-084-6
The Uruguay Round: An Assessment*
Jeffrey J. Schott, assisted by Johanna W. Buurman
November 1994   ISBN 0-88132-206-7
Measuring the Costs of Protection in Japan*
Yoko Sazanami, Shujiro Urata, and Hiroki Kawai
January 1995   ISBN 0-88132-211-3
Foreign Direct Investment in the United States, 3rd Ed.   Edward M. Graham and Paul R. Krugman
January 1995   ISBN 0-88132-204-0
The Political Economy of Korea-United States Cooperation*
C. Fred Bergsten and Il SaKong, editors
February 1995   ISBN 0-88132-213-X
International Debt Reexamined*   William R. Cline
February 1995   ISBN 0-88132-083-8
American Trade Politics, 3rd Ed.   I.M. Destler
April 1995   ISBN 0-88132-215-6
Managing Official Export Credits: The Quest for a Global Regime*   John E. Ray
July 1995   ISBN 0-88132-207-5
Asia Pacific Fusion: Japan's Role in APEC*
Yoichi Funabashi
October 1995   ISBN 0-88132-224-5
Korea-United States Cooperation in the New World Order*
C. Fred Bergsten and Il SaKong, editors
February 1996   ISBN 0-88132-226-1
Why Exports Really Matter! *   ISBN 0-88132-221-0
Why Exports Matter More!*   ISBN 0-88132-229-6
J. David Richardson and Karin Rindal
July 1995; February 1996
Global Corporations and National Governments
Edward M. Graham
May 1996   ISBN 0-88132-111-7
Global Economic Leadership and the Group of Seven   C. Fred Bergsten and C. Randall Henning
May 1996   ISBN 0-88132-218-0
The Trading System After the Uruguay Round*
John Whalley and Colleen Hamilton
July 1996   ISBN 0-88132-131-1
Private Capital Flows to Emerging Markets After the Mexican Crisis*   Guillermo A. Calvo, Morris Goldstein, and Eduard Hochreiter
September 1996   ISBN 0-88132-232-6
The Crawling Band as an Exchange Rate Regime: Lessons from Chile, Colombia, and Israel
John Williamson
September 1996   ISBN 0-88132-231-8
Flying High: Liberalizing Civil Aviation in the Asia Pacific*
Gary Clyde Hufbauer and Christopher Findlay
November 1996   ISBN 0-88132-227-X

Measuring the Costs of Visible Protection in Korea* Namdoo Kim
November 1996 ISBN 0-88132-236-9

The World Trading System: Challenges Ahead
Jeffrey J. Schott
December 1996 ISBN 0-88132-235-0

Has Globalization Gone Too Far? Dani Rodrik
March 1997 ISBN cloth 0-88132-243-1

Korea-United States Economic Relationship*
C. Fred Bergsten and Il SaKong, editors
March 1997 ISBN 0-88132-240-7

Summitry in the Americas: A Progress Report
Richard E. Feinberg
April 1997 ISBN 0-88132-242-3

Corruption and the Global Economy
Kimberly Ann Elliott
June 1997 ISBN 0-88132-233-4

Regional Trading Blocs in the World Economic System Jeffrey A. Frankel
October 1997 ISBN 0-88132-202-4

Sustaining the Asia Pacific Miracle: Environmental Protection and Economic Integration André Dua and Daniel C. Esty
October 1997 ISBN 0-88132-250-4

Trade and Income Distribution William R. Cline
November 1997 ISBN 0-88132-216-4

Global Competition Policy
Edward M. Graham and J. David Richardson
December 1997 ISBN 0-88132-166-4

Unfinished Business: Telecommunications after the Uruguay Round
Gary Clyde Hufbauer and Erika Wada
December 1997 ISBN 0-88132-257-1

Financial Services Liberalization in the WTO
Wendy Dobson and Pierre Jacquet
June 1998 ISBN 0-88132-254-7

Restoring Japan's Economic Growth
Adam S. Posen
September 1998 ISBN 0-88132-262-8

Measuring the Costs of Protection in China
Zhang Shuguang, Zhang Yansheng, and Wan Zhongxin
November 1998 ISBN 0-88132-247-4

Foreign Direct Investment and Development: The New Policy Agenda for Developing Countries and Economies in Transition
Theodore H. Moran
December 1998 ISBN 0-88132-258-X

Behind the Open Door: Foreign Enterprises in the Chinese Marketplace
Daniel H. Rosen
January 1999 ISBN 0-88132-263-6

Toward A New International Financial Architecture: A Practical Post-Asia Agenda
Barry Eichengreen
February 1999 ISBN 0-88132-270-9

Is the U.S. Trade Deficit Sustainable?
Catherine L. Mann / *September 1999*
ISBN 0-88132-265-2

Safeguarding Prosperity in a Global Financial System: The Future International Financial Architecture, Independent Task Force Report Sponsored by the Council on Foreign Relations
Morris Goldstein, Project Director
October 1999 ISBN 0-88132-287-3

Avoiding the Apocalypse: The Future of the Two Koreas Marcus Noland
June 2000 ISBN 0-88132-278-4

Assessing Financial Vulnerability: An Early Warning System for Emerging Markets
Morris Goldstein, Graciela Kaminsky, and Carmen Reinhart
June 2000 ISBN 0-88132-237-7

Global Electronic Commerce: A Policy Primer
Catherine L. Mann, Sue E. Eckert, and Sarah Cleeland Knight
July 2000 ISBN 0-88132-274-1

The WTO after Seattle Jeffrey J. Schott, editor
July 2000 ISBN 0-88132-290-3

Intellectual Property Rights in the Global Economy Keith E. Maskus
August 2000 ISBN 0-88132-282-2

The Political Economy of the Asian Financial Crisis Stephan Haggard
August 2000 ISBN 0-88132-283-0

Transforming Foreign Aid: United States Assistance in the 21st Century Carol Lancaster
August 2000 ISBN 0-88132-291-1

Fighting the Wrong Enemy: Antiglobal Activists and Multinational Enterprises Edward M.Graham
September 2000 ISBN 0-88132-272-5

Globalization and the Perceptions of American Workers
Kenneth F. Scheve and Matthew J. Slaughter
March 2001 ISBN 0-88132-295-4

World Capital Markets: Challenge to the G-10
Wendy Dobson and Gary C. Hufbauer, assisted by Hyun Koo Cho
May 2001 ISBN 0-88132-301-2

Prospects for Free Trade in the Americas
Jeffrey J. Schott
August 2001 ISBN 0-88132-275-X

Lessons from the Old World for the New: Constructing a North American Community
Robert A. Pastor
August 2001 ISBN 0-88132-328-4

Measuring the Costs of Protection in Europe: European Commercial Policy in the 2000s
Patrick A. Messerlin
September 2001 ISBN 0-88132-273-3

Job Loss from Imports: Measuring the Costs
Lori G. Kletzer
September 2001 ISBN 0-88132-296-2

SPECIAL REPORTS

WORKS IN PROGRESS